"Hank writes with a passion for game that few other writers can approach. *Pheasant, Quail, Cottontail* is a joy to read and to cook from. It is entertaining, well organized, and crazy smart—the new gold-standard for small game cookery."

—JOHN CURRENCE, quail hunter and James Beard Award-winning chef of City Grocery in Mississippi

---

"*Pheasant, Quail, Cottontail* is simply the most complete gamebird cookbook I've ever read. It's got it all—dressing birds, flavor comparisons with substitutions, recipes organized by light meats and dark meats, and preparations for giblets and small game charcuterie. Without doubt, Hank's book is the best book to bag this season."

—CHEF JOHN FOLSE, author of *After the Hunt: Louisiana's Authoritative Collection of Wild Game & Game Fish Cookery*

PHEASANT, QUAIL, COTTONTAIL

PHEASANT, QUAIL, COTTONTAIL

UPLAND BIRDS AND SMALL GAME FROM FIELD TO FEAST

HANK SHAW

Photographs by HOLLY A. HEYSER

H|H

For Chris Niskanen and Finn: This is all your fault!

Published by
H&H BOOKS
huntgathercook.com
All H&H books may be purchased for business or promotional use or for special sales.
For information, please write to: Special Markets Dept., H&H Books, P.O. Box 2984, Orangevale, CA 95662; or email scrbblr@hotmail.com, attention Special Markets.

Design and Layout: Laura Shaw Design, laurashawdesign.com
Food and prop styling: Hank Shaw and Holly A. Heyser
Editorial: Richard Feit Editorial, rfeditorial.com
Icons: Allison Meierding, allisonmeierding.com
Photographs on frontspiece and pages 8, 14–15, 18, 24, 40, 59, 60–61, 75, 125 (inset image), 182, 206–7, 209, 210, 216, 234, 277, 284, 286, 287, 292–3 by Hank Shaw; on page 11, by Randy King; on page 63, by Kevin Kossowan.

ISBN-10: 0-9969448-1-8
ISBN-13: 978-0-9969448-1-6

11 10 9 8 7 6 5 4

Printed in the United States of America

Library of Congress Cataloging-in-Publication Data
Shaw, Hank, 1970—
Pheasant, Quail, Cottontail: Upland Birds and Small Game from Field to Feast / Hank Shaw
Pages cm Includes index
Cooking (Turkey) 2. Cooking (Rabbit) 3. Cooking (Game) I. Title.
2017916754

CONTENTS

RECITES

INTRODUCTION

I'm often asked what animal I'd pursue if forbidden to chase all others. It's a way people have of asking what my favorite game animal might be. My answer is, always, the grouse—which strikes some as a bit of a cop-out. Grouse, after all, is an entire clan of birds, occupying nearly every habitat in North America—sage grouse in the Great Basin, ptarmigan on the tundra, sooty grouse in the rain-soaked Pacific Northwest, sharpies on the Great Plains. To me, grouse are a microcosm of the spectacular diversity that makes the world of small game and upland birds so endlessly fascinating—diversity of place, diversity of flavor, diversity of animal, diversity of the people who pursue them.

And grouse are just one example. There are seven different quail in North America, turkeys and pheasants live in most states, and rabbits and hares, from tiny desert cottontails to giant Arctic hares, are everywhere. Coastal marshes hold rails and snipe. Boggy inland alder thickets are home to the woodcock. The Great Plains are a game-bird hotspot, with Hungarian partridge, sharp-tailed grouse, prairie chickens, and pheasants, depending on where you go. Deserts are home to Gambel's, scaled, and Mearns' quail. Our mountains host blue grouse and mountain quail and all kinds of squirrels, and ptarmigan hide on mountain peaks, holed

up above the tree line in quasi-Arctic refugia. No matter where you go in this world, there's some sort of small game.

But you need not travel to the top of the Rockies to experience the world of small game. That's the beauty of it—odds are there's some sort of small game in your yard right now. The cute (and tasty) cottontail is a ubiquitous garden invader, the eastern gray squirrel now ranges as far as the West Coast, the turkey is fast becoming a regular part of the suburban scene (as many of us can attest), and doves and pigeons are everywhere (and I'm here to tell you that the common pigeon, also known as the rock dove, is fine table fare).

These animals are many a young person's entrée into the world of hunting. If you can hunt squirrels where they're truly wild, you can hunt the deer that live among them. If you can sit still enough and quiet enough to coax a turkey close enough to shoot him, you can do the same in the deer blind. I experienced just such an initiation—with a squirrel in a Minnesota woodlot—at the tender age of thirty-two.

So when I'm asked about my favorite small game and then pressed by someone in the know for something a bit more specific than "grouse," I'll admit to the grouse of my dreams: the ruffed, *Bonasa umbellus*. Ruffies occupy deciduous forests from Maine to

California. I've hunted them, with varying degrees of success, on Cape Ann in Massachusetts, in the Northwoods of Minnesota, on the high mountains of Utah, and in the boreal forest of Alberta. Throughout most of their range, ruffed grouse are a challenge to hunt (though oddly enough, I've seen them just sit and stare at you when approached in the bush). They bring you into the kind of woods very much like the mountains I grew up around, the Watchung Mountains of New Jersey.

And they're unmatched at the table.

This is the real reason I love ruffed grouse so much—aside from where they live and how one pursues them. Though a plucked ruffed grouse may look like its Asiatic cousin, the jungle fowl—which we know of as a chicken—it tastes like nothing else. There's a certain beguiling funk to a grouse, a musky, rough aroma that just says *wild*. I can't get enough of it.

Though I do love ducks, geese, and venison, the fact is that they're all red meat, with more similarities than distinguishing traits; in culinary terms, it's fair to say that only skin and fat separate waterfowl from pretty much any red-meat animal. Sure, there are differences. But in general, the culinary experience of the red-meat realm is relatively narrow compared to the world of small game.

No other area of hunting offers such a dazzling array of flavors. Even pheasants, partridges, and quail—the most chickeny of our wild birds—have their own unique flavors. And a mountain quail from California isn't going to taste like a Mearns' quail from Arizona. Add to this the small red-meat animals—the hares, the sharpies, and the ptarmigan, the funkiest grouse of them all—as well as snipe and rails, and you have yet another layer of culinary experience. There's a reason why the great French chefs hold game birds in such high regard—higher even than the big-game animals like deer and boar—and why they positively swoon over the woodcock, one of the few birds that rivals the grouse for my attentions.

Take a step back a moment to consider where small-game hunting stands in the grand story of us. Deer and big-game animals like them may well have helped make humans fully human, but small-game hunting is where human ingenuity really flowered. We *Homo sapiens* aren't the only species of human that chased smaller animals, but we're the only one clever enough to have perfected it.

Those who study such things believe we humans became hunters because of large game. We hunted in groups, developed complex language, refined the spear and the atlatl, and expanded our ability to throw and to run—all in pursuit of something like a deer. The pursuit of small game may have came much, much later, but it is every bit as important to our story.

Evidence exists, albeit not without controversy, of humans hunting big game as far back as one million years ago. Small game seems to really have become part of our skill set only about two hundred thousand years ago. That's still a powerful long time ago, possibly before our species was fully formed and certainly before we were alone as the only member of the genus *Homo* left on this planet of ours.

What took so long? Simple. Ever try to catch a rabbit? Shoot a partridge with an arrow? It can be done, but it's neither easy nor efficient. Other than the slowpokes like turtles and shellfish that we ate very early in our evolution, this so-called "catch cost" of small game meant it was better to focus on the big animals because they offered far more reward for the risk of the hunt.

Climate seems to have been the pivot point. Wherever it changed enough to chase off big-game animals, hunters turned their attention to smaller game. So it stands to reason—and there's ample evidence to support it—that small-game hunting developed independently in many places. At first, it was all about deadfall traps and snares. The bow came later, certainly by twelve thousand years ago, although there is some evidence of bow-and-arrow technology as far back as seventy-one thousand years ago. That said, bows and arrows aren't an efficient way to collect small game, especially with brittle stone points that take hours to make.

Nets were the key. The earliest evidence of net making is about twenty-six thousand years old, and nets were certainly in use by sixteen thousand years ago. What did people catch in their nets? Fish, of course. But also upland birds, notably chukars, Hungarian partridge, and quail. Why these birds? They covey up tight, unlike grouse, pheasants, or hares, which are more solitary. That's why rabbit hunting shows up so late in the game, relatively speaking—about thirty thousand years ago, according to some of the earliest evidence of rabbit hunting from Spain and Portugal.

Small-game hunting continued more or less like this until the gun came along in the 1500s. Most guns back in the 1600s could fire birdshot, and when dedicated "fowling pieces," as early shotguns were called, became available in the 1700s, the pursuit of small game as we know it was on.

But that pesky catch cost never quite went away. Think about it. Is there a more calorie-negative hunt than a day spent chasing snipe? Sure, it's possible to swing into calorie-positive territory hunting small game, especially if you live in a state where you can shoot more than one turkey a day or, if you're lucky enough, to shoot a limit of rabbits or hares. But for the most part, small-game hunting is ceremonial, or at best, supplemental. Where you see small game as a primary food source, you see scarring poverty. The stain on the jackrabbit's reputation, for example, stems from this; during several periods in American history, people in the Great Plains had little access to protein other than the humble jack. The remnants of this experience exist to this day, and in most places, jacks are seen as unfit to eat. In the South, the historic connection between black Americans and the hunting of raccoons and opossum goes all the way back to slavery,

when these were the only animals that owners would let slaves hunt—at night, after their work for master was finished.

Maybe in the end it's this cultural diversity of small game that fascinates me most. From working-class Appalachians and Hmong immigrants chasing squirrels to the fancy-pants woodcock and grouse hunters who take the field in jodhpurs and tweed jackets with leather patches on their sleeves, the world of small game reflects us as a culture—varied and wondrous.

Let me take you through this kaleidoscope, one plate at a time.

HANK SHAW
Orangevale, California
August 2017

HOW TO USE THIS BOOK

Upland birds and small game are special cases in the hunting world: there are myriad species, yet many are interchangeable in the kitchen. Do pheasants and blue grouse taste different? You bet. But as pheasants and blue grouse are both gallinaceous cousins of the chicken, any pheasant recipe can be a blue grouse recipe. And even though squirrels and cottontails taste quite different, they can be used in each other's recipes.

For this reason, Part One, the basics, is in many ways the most important part of the book. This section will give you a foundation of knowledge about how to handle and prepare all sorts of birds and small game, from field to kitchen and beyond. If you take some time to familiarize yourself with the differences between the species, you'll soon be able to make your own decisions about substituting snowshoe hare in a quail recipe or Hungarian partridge in a woodcock recipe. Knowledge is power!

That said, there are a few broad categories to live by as a cook of small game. First and foremost is the distinction between light meats and dark meats. In the kitchen, a light-meat cottontail is closer to a light-meat pheasant than it is to its dark-meat cousin, the jackrabbit. And a dark-meat sharp-tailed grouse is closer, cooking-wise, to a pigeon or a dove (or even a duck) than to its light-meat cousin, the

ruffed grouse. Can you cross over and use dark meat with a light-meat recipe? Sure, but in some cases the flavors might not play well together.

With this most basic distinction in mind, I've organized the recipes in *Pheasant, Quail, Cottontail* in two broad sections: light-meat recipes in Part Two, dark-meat recipes in Part Three.

The light-meat animals in Part Two offer the hunter an unrivaled source of white meat for the table (with the possible exception of wild pigs). Lighter meats are often (but not always) milder in flavor than redder ones, and they tend to make better fare when the weather gets hot. Although the recipes in the chapters that follow feature the animal that I prefer for that particular preparation, substitutions are perfectly fine. If you want to use pheasant or turkey instead of rabbit for the African Rabbit Curry (page 199), for example, you'll still have a great dish.

The meats in the dark-meat section (Part Three) are the most interesting meats in the world of wild game. Some, like jackrabbit, are surprisingly mild. Others, like snipe or woodcock, are oddly gamy but still fun. Still others, like dove or pigeon, are beefy in flavor but not in texture. And some, like squirrel, are utterly unique. Here you'll find recipes that could be appropriate for such animals as woodchucks, beavers, raccoons, muskrats, and opossum. Although I have no specific recipes for these particular animals, they're all so similar to jackrabbit in color and texture that you can use them in these recipes with no trouble.

Beyond the light-meat–dark-meat divide, I do categorize recipes in this book by animal, or at least by broad categories of animals; pheasants, ruffed grouse, and blue grouse are so similar in the kitchen that they're all in one chapter. The same goes for doves and pigeons. In most cases, I pair a recipe with an animal simply because that's the animal I normally use when I make it. In only a few instances is a recipe really best with a particular animal; even then, consider the animal pairing a first choice, not an absolute. You can certainly mix and match.

You'll also notice a preponderance of pheasant recipes in this book. This is because pheasant is one of the most widely hunted species in America and because pheasant is the perfect canvas for a variety of white-meat recipes. But know that every recipe for pheasant can be done with ruffed or blue grouse, wild turkey, or rabbit—even the Honey-Mustard Pheasant Wings (page 105), which you can make with the front or hind legs of a cottontail if you wanted to.

To help you sort through this wide world of substitutions, we've created a series of icons that will appear with each recipe. Each icon is linked with its chapter. If you see a pheasant icon next to a turkey recipe, know that you can use ruffed or blue grouse with it, too. Similarly, if you see a silhouette of a sage grouse, that means any dark-meat grouse will work with that recipe. A handy key to the icons is shown below and also on the inside back cover.

Part Four completes the tour, with recipes for small-game charcuterie—including sausages and smoked meats—and for those often-overlooked parts of the hunt, the giblets and offal.

LIGHT MEAT

Pheasant, Ruffed Grouse, and Blue Grouse

Wild Turkeys

Quail, Partridges, and Chukars

Rabbits

DARK MEAT

Squirrels, Hares, and Others

Sharptails, Spruce Grouse, Sage Grouse, Ptarmigan, and Prairie Chickens

Doves and Pigeons

Snipe, Woodcock, and Rails

OTHERS

Beavers and Woodchucks

Opossums

PART ONE

BASICS

CHAPTER 1

FEATHERS AND FUR

OUR CAST OF CHARACTERS

This book deals with birds and mammals. Here, the term "small game" refers to any game animal smaller than a deer that is not waterfowl. Though turtles, snakes, and frogs could rightly be considered small game, these have not been included, primarily to keep the cookbook to a manageable size.

Our various gallinaceous birds—chicken relatives all—are the most commonly hunted. From the turkey to the quail, these are our most popular upland birds. Most, but not all, have white meat and thin skins. And they run around a lot. Many share a slightly funky "chicken smell" when plucked and gutted.

Following the gallinaceous birds in popularity are doves and rabbits. Dove hunting is wildly popular in the forty-two states that allow it. Interestingly, the ban on dove hunting in those remaining eight states has deep-seated roots in discrimination against black Americans and Italian immigrants, but that's a story for another day. (If you do want the full story, read *Our Vanishing Wildlife: Its Extermination and Preservation*, by William Temple Hornaday. It'll curl your hair.) Yet for all its popularity, dove hunting is a short-lived affair, with most

hunters taking the field only for the traditional Labor Day opening weekend.

Rabbits, however, are ubiquitous and can be hunted many months of the year; in some Western states, they're not even considered game animals. Although there is a strong tradition of snowshoe hare hunting in upper New England and eastern Canada, real rabbit-hunting culture is largely a Southern thing.

All the other animals covered in this book are less popular with North American hunters but are still widely sought after and make first-class table fare.

Here are some of my personal notes on how these animals rate in the kitchen.

FEATHERS

PHEASANT

Any discussion of upland birds must start with pheasants. *Phasianus colchicus*, the common pheasant, is just one of a wide range of pheasants in various genera. Most live only in Asia, where they originated, but oddball pheasants can be seen running around in preserves and in Hawaii, where Kalij pheasant, *Lophura leucomelanos*, introduced in 1962, run wild.

Pheasants were brought to the United States in 1871 by our then-ambassador to China, who thought they might like living in Oregon's Willamette Valley. He was right, and the birds he released multiplied so fast that within a mere twenty years there was a hunting season on them.

Wild pheasants can be found across the northern American states and throughout southern Canada. They don't like the heat of the South or the Southwest, but you can often find them in hunting preserves there. This is one reason why pheasant is king in the United States: hunting at a pheasant preserve is often a new hunter's first experience.

In the kitchen, pheasants resemble chicken—they're cousins, biologically speaking. Pheasant meat is a little darker, denser, and tougher than chicken, however. This will be true with every species in this book that has a farmed analogue.

Pheasants are smaller than most chickens, and they have what's called a "single breast"; nearly every chicken sold for meat in this country is "double breasted," meaning it has been bred to have a breast that is wide and meaty instead of narrow and hatchet shaped and unlike chicken drumsticks, pheasant drumsticks are riddled with tough tendons that will not break down, even after long cooking. This is why you should always separate the drumstick from the thigh (my favorite part of a pheasant). Pheasant drumsticks are best cooked slowly, with the meat pulled away from all those sinews, or tossed into the stockpot.

The flavor of pheasant is very mild—until you age it. A hung pheasant matures into something very special, but hanging must be done right or you risk bacterial issues; see my instructions on hanging on page 25.

You can cook a pheasant any way you'd cook a chicken, so long as you remember those sinews in the drumsticks.

A typical pheasant will feed two people, although I've eaten a whole one easily.

TURKEY

There may well be more turkey hunters than pheasant hunters out there, and in the South, where there are no wild pheasants, turkey reigns supreme. Wild turkeys of various subspecies can be found in forty-nine states as well as in Mexico and parts of southern Canada. And while there are six subspecies of wild turkey, they are all interchangeable in the kitchen.

Although the wild turkey is the bird that most closely resembles its domesticated counterpart, it's really only comparable to the best that money can buy, those hundred-dollar birds I call "Gucci turkeys." A wild turkey bears only a passing resemblance to one that's been factory-farmed.

Like pheasants, wild turkeys will have a narrow breast and gnarly sinews in their drumsticks. I highly recommend that you separate the drumstick from the thigh when you store your turkeys. Many people forget the wings on a turkey, but I urge you not to; they are large, are pure white meat, and, when braised tender, can be a very enjoyable part of the bird.

Can you roast a whole wild turkey for a traditional Thanksgiving dinner? Yes, but it's trickier than you might think (Roast Wild Turkey, page 126). Mostly, I break my turkeys into breasts, thighs, drumsticks, and wings.

Flavor-wise, wild birds are just stronger-tasting versions of their store-bought counterparts. The dark meat of wild turkey is darker, too, almost a red meat when braised.

A whole wild turkey will serve six to ten people (a single thigh can be a healthy portion). You can cook wild turkey any way you would cook domestic turkey—remembering those sinews in the drumsticks.

QUAIL

Quail can be found in most American states and throughout Mexico. There are seven species, six of which live in the United States. In general, the bobwhite is the quail of the South and East and the California quail is the dominant species in the far West. The Desert Southwest is quail mecca with Gambel's, Mearns', and scaled (blue) quail all running around in various habitats. The largest quail is California's mountain quail, which can also be found in a few places in Oregon, Washington, and Idaho.

All quail can be used interchangeably in the kitchen, although mountain quail are large enough to be used in partridge recipes. There are slight differences in flavor, differences I attribute more to diet than to species. All are mild, white-meat birds with just enough wild flavor to let you know that this isn't some flaccid store-bought quail. Store-bought quail are mostly *cotornix*, a species not found wild in North America.

I primarily pluck and cook quail whole, but many people breast them out. This is fine, but it misses what's special about these birds: the perfect balance of mild and gamy that makes quail so popular as table fare. Besides, the legs on a quail are tender and fun to gnaw on.

One quail is a nice appetizer; two are a decent entrée. I've eaten four with no trouble. Quail are delicate, so be extra careful not to overcook them.

GROUSE

Grouse are a hard bird to classify. There are so many species, and some are red-meat birds, some are white, and some are both. Grouse are North America's native "chicken," and each one occupies a different habitat.

Opposite: My friend Alex Blanche hikes up a Colorado mountain in search of ptarmigan.

Ruffed grouse are creatures of the deciduous forest and are the most wide-ranging species, huntable from California to the Canadian Maritimes. They like cooler climates, so in the South they're found only at elevation. They are the most popular grouse to hunt and eat, since they're, essentially, forest chickens. But better. Much better.

The blue grouse—which now comprises two distinct species, the dusky and the sooty grouse—is second on the popularity list. These are birds of the Western forests and are large, white-meat "tree chickens" that love to hang out in big conifers. It's my favorite grouse to eat, and can be alternately frustrating or ridiculous to hunt; in one habitat they can be more elusive than ruffies, and in another they can be so dim that they'll let you kill them with rocks.

There are two grouse of the Great Plains, the sharp-tailed and the prairie chicken (and there's a greater and lesser prairie chicken). Sharpies and prairie chickens are both dark-meat birds and need to be treated in the kitchen more like doves, pigeons, or ducks. Those who deem them to be inferior table fare (and many do) are, more often then not, trying to force a sharpie-shaped peg into a ruffie-shaped hole. Don't do it. Sharpies and ruffies are distinctly different animals and need to be treated as such. Incidentally, there are a total of six sharp-tailed grouse subspecies that range from Alaska and northern Canada through the Mountain West and plains down to about Nebraska.

The funkiest grouse of them all is the ptarmigan, of which there are three varieties. All are deeply dark-meat birds. Ptarmigan are the smallest of the grouse, more like chukars in size.

That leaves the spruce grouse and the sage grouse. Both are oddballs in the kitchen. The sprucey is an amazing bird to eat if shot in autumn before the snow flies. Once snow blankets the ground, the spruce grouse switches its diet to spruce needles, which can give the meat a whiff of turpentine. Not terrible, but very pronounced.

Similarly, the sage grouse tastes like the sagebrush it eats. It's a special bird in that the breast meat is dark, like a sharpie's, but its legs and wings are white meat. It's one of a few "opposite birds" I know of, another being the woodcock. Sage hens are fantastic eating, but a big boomer of a rooster can be a little tough on the tooth. One particularly odd fact about sage grouse is that they don't have gizzards in the traditional sense, so you can't use them in gizzard recipes.

Since sage grouse are in decline, you're likely to eat only one or two a season. Do them the service of plucking them—sage grouse are the easiest grouse to pluck—and serving up every little bit. They'll make a meal to remember.

If you happen to be reading this in Scandinavia, a capercaillie is basically a sage grouse with a different diet, an especially large, dark-meat grouse of up to six-and-a-half pounds each.

Grouse are definitely candidates for roasting whole, especially ruffies and blues. The drumsticks can be a little sinewy, but not terribly so.

One thing to remember with grouse is that there is no other class of birds whose flavor so depends on its skin and fat. A skinned ruffed grouse is essentially a boring chicken. With its skin on and intact, a ruffed grouse may well be the best thing I've ever eaten. They can be tricky to pluck, but I will walk you through it in the pages ahead.

In general, a grouse will serve one or two people, with the exception of a rooster sage grouse, which can run upward of seven pounds and can serve four or more. It's a little sad to serve one ruffed grouse to two people, but if you have other lovely things on the plate, you'll be forgiven.

Grouse can go from amazing to dry in a heartbeat; this is especially true with the dark-meat grouse. For some reason, dark-meat grouse breasts go from rare to gray in seconds. Not to worry—I'll

show you a special way to cook them when we get to the recipes.

PARTRIDGES

There are no partridges native to North America, but the two that have been introduced here, the Hungarian partridge and the chukar, are doing quite well. Both have relatively restricted ranges.

Huns are a northern bird, found primarily in the high desert of eastern Oregon, Washington, and Idaho; in the northern Great Plains states, especially the Canadian provinces that adjoin them; and in bits of Ontario and the western part of the Upper Midwest. They like big, rolling, grassy hills.

Chukars prefer nastier terrain. Native to the Caucasus Mountains, here they are birds of the Great Basin—the rocky, cool deserts of Utah, Nevada, and Idaho. They can also be found in far eastern California and in some parts of eastern Oregon and Washington. You'll find them on rocky mountains with steep inclines.

Huns and chukars are both wonderful to eat— white-meat birds with tender legs and a mild disposition at the table. Think of them as big quail. I usually pluck and serve them whole, although I have a specific way of spatchcocking them that I'll get into later.

Figure on one partridge per person; two is a lot but will be appreciated by hearty eaters. Like quail, their flavor is delicate. Don't overcook them.

DOVES AND PIGEONS

Doves are the krill of the air: everything eats them, and they are one of the most abundant birds in the Western Hemisphere. We have three huntable doves in the United States: the mourning, the white-winged, and the Eurasian collared. The mourning dove is the most common, with the white-winged dove occupying the dry southwestern parts of the country. The Eurasian collared dove, which is a non-native invasive species, is spreading across the country; one great thing about these is that there's often no season or limit on them.

Pigeons occupy a similar space. With one exception, pigeons are unprotected in most states and fair game all year long. The exception is the western band-tailed pigeon, which is still recovering after being overhunted in the 1970s; limits on these fine birds are restrictive, and if you get a brace, make a special meal of them.

All members of the family Columbidae are dark-meat birds that are rarely fat. With meat that is lean and very fine grained, doves and pigeons can be top-notch table fare. Their flavor can be best described as rich and unusually savory for their size. Their legs are tender and best cooked medium. This is important. If cooked any more than medium, the breast meat of pigeons and doves begins to resemble overcooked liver.

Since doves and pigeons are the easiest birds to pluck, I pluck all but the most shot-up. Most often, I cook them whole and on the grill. But I recognize that many people breast out their birds, so I include several recipes for boneless dove breast meat, too, including the venerable popper, a Labor Day tradition (Hank's Dove Poppers, page 253).

One pigeon per person is nice; two are a bit much. Unless it's a Eurasian collared dove, one dove is scanty, even for an appetizer. Two make a good appetizer portion, and four a good entrée. Three Eurasians make a hearty meal.

When cooking, remember the "liver" rule: unless you're stewing it, you want the whole bird cooked medium-rare to medium.

SNIPE, WOODCOCK, AND RAILS

I put these three birds together largely because they are small birds of wet places. They also share many flavor similarities, which is to say they are, shall we say, unique.

Rails are hunted mostly in the South, often from boats. Huntable species include the sora, clapper, and Virginia rail. Aficionados say they are best skinned and cooked like ducks. Snipe and woodcock, along with doves, are the smallest birds we hunt and really ought to be cooked whole. Both are darlings of French haute cuisine, and deservedly so. They look pretty on a plate and have an absolutely enchanting flavor—the best way I can describe it is a cross between duck and grouse. Gamy, but in a good way. When you bite into one, you know you're eating something special.

Snipe are so small that you need two to four per person as an entrée. With woodcock, you can get away with one per person (and you may have to— it's hard to get them in ample numbers). Serving royalty? A brace is best.

FUR

COTTONTAIL RABBITS AND SNOWSHOE HARES

Bunnies. The iconic combination of cute and tasty. Cottontail rabbits are to small mammals what doves are to the birds: krill, bottom of the food chain, eaten by everything. Because they don't tend to live long, they tend to be tender— one of the very few wild animals tender enough to fry like a chicken.

Cottontails come in a range of sizes, from the tiny desert cottontails that average about two pounds to the big northern rabbits that can routinely hit four-and-a-half pounds. There are even a few places in North America, notably Washington State, that have invasive European rabbits.

The snowshoe hare is cousin to the cottontail, and I include them here and not with the other hares because snowshoes have white meat, or at least meat that is whiter than that of jackrabbits. Snowshoes prefer cold places and are found throughout Canada, in all the northern states, and, at elevation, as far south as California, the Rockies, and the Appalachian Mountains. Snowshoes average about four pounds.

Cottontails and snowshoes both have mild, delicate meat. Along with pheasant and quail, they are the most approachable small-game meats for newcomers.

One little rabbit will serve one person; a normal bunny will serve two. Snowshoes can serve up to three, but one snowshoe for two people is a nice, hearty meal. Rabbit is prone to drying out, so be careful if you cook it hot and dry, as you would on a grill. Stews and braises are my go-to here, although I do love me some chicken-fried cottontail.

HARES

Ah, the unloved jackrabbit. Jacks are hares, and hares are a popular game meat all over Europe. How did they get so despised here? I mentioned the legacy of poverty in my introduction (page 11), but there is also the question of parasites. Yes, hares carry them. Often. I delve more into this on page 49.

Still, hares are great table fare—red meat, mild, and rich. Think of jacks as little deer. They can range from four-pound leverets (young hares) to massive, fifteen-pound brutes. The largest are the Arctic hares of the north and the antelope jackrabbit of the Desert Southwest. Yes, there really is a jackalope: *Lepus alleni* (no antlers, though). We also have black-tailed and white-tailed jackrabbits scattered throughout North America.

White-tailed jacks are a northern animal, common in the northern Great Plains into Canada, although they're found from eastern Washington out to the northern Great Lakes. Black-tailed jacks are their hot-weather cousins, ranging from California to the southern Great Plains.

And, like the European rabbit, the European hare can sometimes be found in North America, notably in Ontario and New York. They're also in New Zealand and Australia.

Hares are a dark-meat animal, and, since they can live several years in the wild, they can be tough. Braises and stews are the rule here, with the exception of the hare's backstrap, which on a large animal can be removed like a tiny deer loin. This cut is excellent in stir-fries or any way you want to serve red meat medium-rare.

One typical hare will serve two hearty eaters; in a stew or braise, a hare can serve four, a big one even more.

SQUIRRELS

My friend Steven Rinella calls squirrels "the thinking man's chicken." Another friend, Arkansan Chef Jonathan Wilkins, calls them "tree ninjas." Both nicknames are true. Squirrels are their own thing. Neither white meat nor dark, squirrel meat is grayish, like the thigh meat on a heritage chicken. It's dense, sweet, and nutty—in short, amazing. Squirrel is my favorite small mammal to eat, hands down, no contest.

There are a great many huntable squirrels in the United States, the most common being the eastern gray squirrel, followed by the fox squirrel. The eastern gray comes in three colors: ruddy gray, black (often called Algonquin blacks), and, rarely, white. Fox squirrels are larger and are mostly reddish, but they can come in all sorts of colors; in the Deep South, there's a black-and-white variant.

Out West, the squirrel stars are the western gray, whose coat is a cooler blue-gray than that of the eastern gray, and the Abert's squirrel of the southern Rockies. Both are excellent eating.

Determining age in squirrels can be tricky. Looking at the teeth is one way: old squirrels have yellow teeth with a gap in between. Size is a better clue. Young squirrels are small. These are the only ones that can be chicken-fried without parcooking (cooked partially for finishing later). Mostly, I stew or braise squirrels, though. A squirrel is a single-serving animal.

Yes, there are several red squirrel species that are legal game, but I find them too small to bother with, and besides, most are pine eaters and can taste of turpentine.

SMALL GAME IN THE SUPERMARKET

A wonderful thing about small game is that it's easily accessible to a non-hunter. Every supermarket in America carries turkey, and most carry quail. Increasingly, a look in the freezer section will turn up rabbit, pheasant, and sometimes even squab.

True wild game is harder to come by. It must be imported from the United Kingdom, and, while excellent in quality, it isn't cheap. A dedicated non-hunter who wants to eat a real hare or a Scottish grouse or a red-legged partridge can do so—but it'll cost you. By far the best source for this sort of game is D'Artagnan Foods in New Jersey. Their website offers a variety of British wild game via mail order. My advice: pounce on their freezer specials, which will save you tons of money.

And one fascinating note: the Scottish grouse that D'Artagnan sells is essentially a ptarmigan.

Dark, rich, and definitely gamy, it's a deep dive into the world of exotic upland birds.

If you're reading this in the United Kingdom, note that the rules are different there than in the States. Sale of true wild game is still legal in the UK. Most of the animals I write about in this book can be bought in your local supermarket—even gray squirrels, which are considered an invasive pest in Britain.

When considering these store-bought facsimiles of true game animals, there are a few things to keep in mind. First, they are all younger and weaker than their wild counterparts, lacking the depth of flavor and muscle tone of wild ones. For example, while most wild roosters live only a year, it's not uncommon to shoot two- and three-year-olds. A store-bought (or pen-raised) pheasant is normally about three months old—yet even this is a far more mature bird than the typical fryer chicken, which is slaughtered at six to eight weeks. That difference can be dramatic in the kitchen.

Farmed animals are normally larger and fatter than wild ones. This is definitely the case with pheasants, rabbits, and squab. I've seen plenty of twenty-pound-plus wild turkeys, but they are invariably old and lean compared to their fat, farmed cousins, and I've seen some farmed pheasants every bit as big as a chicken. An exception on size is quail. Most store-bought quail are a Japanese breed called *Coturnix japonica*; they're tiny compared to California or mountain quail, and are even smaller than eastern bobwhites.

Partial exceptions to these general farmed-versus-wild rules can be found at the farmer's market. As more and more people get into small-scale livestock farming, we're seeing better-quality animals for sale. A rabbit from a farmer's market will almost always be of better quality than one from the supermarket, and if you can find someone raising bobwhite quail for the market, buy all you can.

The pinnacle of this phenomenon are those "Gucci turkeys," old-school heritage-breed birds normally ordered in spring and slaughtered for Thanksgiving. These turkeys, which are typically about seven months old, are very similar to good, young, wild turkeys—like jakes (young males)—except that they will be heavier and more tender. They aren't cheap, but if you want a taste of the wild, this is the closest thing to it.

Know that if you're using farmed animals for the recipes in this book, you'll almost always need to decrease cooking time to account for the younger age and the less athletic careers of store-bought critters. Just have your wits about you at the stove and you'll be fine.

A word on furbearers and other small creatures. I've seen oddities like raccoon and opossum for sale in markets in places as disparate as Los Angeles and St. Louis, and I distinctly remember my shock as a teenager seeing quartered armadillos in New York's Chinatown. Muskrat is a fairly normal market item from southeast Pennsylvania through Maryland and Delaware. Keep your eyes open. You never know what you'll find.

CHAPTER 2

SMALL GAME FROM FIELD TO KITCHEN
HANGING, SKINNING, GUTTING, AND BREAKING IT DOWN

HANGING GAME

For several years after I began hunting, I recoiled at the idea of hanging game birds. The notion of hanging shot pheasants or partridges undrawn and in the feathers for days and days just didn't seem terribly hygienic or sane to me. Old texts wax rhapsodic about the sublime flavor of "high" game, which usually means pheasants and usually means birds that have hung for more than a week. This, I decided, was madness.

I was wrong.

So I took a careful, systematic look at the science of hanging game birds. Happily, among the scores of game cookbooks in my library (I'm a bit of a collecting fanatic for these tomes of culinary wisdom), there are several that discuss hanging game.

Nearly everyone who reads this would probably agree with me that dry-aged beef is the finest expression of that meat. It's concentrated, savory, and tender. It's also very expensive, because dry-aging necessarily means a layer of crusty, slightly moldy ick on the outer edges of the meat, which is removed before selling or serving.

Hanging beef is important, in part because these animals tend to be dispatched when they're between eighteen and twenty-four months old—old enough to get a tad tough for the teeth. The same holds true for venison, only more so. Think about it: a whitetail buck sporting trophy antlers is likely to be four to seven years old. Conversely, we don't hang pork—or chickens, for that matter—because hogs and chickens are slaughtered young. Young animals are already tender, so the tenderizing function of aging isn't needed.

Enter the pheasant. A pheasant really is a "ditch chicken." It's a close cousin of the domestic chicken, and when eaten fresh, it has, as the great gastronome Jean Anthelme Brillat-Savarin puts it in his *The Physiology of Taste*, "nothing distinguishing about it. It is neither as delicate as a pullet, nor as savorous as a quail." Those who have eaten fresh pheasant—and by fresh, I mean un-hung—can't help but wonder what all the fuss is about.

Brillat-Savarin doesn't give a specific timetable for aging, but says that "the peak is reached when the pheasant begins to decompose; its aroma develops, and mixes with an oil which in order to form must undergo a certain amount of fermentation, just as the oil in coffee can only be drawn out by roasting it." Sounds pretty hardcore.

American game cook Roy Wall wrote in 1945, "The flesh of either wild game or domesticated animals and fowl can certainly be improved by aging, but it is my opinion that there must be a limit to the aging process.... Aging in the open air for 10 days or a month, according to weather conditions, is, in my opinion, most beneficial to domestic and wild meat alike."

Don't panic. Roy doesn't specify what game he's talking about there, and aging an old buck deer in proper conditions for a month isn't such a crazy idea, although I'd probably take it down after three weeks. More recently, Clarissa Dickson Wright, one of the *Two Fat Ladies*, my favorite TV food personalities, says of pheasant, "Hang it you must, even if for only three days, for all meat must be allowed to rest and mature." Clarissa's preference is a week to ten days.

Another Briton, Hugh Fearnley-Whittingstall, in his *The River Cottage Meat Book*, says, "Four or five days would be about right for me" if a bird is hung at 55°F.

This is what the food writers say. What about science?

Fortunately, science exists on the topic of hanging game birds. My best source is an Australian government publication that did some rigorous experiments. For example:

> *Pheasants hung for 9 days at 50°F have been found by overseas taste panels to be more acceptable than those hung for 4 days at 59°F or for 18 days at 41°F. The taste panels thought that the birds stored at 59°F were tougher than those held for longer periods at lower temperatures. Pheasants hung at 50°F became more 'gamy' in flavor and more tender with length of hanging.*

One issue solved. Food writers rarely talk about hanging temperature because most of them think about hanging pheasant outdoors, which is fine if you don't live in a warm place. It seems that 50°F is ideal and 55°F is acceptable.

Furthermore, an English study from 1973 found that *clostridia* and *E. coli* bacteria form rapidly at about 60°F, but slowly—or not at all in the case of *clostridia*—at 50°F. That same study found that field care of the birds is vital. Under no circumstances should you allow pheasants to pile up in warm conditions, because doing so will slow cooling so much that the dead birds will develop bacteria in their innards. This is *no bueno*.

Also note that the study's 39°F upper limit corresponds with the maximum storage temperature allowed by the European Union. Although storing birds at this cool a temperature, even for up to a week, won't develop much of the hung flavor that European food writers rhapsodize over, it will result in a more tender bird.

All the tests for bacteria and taste converge on two things: a temperature range of 50°F to 55°F and a hanging period of three to seven days. That's your takeaway, folks.

Over the years, I've come to these conclusions on hang time:

- Pheasants, grouse, and partridges I hang whole and in the feathers for three to seven days, depending on how old they were. Because turkeys are so large, I *always* gut them before hanging so the carcass can cool faster, and I hang them anywhere from one to five days, depending on age.

- Pen-raised pheasants, quail, woodcock, and snipe I age for only one to three days—again, depending on size and age. The smaller the bird and the younger the bird, the shorter the hang time.

Left undiscussed is the importance of feathers and innards. A 2008 study showed measurable loss of quality in *ungutted* pheasants hung at a fairly low 39°F for more than a week, suggesting that a week is the upper end of hang time in terms of absolute food safety. Data suggest that gutted pheasants, with the cavity wiped dry with paper towels, can hang longer. I myself am on the fence about guts. I think they do add something: fish guts will affect the fillets because of the animal's digestive enzymes. And data suggest that enzymes in the bacteria within the animal's innards do play a role in creating that hung flavor, although at 50°F to 55°F this is going to take some time to develop (for what it's worth, a living pheasant's body temperature runs about 105°F).

To eat the giblets or not? For birds aged up to three days that have not been shot up, I'd say go for it. If there's any sign of ickiness in the innards, toss them. If you're unsure, one way to tell is to use your nose: If the giblets stink, toss it.

As for feathers, Brillat-Savarin speaks about a mysterious "oil," and Wall talks about bacterial decomposition. Here's my take: the feathers provide protection for the skin against drying out during aging. Pluck the feathers right away and you can still age the bird, but the skin will be unacceptably dried out and therefore unusable. But don't try to wet-pluck an aged game bird. You must dry-pluck these birds because the skin gets looser and scalding does not seem to help with the feathers. The good news is that aged birds pluck much more easily than fresh ones.

So, to wrap up:

- Keep your birds as cool and as separated as possible in the field. If the weather is warm, try to use a game strap, not the game bag in your vest. Separate your birds in the truck or put them in a cooler. And do not get them wet.

- Hanging your birds by the neck or feet does not matter (several studies confirm this).

- Hang the birds between 50°F and 55°F for at least three days and up to a week with an old rooster. Old roosters will have horny beaks, blunt spurs, and feet that look like they've gone the distance. They will also have a stiff, heavy keel bone. Pen-raised hen pheasants need only three days.

- Do not hang any game birds that have been gut-shot or are generally torn up. Butcher these immediately.

- Dry-pluck any bird that has hung for three or more days.

- Wash and dry your birds after you pluck and draw them. Only then should you freeze them.

One more thing. Every so often you'll see what I call "green butt." This happens when you've hung gut-shot birds. It's caused by bacteria in the perforated guts going to work on the surrounding tissue. Hydrogen sulfide is one of its byproducts—that's the stink in your nostrils—and it's a sign of spoilage. Not great, but you can still salvage any meat not associated with the greening; typically this means breast meat. That Australian government publication suggests wiping down the plucked carcass with vinegar in cases of greening.

Can you hang rabbits, hares, and squirrels? Yes, but I rarely do. The awful smell of the guts, even after just a couple of days, will lodge itself in your nostrils for hours. And since you're typically braising these animals anyway, hanging doesn't do much good.

SKINNING, PLUCKING, AND GUTTING SMALL GAME

SKINNING RABBITS AND HARES

Rabbits and hares are the easiest to skin. They have a very loose pelt that comes off quickly; all you need is a pair of stout kitchen shears (I like the Wusthof breakaway shears with the bone notch). Use that bone notch on the shears to snip off the feet, the tail, and the head, either before or after skinning. Now pull up the pelt on the center of the rabbit's or hare's back and snip it perpendicular to the backbone. Jam the first two fingers of each hand into the opening you just made and yank in opposite directions. The pelt will come off easily. You might need to finish it off on the belly, which sometimes stays on after the initial yanking. But it's a quick process, no more than a minute or so.

Note: In these photos, I'm working with a wild New Zealand rabbit, which doesn't have the same parasite risk as rabbits in North America and elsewhere. Unless you happen to be down under, consider wearing gloves when butchering rabbits.

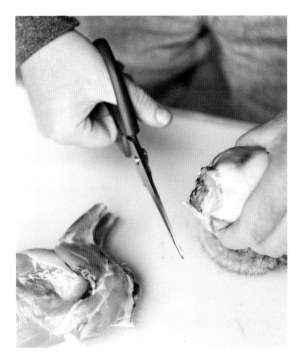

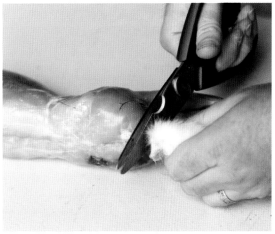

SKINNING AND GUTTING SQUIRRELS

Skinning a squirrel, with its thick, dense hide, is a bit harder than skinning a rabbit. Start by snipping off Mr. Squirrel's head, feet, and tail with the shears using the bone-cutting notch at the base of the shears (just as for a rabbit). Some people like squirrel brains, but I'm not one of them. I toss the head.

You are now left with a sad-looking, tailless, headless squirrel. Take your knife in one hand, and with the other, pinch up the loose skin at the center of the squirrel's back. Just like with the rabbit, use the knife to make an incision perpendicular to the squirrel's backbone about an inch long.

To skin the squirrel, work the fingers of each hand under the skin through the incision you just made. Now pull—I mean really pull!—and the skin will come off in each direction. You'll get it most of the way, but the skin will hang up under the legs and at the center of the belly. Poke your finger through under the legs to free the skin from them. Use the knife to carefully start the belly skin going, then pull it, too. It takes a little practice, but you'll get the hang of it.

There are people who do the tail-yank method, and while I've seen it work on video, I've never been able to master it. Basically, you take a knife, cut through the bone at the base of the tail, and then stand firmly on the tail. Grab the squirrel's hind legs and stand up. If you're lucky, this will wrench most of the skin off the carcass. Except, of course, for the skin on the hind legs, which you'll need to pull off separately.

Gutting small mammals is more or less like gutting a larger animal, only smaller.

Use the knife, with the blade facing away from the guts, to open up the paunch. Its guts will spill out. With your fingers, reach upward toward the heart and lungs and wrench them out. Save the heart. If you want, save the liver and kidneys, too— although I never save livers from wild rabbits or hares (see Food Safety, page 48). Use the kitchen shears to split the pelvis so you can get the remaining bits of poop chute out.

Incidentally, rabbits are the only animal I gut while wearing nitrile or latex gloves. While the chance of my catching a parasite or disease is small, it's higher than the chances of getting sick while gutting, say, a deer or a pheasant.

Wash the animal well under clean, cold, running water. Now you're ready to break the animal into serving pieces.

 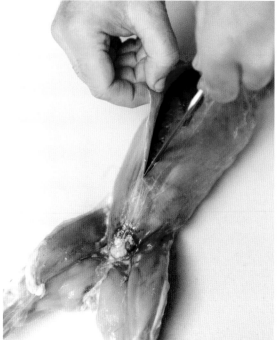

PLUCKING AND SKINNING BIRDS

Not every bird needs to be, or even should be, plucked. I prefer plucked birds, to be sure, but even I, a self-avowed plucking evangelist, don't pluck all my birds. Here are the guidelines I use to determine which birds get skinned and which get plucked.

Let's start with the obvious: skin your center-patterned birds (see the sidebar on page 34, What to do with a Blown-Up Bird, on what to do with such a mess). Skin birds that your dog or, God forbid, someone else's dog, mauled on its way back to you. Mauled birds will still be fine to eat, but with broken bones and bruised skin or meat, there's no real point in spending the time to pluck them.

Pluck all your doves and pigeons—unless they're mangled, of course. Plucking doves and pigeons is easy. Once you get the hang of it, you can pluck a dove in about ninety seconds; its feathers just fall away (which is one reason many dogs don't like picking up doves—the feathers get stuck in their mouths).

Beyond that, things get more subjective. For the most part, I pluck all my upland game birds that are well shot—wingshot, head shot, or otherwise "lightly killed." I do this because I rarely ever kill that many in a day. Five grouse, ten quail, a trio of pheasants—typical upland bag limits are small enough so you'll never face the scary task you can face in waterfowling, where you might come home with seven ducks and several dozen geese. The only exception to this is on those rare occasions when I find myself on a preserve where there's no limit on pen-raised birds. I've shot a half-dozen pheasants at such places, and I know people who routinely shoot many times that number. In those cases, my advice is to pick and choose: pluck a few choice birds and skin the rest.

With turkeys, I pluck jakes and hens and skin old toms. I find that the skin on an old tom can be overly thick and leathery, and while I can make even that skin taste great, for me, the eating payoff versus the time invested to pluck a tom isn't worth it. A jake or a hen is a different story. They are typically younger, and their skin is much more like that of a store-bought turkey. And if you aren't one of those people fighting over the Thanksgiving turkey skin, you need to get into that scrum. You don't know what you're missing.

Ultimately, whether to pluck or not to pluck is up to you. The skin on upland birds is delicious, it provides protection to the meat, which is prone to drying out, and it's the center of any given bird's character in the kitchen. A skinless grouse breast is OK, but not so different from a skinless chicken breast. But add the skin, and you'll suddenly understand why the grouse is the king of all game birds.

ON PLUCKING GAME BIRDS

Plucking upland game birds can be tricky. Their skin is thinner and far looser than that of a duck or a goose, and the feathers cling to the skin more tightly than they do on a dove or pigeon. Chances are you've wanted to pluck and roast a pretty grouse or pheasant, tried to do it, ripped the skin, cursed a few times, then skinned the bird out of frustration. It happens.

Plucking a bird is an act very much like unearthing an archaeological treasure. It can be a painstaking business—frustrating and messy—and yet, when you're done, it can be deeply rewarding. In an odd way, it's an act of love. You're working hard to bring out the best in your birds. For me, plucking a bird is a calming process, a task I can Zen out on, focusing only on the next feather. Plucking occupies the same mind space for me as making pasta: mindless yet highly focused.

Yes, I'm good at it. Repetition will do that for you. But I'm here to help you build this skill.

Why bother? Because a bird's distinctiveness resides primarily in the skin and fat. I've written extensively about the relationship between fat and flavor, but suffice to say that if you skin your birds, you'll have a hard time telling a bite of factory-farmed chicken breast from a bite of pheasant breast. Really. Trust me. I've done blind tests.

From a cook's perspective, dry-plucking is by far the best method of removing feathers from an upland bird. Dry-plucking is what it says it is: you sit with a bird and pluck off all its feathers. This is most likely what you've tried before, with varying degrees of success. Let me walk you through it.

To start, you need patience and a good, sharp set of kitchen shears. The shears are used to clip the wingtips and to remove the bird's head and feet. Find yourself a place outside or in a garage where you can clean up all those feathers. Don't do this in a kitchen.

In most cases, you'll be plucking your birds before gutting them. The most common exception is for a turkey that has been hung for several days. Can you pluck a gutted bird? Sure, but it's a lot harder. Intact skin, and the tension you can create working with that intact skin, will make the job easier.

If you can, begin your plucking adventure in September, with dove season. Doves are easy to pluck, and so long as you don't manhandle the birds as you're plucking, things will go quickly. Don't rub off the feathers the way you might do with a duck; that will tear or bruise the skin. Pluck. I tend to slip my thumb across the bird's skin and pluck by snatching feathers between my forefinger and thumb in quick little wrist snaps. You're not *pulling* feathers, you're *plucking* them. No feathers on a dove or pigeon are held in so tight that you'll need to worry about ripping the skin. Have a light hand and you'll get the hang of it in a few tries.

Moving on to upland birds, I can tell you in no uncertain terms that dry-plucking an upland game bird is something of an art; you will absolutely mess up birds before you master this skill. But it's not wizardry. All you need is a touch of finesse. And a plan.

Here's the plan. Start on the back and the wings. Remember: *pluck*, don't pull. Use a quick snap of the wrist to yank the feather out quickly while anchoring that loose skin at the base of the feather with the thumb of your other hand. Under no circumstances should you try to grab more than a few feathers at a time. You *will* tear the skin.

The tail and back are the easiest. Start by pulling out each tail feather individually (you can grab a few at a time when you get better at it), pulling directly away from the body of the pheasant. These and the flight feathers of the wings are the only feathers you actually pull.

Use that same thumb-and-forefinger action you use with doves on the back feathers, plucking them out from the tail toward the head—in other words, against the grain. You'll soon notice fluffy little under feathers, often gray. These come out very easily by gently sweeping them off with your thumb and forefinger—*gently* being the operative word. This action is where a lot of hunters bruise skin.

Clip the wingtips. On large birds like pheasants and big grouse, I keep two sections of the wings; on smaller birds, I keep only the drumette. Chances are you'll have at least one wing that was broken. Clip that off to the undamaged portion; for example, if you broke the wing farther out than the drumette, clip to save the drumette.

Yank out the flight feathers on the wings one at a time. Now use the thumb-and-forefinger method to remove the other feathers on the wing, going against the grain. The very small feathers on the leading edge of the wings need to be removed almost one at a time, plucking in toward the body of the bird while holding the wing taut and outstretched with the other hand.

Moving on to the body, I like to begin with the drumsticks. Hold the bird by its feet and pluck down toward the body. Stop when you get to the big feathers on the thighs. You can pluck the area around the anal vent now, too. You'll probably also need to spend a few seconds focusing on where feathers meet feet. On grouse, which have fuzzy feet, this is especially true.

Go to the neck. You'll now see those two types of feathers clearly. There are larger, quill-type feathers overlaying those little fuzzy under feathers. Start with the under feathers, as they are easier. Anchoring the base of the neck with your off hand, pluck off the larger feathers one or two at a time, moving from the base of the neck toward the head. The neck is a little rippy, but don't sweat it.

Look at the breast and thighs. You'll see some very long quill feathers. To pluck these quill feathers correctly, anchor the skin above the feather near the base and pluck each feather in the same direction as it's attached, that is to say, *with* the grain. It's very important to do only one or two feathers at a time when you get to these feathers, which are on each side of the breast and the flanks of the bird. Take your time here, and don't despair if you get little rips.

Save the center of the breast for last: the little feathers are a breeze, and you get a satisfying

PLUCKING SNIPE: A SPECIAL CASE

Snipe are an odd bird in many ways, not least of which is the process used to get their feathers off. Snipe are a shorebird, and plucking them is a sort of hybrid experience between an upland bird and a duck. Why? Snipe have down, like a duck.

I have dry-plucked more than my share of snipe, and it works fine. But you have thousands of tiny black down feathers that you need to deal with. A half-plucked snipe looks like a man's legs in winter. Not appetizing. Picking these little feathers one by one is a massive pain.

The answer is to wax them, the way you'd wax a duck. Add a standard block of paraffin canning wax (about four ounces) to a pot of scalding water (between 140°F and 150°F). While the wax is melting, carefully pluck the snipe's tail feathers and some of its largest flight feathers. Dip the partially plucked snipe into the melted wax to coat it, and then toss the bird into a bucket of cold water to set the wax. You want the wax to be hard, so let the bird soak for a good few minutes.

Once the wax hardens, remove the snipe from the bucket and carefully crack and remove the wax coating. The feathers will come away with the wax.

A few tips: first, you don't want a very thick coat of wax—if you entomb the snipe in wax, it will be harder to remove the wax without ripping the skin; second, always move the skin away from the wax, using your thumb or forefinger—do not tear away the wax or you will rip the skin. Free the skin from the wax, not the other way 'round.

WHAT TO DO WITH A BLOWN-UP BIRD

It happens to the best of us. An upland bird flushes close—sometimes you almost step on them—you get flustered, forget to wait, and *crack!* You annihilate the poor thing at five yards. What to do? It's part of your bag, after all.

If you have a particularly adventurous cat, this will be a nice treat for her. But a better fate for your "pillowed" bird is the soup pot. Yep, make soup. Pull off as much skin and feathers as you can, remove the guts, and rinse the bird. You can then either pat it dry(ish) with paper towels, coat the carcass in oil, salt it, and roast it for a soup base; or you can just toss it into the soup pot as is. If you do that, when the water comes to a simmer, a froth will form at the surface; this is blood and other proteins coagulating. Skim this off and go from there.

If this sounds odd, think for a moment: most chicken, pheasant, and turkey broths are made with the leftover carcasses of whole birds (see chapter 4, page 51). This method will make an even better broth because the meat (well, most of the meat) is still on the carcass. Try it. You'll see.

"reveal" when the whole bird magically transforms from feathery carcass into something that looks like something you'd want to eat.

This method takes time, about five to ten minutes for a quail, twice that for a pheasant or grouse. But it results in beautiful birds for the table that look as good or better than birds bought at the market.

WET-PLUCKING

There is another way. Wet-plucking is how most chicken farmers de-feather their birds, and, when you consider that most upland birds are all chicken relatives, this method works well with hunted birds as well.

Wet-plucking basically means scalding the bird before plucking. To do this, you need to get a large pot of water and get it to scalding temperature. What is scalding temperature? Steaming, but not boiling—not even simmering. Shoot for between 140°F to 150°F.

Do one bird at a time. The scalding process works only when the feathers and skin are warm. Once they grow cold, you'll have a soggy mess. Work quickly and efficiently.

Heat the water before you start plucking. Once you have the water hot enough, pluck out the bird's tail feathers, one by one. Then grab the bird by the head or feet (I hold the feet) and plunge it into the scalding water. Hold it under for three to five seconds. Lift it out, and holding the bird above the pot, let it drain until the water stops coming off in a stream. Repeat this as many times as you need until a flight feather on the wing comes out easily. Three dunks is minimum, I find; I've needed six for some older birds.

Pluck the bird while it's still warm (wear a long apron or pants you don't care about). Start with the wings. Next, pluck the large feathers along the outer edges of the breast—carefully, as they can easily tear the skin, even when scalded. Then work on the flank feathers on the bird's thigh, go to the neck, and finish with the back and the rest of the legs. Take your time. Go feather by feather if need be, especially around the breast—you want it to look pretty, not torn.

TIPS AND TRICKS

If you have the opportunity to pluck a bird in the field while it's still warm, do it. The feathers will come off very easily, making even dry-plucking a breeze.

Cool birds and day-old birds are the hardest to pluck, but sadly, these are what most of us are faced with. A bird hung for several days (see Hanging Game, page 25) needs to be dry-plucked, but birds hung three days or more will pluck *way* more easily than one shot the day before. And by "hung" I mean stored. I've kept quail whole and in the feathers in the fridge for four days before plucking, and I found the going pretty easy.

Shot holes happen. This is hunting, after all. When you find one, anchor the skin all around the hole with the fingers of one hand and pluck away one feather at a time with the other. It's the only way to get feathers off without tearing the skin.

September grouse will have lots of pinfeathers. You just need to pick them all out one at a time. They come off easily, but can be a pain. Just focus on pulling the pinfeather, not the skin around it.

When you're finished plucking, gut the bird (save the giblets!) and wash it well. Dry the bird thoroughly with a paper towel, stuff a clean paper towel into the cavity, and then set him on another paper towel in the fridge for two to seven days. This cold-aging will help tenderize the bird, and because the bird will dry out a bit, its flavor will concentrate as well.

BREAKING DOWN SMALL GAME

HOW TO CUT UP A RABBIT OR HARE

Butchering a rabbit is a bit harder than cutting up a chicken. That and a higher feed-to-meat ratio is why America became a nation of chicken eaters and not rabbit eaters, a statistic that was actually in doubt a century ago.

All lagomorphs—rabbits and hares—are built alike, so you can use these steps for any variety of bunny you might have on hand.

Why butcher your own rabbits? If you're buying them, it's because whole rabbits are cheaper—sometimes a full $1.50 less per pound—than pre-portioned bunnies. And of course, hunters and livestock farmers need to know this skill.

First you need a very sharp knife; I use a boning knife, but a paring knife or a fillet knife will also work, as will a chef's knife. I also use a pair of kitchen shears. Have a clean towel handy to wipe your hands, and a bowl for trimmings. And for cottontails, wear gloves. As I'll explain below in the section on food safety, I routinely wear gloves when I butcher wild rabbits.

I often start cutting up a rabbit by removing the front legs, which are not attached to the body by bone (1). Slide your knife up from underneath, along the ribs, and slice through (2).

Usually there's some schmutz attached to the front leg that doesn't look like good eats: fat, sinew, and general non-meaty stuff. All this can go into pâté if you're so inclined. Or you can toss it.

Next comes the belly. (Sometimes I start with this.) A lot of people toss this part, but if you think about it, it's rabbit bacon! And who doesn't like bacon? In practice, this belly flap becomes a lovely, boneless bit in whatever dish you're making. It's also good in pâté or terrines.

Turn Mr. Bunny over and slice right along the line where the saddle (or loin) starts, then snip along that edge to the ribs (3). When you get to the ribcage, snip away from the body (4). Finish by trimming any schmutz off the edge; if you're using this part for pâté or terrines, leave the schmutz on.

1

2

Up next: the hind legs, which are the money cuts in a rabbit. Hunters take note: aim far forward on a rabbit, because even if you shoot up the loin, you really want the hind legs clean—they can be a full 40 percent of a gutted carcass's weight.

Start on the underside, slicing gently along the pelvic bones until you get to the ball-and-socket joint (5). When you do, grasp each end firmly and bend it back to pop the joint. (6) Then slice around the back leg with your knife to free it from the carcass (7, 8).

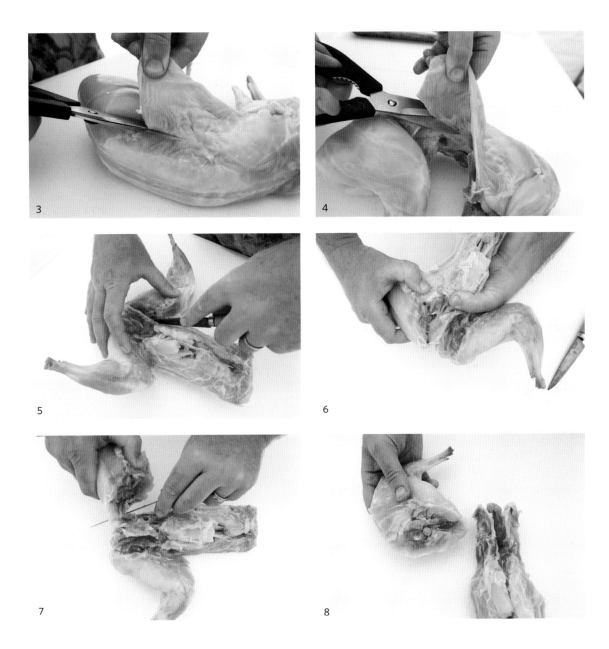

9

10

Once you've done both legs, you'll be left with
the loin. The loin is the part of the bunny that
really sealed its fate in not achieving the status of a
major meat animal when compared to the chicken.
Though both have a tendency to dry out, the
chicken won by virtue of its larger swath of boneless meat. And then, of course, there's that delicious chicken skin.

Now is a good time to remove silverskin. The
back of the loin has several layers, and most need to
be removed. The final layer is very tough to cut off,
and I often leave it. On a large hare or jackrabbit,
however, this layer needs to go, too (9, 10).

11

You're now ready to portion the saddle. Ever
heard the expression "long in the saddle?" It's an
animal husbandry term: a longer stretch of saddle
or loin means more high-dollar cuts come slaugh-
ter time. And meat rabbits have been bred to have a
very long saddle compared to wild cottontails.

Start by removing the pelvis, which is really
best in the stockpot. I do this by severing the spine,
which I do by setting the edge of a cleaver on the
spine and banging it with my palm. Good kitchen
shears will do the trick, too (11).

Now you grab your kitchen shears and snip off
the ribs, right at the line where the meat of the loin
starts. The ribs go into the stockpot, too (12).

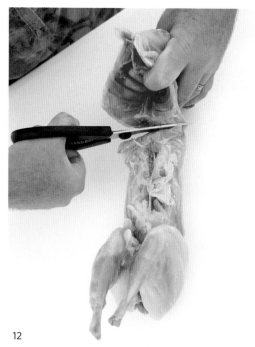

12

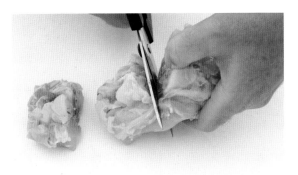

13

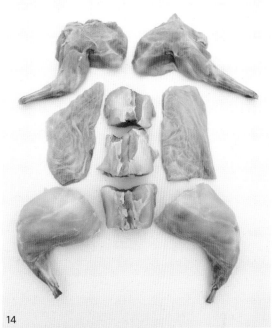

14

Guess what? There's more silverskin to slice off. Could you do it all in one fell swoop? You bet, but it's delicate work and I like to break it up to keep my mental edge. The reason for all this delicate work is that the loin is softer than the silverskin, and if you cook it with the skin on, it will contract and push the loin meat out either side. Ugly. And besides, if you're making Buttermilk Fried Rabbit (page 185), who wants to eat sinew?

Your last step is to chop the loin into serving pieces. I do this by using my boning knife to slice a guideline through to the spine. Then I give the spine a whack with the cleaver, or I snip it with kitchen shears (13).

And *voila*! A bunny cut into lots of soon-to-be-delicious serving pieces (14).

What about the offal, you ask? More on that later (chapter 13, page 294), but suffice it to say that the livers and hearts of a rabbit are pretty much like those of a chicken. The kidneys are delicious, too. Remove the fat (rabbit fat tends to be foul tasting) and peel the nearly invisible membrane off the kidney before cooking (15, 16).

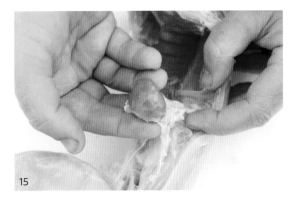

15

16

HOW TO CUT UP A SQUIRREL

Squirrel butchery is like all butchery—different people do it different ways. Some simmer them whole. The Hmong hunters I know like the skin, so they scald their squirrels and scrape off the hair or just toss them into the fire to burn it off. I admit that I have yet to try this.

So I will assume you're starting with a skinned squirrel (page 29). Start by washing the squirrel in cold water, then dry the carcasses with paper towels.

I start by removing the legs. The front legs of most mammals are completely free of the rest of the skeleton. Not ours—our "front legs" are attached by a collarbone. And so are Mr. Squirrel's. He's the only game animal I know of that is so endowed. Even so, use your knife to slice down to the ribcage behind the front leg, then slice along the bones toward the squirrel's neck until you free the foreleg; you'll have to slice through a skinny little collar bone at the end. Do this on both forelegs.

The hind legs on pretty much everything, including us, are attached with a ball-and-socket joint. So, too, are a squirrel's. Use your knife to slice the meat on the inside of the squirrel's leg where it attaches to the body until you can see the ball joint. Bend the leg backward until you pop that joint out. Slice around it to free the legs. Do this with both sides.

You're almost done.

You're now left with the torso and belly flaps. I slice off the belly flaps and save them for either stock or stir-fries. That leaves the ribs and backstraps.

Use kitchen shears to snip off the ribs (save them for stock). Then portion out the backstrap. A big squirrel might give you two pieces, but most will yield just one. You can use either your shears to cut it (which requires a bit of strength) or your cleaver to whack it into pieces. One thing you definitely want to do is chop off the hips and the neck portions, as there isn't much meat there; again, save these bits for stock.

Don't worry if you mess up the first few attempts or if it takes you a while to complete. You'll get the hang of it, and when you do, this process can be done in less than five minutes per squirrel.

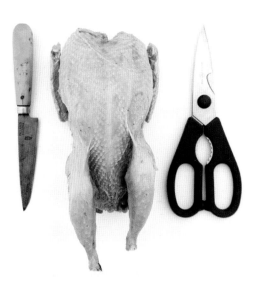

HOW TO CUT UP AN UPLAND BIRD

Cutting up an upland bird, whether it's a pheasant, a quail, or a turkey, is almost exactly the same as cutting up a chicken. If you know how to cut up a chicken, you're on your way. If you don't know how to cut a chicken into serving pieces, here's how I do it.

Have a sharp boning or paring knife at the ready. If you don't have one, a good alternative is a fillet knife for fish; it may be a little thin, but it's better than a chef's knife. And make sure your blade is sharp! Remember, a dull knife is a lazy servant. You'll want a pair of good kitchen shears, too.

Start with the legs. I press on the gap between the legs and the breast to push as much skin toward the breast as I can; a covering of skin keeps the breasts juicy and tender when you cook them. Slice down into the gap and you'll notice that you just sliced skin, not muscle—that's the key. Gently cut downward until you reach the ball-and-socket joint where the leg is attached (1).

Pop the joint (2). As you slice down around the joint, arc the knife under the back of the bird to get all the meat off the thigh (3).

Cut the leg free. As you cut past the socket joint, don't forget to arc the knife around the little pocket of meat, which in birds is known as the "oyster." This is the best part. The oyster is small in partridges and quail and large in turkeys and pheasants.

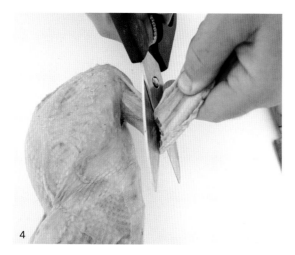

4

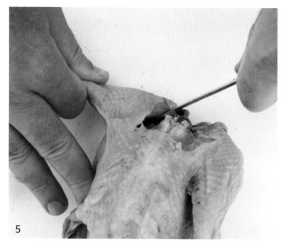

5

6

Now move to the wings. If your bird still has wings (you often lose one when wingshooting), clip the second digit off with shears (4). Turn the bird upside down and look for the place the drumette attaches to the body. Slice through this toward the neck and through the joint (5).

If you cut in the right spot, you'll go right through the soft cartilage and free the wing from the body. Don't worry if you mess it up a few times; it takes practice to know exactly where that spot is (6).

Finish with the breasts. Upland birds are built differently from waterfowl, and when you remove the legs, there's a gap in the skin coverage that leaves some of the breast open (7). Because of this, if I'm filleting the breast meat off the bone I pull off the skin and fry it up crispy separately (see Crispy Bird Skin, page 301) (8).

I then gently slide the knife along the keel bone toward the bird's tail end (9). To get all the meat, you need a sharp knife and the knowledge that upland birds have narrow breastbones but very high keel bones under their breasts—think of the structure as an upside-down Y. Anchoring your blade on the keel bone, slice toward the wishbone, and work the knife around it (10).

Once you've freed one side of the breast, pull off the tender. I save them either as a cook's treat or cut them up for Chinese food, like General Tso's Pheasant (page 81) (11).

In this process, think about "freeing" the meat rather than "slicing" or "cutting" it. That way you will lose less meat off the carcass.

Once you've done this on both sides, you're good to go. Take your time and study the pictures. Each bird you butcher will be easier than the last. And this technique for cutting up a carcass works with any bird: pheasants, pigeons, turkeys—even ducks and domestic chickens (12).

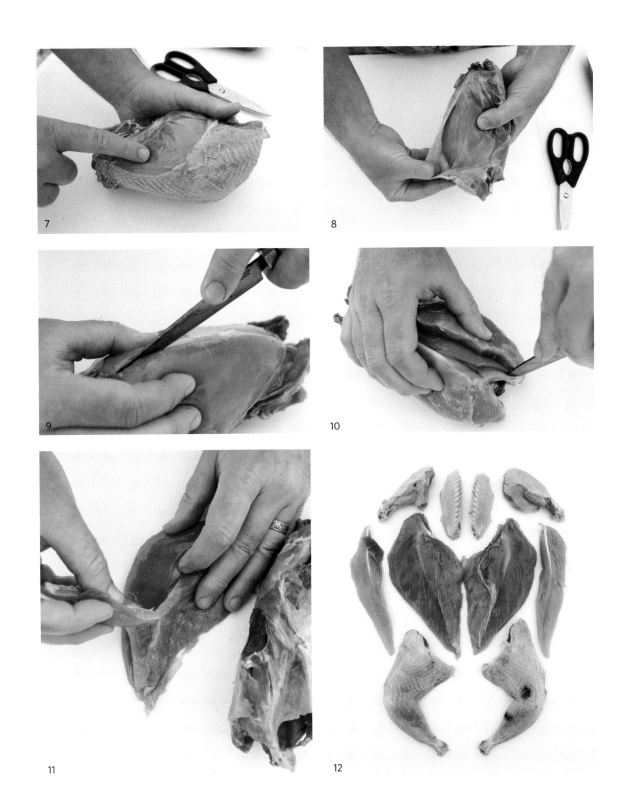

GROUSE CAMP ESSENTIALS

I'm often asked for recipes that can be made in a makeshift kitchen, either in the field or in a cabin in the woods. My advice is always the same: as long as you have a few staples on hand, you can always make a great meal after a long day outside. Here's what I'd want to see in the cupboards of every hunting shack:

- **Salt and pepper.** You'd be surprised how many times people forget these most basic of ingredients. And while you're at it, get kosher salt and one of those built-in pepper grinders in the supermarket spice rack so you can get freshly ground pepper easily.

- **Onions and garlic.** Almost every recipe in this book uses these two staples, and they keep for a long time in the pantry.

- **Stocks.** Yes, homemade stock is better, and you can make shelf-stable stock if you pressure-can it (page 53). But having a few boxes of store-bought chicken and beef broth around will greatly improve your camp cooking.

- **Wine, Port, and brandy.** For obvious reasons, but also to add flavor to sauces and stews.

- **Jelly, honey, syrup, or molasses.** Game birds often benefit from some sweetness.

- **A few packages of dried chiles and dried mushrooms.** Every decent supermarket sells them. They're lightweight and last for years. A few in a stew make everything better.

- **Vinegar.** Any kind except distilled. A splash brightens any dish.

BACKCOUNTRY ESSENTIALS

Going even further into the field? Cooking on an open fire instead of a cabin stove? Here's a stripped-down set of essentials to tuck into your pack. With the exception of the brandy in a flask, everything can be carried in resealable plastic bags.

- **Salt and pepper.** You'd be surprised how even a little salt makes food taste so much better in the wild places of this world. My advice: nice salt, like good sea salt or smoked salt. It will make things happier when all around is cold or dreary.

- **Garlic powder.** I normally don't love this stuff, but it does have a lot of flavor.

- **Bouillon cubes.** Not great, and really salty, but compact and easy to carry.

- **Brandy in a flask.** It gets cold out there!

- **A bit of white or brown sugar.** You'd be surprised how much you'll be craving sweetness after a few days in the open.

- **Dried chiles and dried mushrooms**. Lightweight flavor bombs.

- **A bit of citric-acid powder.** I know, this sounds odd. But you'll want something acidic to brighten flavors of your camp food, and this will do it. Lighter than vinegar and less perishable than citrus, you can find it sold as "fruit fresh" in the canning section of your local supermarket.

CHAPTER 3

STORING YOUR SMALL GAME

Hunt enough and you'll eventually find yourself with more game than you can reasonably eat in a week. In the old days, that meant some serious salting, drying, pickling, and (later) canning. All of those methods are great, but freezing beats them all: it's the only way to eat "fresh" game months after the season has ended.

Once you have your birds plucked and your small mammals skinned, you'll want to age them a bit in the fridge. I do this in large plastic containers with paper towels set underneath the carcasses to soak up the juices that slowly seep from the meat. Cold-aging like this will concentrate the flavor of the meat and tenderize it a bit without developing the hard rind of dry-aged meat. I find that letting birds or squirrels sit in the fridge for up to a week helps their flavor. You can skip this step if you're short on space. Note again that for game birds, cold-aging is done *after* plucking and gutting; it's different from hanging, which is done *before* plucking and gutting (see page 25.)

Generally, seven to ten days is about as long as you want any piece of fresh meat to sit in a fridge. After that, things start to get funky, and the meat can oxidize and turn grayish. You can extend this to about two weeks if you vacuum-seal the meat—essentially wet-aging it like they do in the supermarket. Freezing is the real long-term solution. And while there are other methods of freezing, nothing beats the vacuum sealer. It will radically change how you look at fish and game. By sucking out all the air from the package, vacuum-sealing will prevent freezer burn and moisture loss, thus tripling the effective life of the meat in the deep freeze. I once thawed a two-year-old pheasant I'd lost in the bottom of the freezer, and because the seal had never broken on the vacuum package, it was fine. Apparently, you can even go as long as two-and-a-half years, according to the folks at Weston, a popular maker of vacuum sealers.

There are two kinds of vacuum sealers: suction and chamber. Weston, Food Saver, and other consumer companies make suction-style sealers, which are fine for most of our purposes. But know that the suction method is inferior to the chamber method and that the bags for these sealers are relatively expensive (selling you bags is how they make their money).

Restaurants and serious processors use chamber sealers, which work by creating a vacuum in the chamber holding the meat and bag rather than by sucking out air. The difference between chamber sealers and suction-style sealers is twofold: first, chamber sealers seal liquids or really moist foods, like liver, without seepage; second, chamber sealers can seal much more tightly than suction-style sealers, actually compressing the food for an almost indestructible seal. Suction sealers have a tendency to "break seal," and if you notice that this has happened in your freezer, you must either reseal immediately or thaw and eat.

The downside of chamber sealers is their expense: a good one is never less than $750, whereas a top-of-the-line suction type costs closer to $425. My advice: buy the best suction sealer you can afford. But if you plan on killing whole flocks of pheasants or are an outfitter, a chamber sealer is for you.

Not all animals fit into the vacuum bags. With whole birds that I don't want to squash into a vacuum-sealed bag, I do a multi-step process. First, I stuff the cavity with paper towels so there's no air trapped inside. Next, I wrap the bird in plastic wrap, often several layers, around which I wrap butcher's freezer paper—the kind with one waxed side—and tape it down well. That will keep the meat in good shape for about six months.

A final word on freezing game: buy a chest freezer. If your hunting habit is anything like mine, you'll want the extra space. Chances are that most of you reading this already have at least one chest freezer, but it's worth stating nonetheless. Other than issues of space, which are serious if you kill multiple deer plus small game every year, there's the temperature factor. Chest freezers keep meat much colder—often –10°F or colder—than kitchen freezers, whose lows are usually 0°F at best, and often 10°F.

HOW TO THAW MEAT FAST

Here's a restaurant trick: the fastest way to thaw anything is in a big pot of *cold* water. Sounds counterintuitive, but it works. You use cold water from the tap, and when you add the frozen thing, it acts like an ice cube and chills the water. But unlike an ice cube that melts away, your frozen food thaws quickly but stays cold, so you needn't worry about nasty bacteria. Never use hot or warm water, which can cook the outside of your meat before the center has thawed and can definitely encourage bacterial growth.

You do need to use vacuum-sealed meat for this trick, however. Meat wrapped in butcher paper will get soggy. I've seen people improvise by unwrapping the frozen meat and putting it in a sealable plastic bag, but plastic bags tend to leak, and you need to get all the air out or the meat will float, thawing unevenly.

Want to thaw even faster? Set the pot in the sink and run cold water into it in a slow, steady stream. This moving water will thaw a whole turkey in less than forty-five minutes.

"The highway of life is filled with flat squirrels that couldn't make a decision."

—JOHN C. MAXWELL

NEVER REFREEZE UNCOOKED MEAT

Why? Mostly because of meat quality, but there is also a potential health risk.

The taboo on refreezing uncooked meat is best explained by the renowned food scientist Harold McGee, who wrote in his *On Food and Cooking*:

> The intercellular spaces [in meat], which are often large and which contain some water but very little else, freeze first, and then draw water out of the cells by osmosis. This in turn increases the concentration of dissolved substances within the cell, which further lowers the freezing point. Parts of the cell interior do not freeze at all.

Put simply, freezing damages meat. And when you thaw it, that damage manifests itself as the blood-like fluid that seeps out of the meat. It's not actually blood but rather cell fluid weeping from the damaged cells. The meat's still fine, just not as good as fresh.

Now, if you put that same piece of meat through the whole freezing and thawing process again, well, let's just say you'll notice it. The meat will be even dryer and mushier than once-thawed meat. This will be especially noticeable if all you have is a regular stand-up freezer and not a deep freeze. This is because the longer it takes to freeze something, the larger the ice crystals that will form within its cell walls. The larger the ice crystals, the more damage done to the meat. This is why commercial processors use blast freezers, which can get as low as −100°F. That freezes meat so fast that the ice crystals are tiny, resulting in a lot less meat damage. Your home freezer won't get much colder than about 0°F, and even a home box freezer won't get colder than −25°F.

Depending on how you thawed the meat in the first place, you also might be opening yourself up to some nasty bugs. If you thawed the meat from freezer to refrigerator, you're good—everything's stayed cold enough to inhibit bacterial growth. But if you thawed that pheasant on the counter (which you should *never* do), there's a distinct chance that the exterior will be covered in bacterial nasties. If you then refreeze that bird and then thaw it one more time, once the meat temperature rises to about 45°F, the bacteria will become active again and will have even more cell-wall fluid to feast on. This is not good.

Cooking meat alters its cell structure, so it's OK to refreeze meat that's been cooked. I often make sausages from frozen meat, but I will then hot-smoke or poach them so they're fully cooked before I refreeze them.

DEALING WITH FREEZER BURN

If you don't use a vacuum sealer, sooner or later you'll encounter the dreaded freezer burn (which you'll also experience with vacuum-sealed food whose seal has broken). Freezer burn happens when the ultra-cold, ultra-dry air in the freezer comes in contact with meat or fish for an extended period of time. There's nothing harmful about it, but no one wants to eat freezer-burned meat.

Simply slice off the freezer-burned portions of the meat, feed them to the cat or dog, and cook the rest. Or use the whole thing for stock or broth. And next time, be sure to seal your meat better.

CANNING SMALL GAME

To be honest, I don't can game meats by themselves; they stink like dog food when you open the can. I do, however, can ready-to-eat meals, like spaghetti sauce or stew, which are handy when I'm too busy to cook during the week. And I like canned stock for its great convenience, even though it loses some quality in the canning process.

Here's how it's done. First, you absolutely must have a pressure canner. *You cannot safely can meats with the standard boiling-water bath. A standard boiling-water bath won't get hot enough to kill any dangerous bacteria that may be lurking in your soup.* Every so often, you'll hear reports about people getting sick from home-canned meats. The cause is almost always failure to properly pressure-can it.

As a cook, you need to think of your canned stew as a base, not a finished product. This is because you can't add noodles, pasta, rice, flour, cream, milk, or other thickening agents to home-canned soups, as they can mess up the chemical balance of the stew while you pressure-can it. Add those ingredients later. Also, if you're using dried beans or peas, you need to fully rehydrate them first. Once you've decided to pop open a can and you have it simmering, a handful of freshly chopped herbs added right before you serve the stew helps brighten things up, too.

As for procedure, you brown the meats and onions first, then cook with broth, herbs, and spices for an hour or so—an old hare or tom turkey can take a while to get tender in the pot. After an hour, add the vegetables, bring the stew to a simmer, and turn off the heat.

Prepare your jars (I prefer to use pints), fill them, and hand-seal the lids. Make sure the jar rims are scrupulously clean. Put them in your pressure canner, tighten the lid, and vent for seven to ten minutes before putting on the weight to build pressure. Once you get to pressure—10 psi if you live up to 1,000 feet in elevation, 15 psi if you live at elevations greater than 1,000 feet—pressure-can

your stew for ninety minutes. Bottom line: be sure to follow all the details in the directions that came with your pressure canner; each one works a little differently.

FOOD SAFETY AND SMALL GAME

OK, ladies and gentlemen, here's where we get real.

If you've read my last two books, *Duck, Duck, Goose* and *Buck, Buck, Moose*, you'll remember that there are virtually no health issues related to waterfowl or venison. In terms of parasites or diseases, waterfowl and venison are some of the safest meats to eat. I wish I could say the same for small-game mammals.

FOOD SAFETY AND UPLAND BIRDS

First the good news: upland birds are indeed super safe—*if they're wild*. Virtually no incidences of food poisoning can be traced to wild upland birds, according to an analysis of data collected by the Centers for Disease Control and Prevention (CDC). A 2007 British survey of scientific literature showed that "the available evidence suggests wild birds play a limited role in human infectious diseases. Direct transmission of an infectious agent from wild birds to humans is rarely identified." The same paper reports that the only direct case reported in the literature is "[a] cluster of H5N1 human cases in Azerbaijan where the affected patients were plucking feathers from mute swans that had succumbed to H5N1 infection."

That said, the CDC does report two incidents of *Campylobacter* poisoning involving quail, one in Washington in 2001 and one in Colorado in 2005. The same data show one case of *Staphylococcus* poisoning involving rabbit jerky in Ohio in 2001. Neither reveals whether the quail or rabbit was farmed or wild.

Turkey is another story. According to the CDC, there were 343 outbreaks of various food poisonings involving turkey from 1998 to 2015, sickening 10,846 people, 369 of whom went to the hospital, and 21 of whom died. As you might imagine, such incidents spike significantly between Thanksgiving and Christmas. There's no official data breakout of wild birds versus farmed birds, but every single case I read involved store-bought turkeys. I gave up reading after the 228th case in row.

Similarly, while *Salmonella* is relatively common in factory-farmed chickens, the pathogen has never been detected at the nation's largest pheasant farmer, MacFarlane Pheasants, in Janesville, Wisconsin. And according to a 2011 article in *Veterinary Research*, there has never been a case of human *Salmonella* associated with pigeons or doves.

Although the West Nile virus is contractible by nearly every bird that North Americans hunt, there is no evidence of bird-to-human transmission of the disease. If a person is going to get West Nile, it will be from a mosquito.

Interestingly, in the United Kingdom, pheasants appear to be a vector for the bacteria that causes Lyme disease. So when a tick lands on and munches a pheasant, the tick becomes a Lyme carrier, and if that tick attaches to a person, that person can get Lyme.

FOOD SAFETY AND SMALL-GAME MAMMALS

Now for the bad news: the small mammals. The fact is, they're kinda scrungy. I'm not exactly sure why, but lagomorphs—the rabbits and hares—seem to be beset by a host of potential problems, some of which actually do matter to you.

A list of some of the most common would include ticks, fleas, tapeworm cysts, tularemia, botfly larvae, *E. coli*, fibromas, and rabies. Both squirrels and rabbits have been known to carry *Leptospirosis* and *Salmonella* in their droppings. It's not common, but it happens. The three most common parasites I see in the rabbits and hares that I hunt are, in order of frequency, fleas, tapeworm cysts, and botfly larvae. I've never seen

tularemia in a rabbit, despite its being named for California's Tulare County, just a few hours south of where I live.

Fleas. Jackrabbits seem to have them in spades, especially in hot, dry areas (fleas seem to affect rabbits and squirrels to a far lesser extent). Since I skin my jacks in the field, I've never been really bothered by fleas. But if they do show up for you, wash your game vest. You don't want fleas in your house.

Tapeworm cysts are mostly caused by a tapeworm hoping that its bunny host gets eaten by a coyote. Diabolical, isn't it? The tapeworm in question, *Taenia pisiformis,* can't complete its life cycle inside a lagomorph, but it can inside the guts of a canine, either wild or domestic. This sort of tapeworm is primarily found in cottontails and primarily in the gut cavity. You need not worry about them.

Snowshoes and jackrabbits, on the other hand, can be infected with *Multiceps serialis*, which, when large, can be seen in the meat as a fluid-filled "blister" with little white dots inside. They are not common, but when they are around, I tend to see them in the hare's backstrap. According to the Michigan Department of Natural Resources, "Cysticercosis does not harm the meat of rabbits and hares, or make it unfit for human consumption. Adult tapeworms of these species do not occur in humans. Cysts are usually removed when rabbits are dressed out; any that might be overlooked are destroyed in cooking the meat." Be that as it may, there's no way I want to cut into one of those sacs at the dinner table! Do a search when you're breaking down your jackrabbit. If you find one, cut it out completely. The rest of the meat will be fine.

Botfly, also known as warbles or wolves, is the most horrific of all the parasites that affect North American game. It's a large grub that starts as an egg deposited in the skin of a small mammal—this one can affect squirrels, too—and it grows just under the skin. I can't imagine how nasty this would be for the poor rabbit. And I'm thankful that there are no botflies north of Puebla, Mexico, that affect humans. But as evil and horrid and appalling as they are, botflies do not affect the meat. They live between the meat and the skin. So when you skin an animal with a botfly, it won't stay in anything you plan to eat. Just do me a favor? Burn or squish that bastard when you see it, will ya?

Lower in frequency but higher in seriousness is tularemia. Caused by the bacteria *Francisella tularensis*, tularemia can be found all over North America. The CDC tracks tularemia and reports about two hundred cases a year, centering on Missouri, Arkansas, Oklahoma, and Kansas. Ninety percent of cases come from cottontails.

If you catch tularemia, your symptoms can range from something like a flu with a fever to skin ulcers to trouble breathing. For the most part, it can be treated with antibiotics, but you don't want to catch it, so better safe than sorry. And you *can* catch tularemia through skin contact. That's why of all the animals I hunt, I only wear gloves routinely when I butcher rabbits (though I also wear gloves if I have an open cut on my hand).

A tipoff to tularemia infection in game is the liver, which will be spotted and weird looking. This is why I don't keep livers from cottontails. Despite the rarity of this disease—my state of California had only twenty-eight cases between 2006 and 2015—I'd rather be cautious. And because the bacterium that causes tularemia dies at cooking temperatures, a rabbit infected by it is safe to eat.

Even rarer than tularemia, but potentially nastier, are *E. coli* and rabies.

Escherichia coliform bacteria have been detected in rabbit pellets, but little is known about its prevalence. A 2004 British report shows that rabbits can become infected with *E. coli* when in close proximity to infected cattle. Just over 8 percent of tested rabbits had *E. coli O157* (a particularly virulent type of the bug) in their droppings when in proximity to an infected cattle herd. Interestingly, there seems to be a higher prevalence of this in summer than in winter.

Finally, there is the specter of rabies. Despite legends of rabid squirrels terrorizing parks and yards—do a Google image search; you won't be sorry—this is the final word, from the CDC: "Small mammals such as squirrels, rats, mice, hamsters, guinea pigs, gerbils, chipmunks, rabbits, and hares *are almost never found to be infected with rabies* and have not been known to cause rabies among humans in the United States" (emphasis mine).

And one more thing: remember that infamous 1997 study in the British medical journal *Lancet* that marked a correlation between eating squirrel brains and Creutzfeldt-Jakob disease, which is like mad cow, only for humans? Well, it has since been discredited. Just the same, I'm going to hold off on that big plate of squirrel brains and eggs.

So what's the takeaway? Upland birds are, in general, free of parasites or diseases that can hurt you—but I would still exercise common sense. Small mammals can be affected by more things that can affect you, but a simple pair of nitrile or latex gloves—and, in the case of those botflies or tapeworm cysts, a strong stomach—will serve you well.

CHAPTER 4

STOCKS, BROTH, AND MARINADES

STOCKS AND BROTHS

Making stocks and broths—or, if you're adventurous, French *glace de viande*—are important skills every hunter should have. Making your own broths is one of the easiest ways to get more out of your animals, and is a great use for the bones and trim that are left over after butchering—or for animals you hit too squarely with your shotgun pattern. Beyond utility, the satisfaction of making something you simply can't buy anywhere, perfectly suited to your own tastes, is worth every moment of the time it takes to make a good broth. A house where broth simmers on the stove is a happy one. There are several ways to go about making your own stocks and broths, and I'll walk you through them here.

You can, of course, substitute beef broth or veal stock or chicken stock for homemade dark and light stocks, but there's something special about homemade broths that will elevate your cooking. And telling your guests they're eating snipe broth is a sure-fire conversation starter.

Any bones will work for stock, and I like to keep some meat on them, which makes for a better stock. Blown-up birds or rabbits are good choices—just make sure to wash them well. As for innards, gizzards and hearts are great for stock. Liver and kidney are not. Don't forget the necks of your birds, either.

Freshly made stock is the best-tasting stock, and its quality is an order of magnitude better than that of frozen stock, although frozen is still good. One step below freshly made or fresh-frozen stock is pressure-canned stock (page 53), which isn't as good as fresh or frozen, but which has the significant benefit of being shelf stable and convenient. I use all three methods, depending on the circumstance.

Fresh broth is best for fancy dinners for which the broth is served as the star of a dish, as in the Tortellini en Brodo on page 122 or the Hmong Squab Soup on page 272. Frozen stock is perfectly good for these dishes, and it's also excellent for soups that have other things in them. Pressure-canned is best for sauces, braising liquid, and thick stews with are other big flavors, like the Sage Grouse, Hunters Style (page 247).

A STOCK PRIMER

Making stock is among the core skills of any good cook, and it is a labor of love I embrace wholly. Some cooks make stock without vegetables, but I rarely do that. Vegetables add so much to the final flavor of a stock and can transform it from an additive into a full-fledged broth suitable for drinking on cold days. Incidentally, while I use stock and broth interchangeably, technically a stock is a base and a broth something you can serve on its own; generally a broth is more flavorful and better seasoned than a stock.

My essentials: onions or leeks, carrots, celery, bay leaves, and parsley. I will add other herbs as appropriate, most often rosemary and thyme. With wild game, I often add rosemary and juniper berries. My secret weapon for any dark stock: parsnips. Their sweetness brings a lot to the party.

The first step is roasting the bones. I like darker, fuller stocks, and this is what does it. A classic Asian-style broth doesn't use roasted bones, and I will occasionally make stock without roasting. But not often. So I roast my carcasses at 400°F for an hour or so, until they're well browned and yummy looking.

Next, cram your carcasses into the stockpot and cover with cold water. Cold water will give you more collagen, and it's collagen from the joints, cartilage, and skin that builds body in your stock by making it thicker than water. You only get this by letting the water heat gradually. Want to make a better broth? Go buy a pig's or calf's foot from your local butcher or Asian or Latin market and add it. These cuts have lots of collagen and are a secret to great broth.

Bring the stock to a simmer, and skim off any scum that floats to the surface. After the surface is clear, reduce the heat to a bare simmer. You want it to shimmy, not roil, not even bubble too much. A boiled stock will turn cloudy, and the higher temps can extract bitter flavors from the bones. Let it do this for several hours. How long? Up to overnight.

After the meat has infused the water to your liking—four hours is a minimum for me—add your vegetables, coarsely chopped. You don't want to use anything spoiled or rotten, but the ends of things like carrots or parsnips make great stock, as do onion skins, which will help turn a broth an inviting brown. Stir in your vegetables, and let the broth cook another ninety minutes to two hours, no longer. After about two hours, those bright flavors you added will muddle and become murky.

Now strain everything out. Set a paper towel into a fine mesh sieve. Ladle your stock through this into a large bowl or plastic bin. Is all of this necessary? Yes. Unless you want a mucky, cloudy stock. And it's more than aesthetics: the impurities are just that—impure, and they'll add off-flavors to your otherwise wonderful brew.

Once your stock is strained, clean the stockpot or pour the strained liquid into another one. Now you can reduce it if you want to. This is also the time you can salt the stock. Stock gets saltier the longer you cook it down because salt doesn't evaporate with the water. So add it close to the end, and you will know what you're getting. If you're making demi-glace, don't salt at all.

All of this takes time, but not a lot of it is active. And the process is as comforting to me as the reward.

PRESSURE-CANNING STOCK

All these broth recipes can be stored in your pantry if you pressure-can them. You'll need to follow your canner's directions, but the general procedure is as follows:

- Once your stock is ready to go, keep it hot—a low simmer is just right.

- Get your pressure canner ready. You'll need the tray in the bottom to keep your jars up off the bottom and enough hot water to come about one-quarter of the way up the sides of your jars.

- Use clean pint or quart Mason jars. Use new lids; old lids won't seal (old rims are fine). You'll want a jar funnel, too, so stock doesn't splash the glass rim of the jar during transfer.

- Ladle your stock into the jars, leaving a solid inch or inch-and-a-half of headspace. Make sure the glass edge of the jar is clean and dry. Attach the lids, and put the jars in the canner.

- Seal the canner, and turn the heat to high. Once you get a noisy jet of steam coming out of the vent, let this vent for seven minutes.

- Put the weight on the vent, or otherwise start to build pressure. Around sea level, you need about 10 psi; if you're at elevation greater than 1,000 feet, 15 psi is necessary. When you hit the target pressure, set the timer: twenty-five minutes for quarts, twenty minutes for pints. While this is cooking, you want the weight to jiggle about three times per minute. Adjust your heat accordingly.

- When you're done, turn off the heat and let the pressure drop naturally. Don't take the weight off the vent or remove the lid! Only when the pressure is at zero can you remove the lid.

Canned this way, stock will keep at room temperature indefinitely.

BASIC BROTH FOR LIGHT-MEAT ANIMALS

This is my go-to broth for pheasants, rabbits, turkey, and quail. It can stand alone as a broth for pasta or, if you clarify it later, as a consommé. It's stronger in flavor than store-bought stock, so if you use it as a base for stews or soups, remember that—and label your jars accordingly. Making a good stock or broth is an all-day affair. Don't take shortcuts, or your broth will suffer. Relax and let things happen as they will.

A note on the carcasses. Your stock will be better if there's some meat on them. I'll often leave some wings in there, or the front legs of rabbits or squirrels. Don't forget turkey necks, or gizzards and hearts. All are good in stock.

Makes about a gallon | **Prep Time: 10 minutes** | **Cook Time: At least 6 hours**

4 pounds carcasses (see above)

4 tablespoons olive oil

Salt

1 pig's foot (optional)

1 tablespoon crushed juniper
    berries (optional)

2 tablespoons fresh rosemary

1 tablespoon black pepper,
    cracked or coarsely ground

1 tablespoon dried thyme,
    or several sprigs of fresh

4 bay leaves

2 large onions, chopped

2 large carrots, chopped

4 celery sticks, chopped

1 fennel bulb with fronds,
    chopped (optional)

About ½ a bunch of parsley, chopped

Coat the carcasses with olive oil and salt well, then roast in a 400°F oven until brown, about an hour. Put the bones in a large stockpot. If you want, cut the carcasses into large pieces with kitchen shears; this lets you fit more in the pot, making a richer broth. Cover with water by an inch or two, add the pig's foot, and bring to a simmer over medium-high heat.

While the water is heating up, add more water to the roasting pan, and let it sit for a few minutes to loosen up the browned bits on the bottom. Use a wooden spoon to scrape up those bits and pour it all into the stockpot.

Skim any froth that forms on the surface, and simmer very gently for at least 4 hours; I let it go overnight, slightly covered. You want the broth to steam and burble a little, not roil.

Add the remaining ingredients and simmer for another 90 minutes.

Using tongs, grab out all the bones and large bits and discard. Set a paper towel in a fine-mesh sieve that is itself set over another large pot or plastic bin. Ladle the broth through the paper-towel-lined sieve. Discard the dregs in the broth pot, which will be loaded with sediment and other bits.

Add salt to the clarified broth to taste, and pour into quart jars and freeze (or pressure-can, see page 53). If you freeze, leave at least 1½ inches of space at the top of the jar or the jars will crack when the broth freezes. Use within a year.

BASIC BROTH FOR DARK-MEAT ANIMALS

This is a darker, richer broth that is a bit burlier than the previous recipe. Use this one for hares, dark-meat grouse, doves, and pigeons. Squirrels are on the fence—they can be used with either broth recipe.

   A note on the carcasses: your stock will be better if there's some meat on them. I'll often leave some wings in there, or the front legs of hares or squirrels. Don't forget necks, gizzards, and hearts. All are good in stock.

Makes about a gallon | *Prep Time: 10 minutes* | *Cook Time: At least 6 hours*

3 pounds carcasses (see above)

1 pound chopped random meaty bits

7 tablespoons olive oil, divided

Salt

1 pig's foot (optional)

1 large onion, chopped

2 large carrots, chopped

1 parsnip, chopped (optional)

2 celery sticks, chopped

4 tablespoons tomato paste

Skins from the onion

1 tablespoon crushed juniper
   berries (optional)

2 tablespoons fresh rosemary,
   or 1 large sprig

1 tablespoon black pepper,
   cracked or coarsely ground

1 tablespoon dried thyme,
   or several sprigs of fresh

4 bay leaves

2 star anise pods (optional)

About ½ a bunch parsley, chopped

Coat the carcasses and meat with 4 tablespoons of the olive oil and salt well, then roast in a 400°F oven until brown, about an hour. Put the bones and meat into a large stockpot. If you want, cut the carcasses up with kitchen shears; this lets you fit more bones in the pot, making for a richer broth. Cover with water, add the pig's foot, and bring to a simmer over medium-high heat.

While the water is heating up, add more water to the roasting pan, and let it sit for a few minutes to loosen up the browned bits on the bottom. Use a wooden spoon to scrape up those bits, and pour it all into the stockpot.

Skim any froth that forms on the surface, and simmer very gently for at least 4 hours; I let it go overnight, slightly covered. You want the broth to steam and burble a little, not roil.

When you're almost ready to add the remaining ingredients, heat the rest of the olive oil in a large sauté pan, and brown the vegetables over medium-high heat. Stir occasionally. This should take a solid 10 to 15 minutes. Stir in the tomato paste, and let this cook another 4 or 5 minutes. Add all this to the stockpot, and ladle some of the broth into the sauté pan to get every last bit of goodness out of the pan. Return that bit to the pot.

Add the remaining ingredients to the stockpot, and simmer for another 90 minutes.

Using tongs, grab out all the bones and large bits and discard. Set a paper towel in a fine-mesh sieve that is itself set over another large pot. Ladle the broth through the paper-towel-lined sieve. Discard the dregs in the broth pot, which will be loaded with sediment and other bits.

Add salt to taste to the clarified broth, and pour into quart jars and freeze (or pressure-can, see page 53). If you freeze, leave at least 1½ inches of space at the top of the jar or the jars will crack when the broth freezes. Use within a year.

ASIAN-STYLE STOCK

While not strictly needed, making a special Asian-style stock adds something special when you're making Asian dishes that need stock, like the Hmong Squab Soup on page 272.

You can make this soup with either dark- or light-meat animals. And, as with the other stock recipes in this chapter, adding some meat will make a better broth.

Makes about a gallon | **Prep Time: 10 minutes** | **Cook Time: At least 6 hours**

3 pounds carcasses (see the headnote in the previous recipe)

1 pound chopped random meaty bits

1 pig's foot (optional)

1 large leek, chopped (both white and green parts)

2 bunches green onions, chopped (both white and green parts)

One 4-inch piece of ginger, sliced (not peeled)

2 star anise pods (optional)

2 cups Shaoxing or other rice wine

About ½ a bunch of parsley, chopped

Salt

Unlike Western stocks, this stock doesn't rely on roasted bones. Instead, put the carcasses, the random meaty bits, and the pig's foot into a large stockpot, and cover with cold water by at least 4 inches. Slowly bring this to a boil. When it does boil, drop the heat to a bare simmer, and skim all the scum that will have accumulated on the top. This will take a bit of doing. Use a shallow spoon to skim into a little bowl.

Let this simmer very gently as long as you can stand it, at least three hours. I go overnight with the pot halfway covered.

In the last 2 hours of cooking, add the remaining ingredients, and continue to simmer gently.

Using tongs, grab out all the bones and large bits and discard. Set a paper towel in a fine-mesh sieve that is itself set over another large pot. Ladle the broth through the paper-towel-lined sieve. Discard the dregs in the broth pot, which will be loaded with sediment and other bits.

Add salt to the clarified broth to taste and pour into quart jars and freeze (or pressure-can, see page 53). If you freeze, leave at least 1½ inches of space at the top of the jar or the jars will crack when the broth freezes. Use within a year.

SMALL-GAME GLACE DE VIANDE

Glace de viande, essentially meat jelly, is a secret ingredient of many professional chefs. It's cooked-down stock that has some added source of gelatin in it. A spoonful here and there makes everything better. *Glace* (pronounced glah-ss) freezes really well, too. It takes a long time to make, so make a big batch and freeze it for the rest of the year. Any of the animals featured in this book can be used, and you can combine them if you want. Note: the pig's feet are not optional here. You need them to set the *glace*.

Makes 6 half pints | Prep Time: 10 minutes | Cook Time: Overnight

4 pounds carcasses

4 tablespoons olive oil

Salt

2 pig's feet

1 tablespoon crushed juniper berries

2 tablespoons fresh rosemary, or 1 large sprig

1 tablespoon black pepper, cracked or coarsely ground

1 tablespoon dried thyme, or several sprigs of fresh

4 bay leaves

1 large onion, chopped

2 large carrots, chopped

2 celery sticks, chopped

About ½ of a bunch of parsley, chopped

Coat the carcasses with olive oil and salt well, then roast in a 400°F oven until brown, about an hour. If you can stand it, keep some meat on the bones—wings and front legs are ideal for this. It will make a better broth. Put the bones in a large stockpot. If you want, cut the carcasses into pieces with kitchen shears; this lets you fit more bones into the pot, again, making a richer broth. Add the pig's feet. Cover with cold water and bring to a simmer over medium-high heat.

While the water is heating up, add more water to the roasting pan and let it sit for a few minutes to loosen up the browned bits on the bottom. Use a wooden spoon to scrape up those bits and pour it all into the stockpot.

Skim the froth that forms on the surface and simmer very gently for at least 4 hours; I let it go eight hours. You want the broth to steam and burble a little, not roil. Add the remaining ingredients and simmer for another 90 minutes.

Using tongs, grab out all the bones and large bits and discard. Set a paper towel in a fine-mesh sieve that is itself set over another large pot. Ladle the broth through the paper-towel-lined sieve. Discard the dregs in the broth pot, which will be loaded with sediment and other bits.

Clean the stockpot, return the clarified broth to it, and set it over very low heat on a weak burner. Put the pot a little off center on the burner, which sets up a circulation pattern that concentrates all the impurities on one side of the pot. This makes them easier to skim off. Let the stock reduce by half or more, very slowly, skimming the surface from time to time. By the time I'm at this point, it's usually nighttime, so I let it go overnight.

The next morning, pour the reduced stock through the same set up as you did before—the strainer with the paper towel in it—into a container. Now's the time to pour it into small glass jars, leaving about half an inch of headspace or so (*glace* doesn't expand as much as stock). Set the jars in the fridge to cool for a day.

The next day, if the stock has set up and is a gelatin, label the jars and put them in the freezer. They'll keep for more than a year.

MARINADES

"What marinade do you use?"

This is perhaps the most common question I get when people ask me about cooking wild game. Truth is, I don't always use a marinade—a quail or a ruffed grouse needs little more than fire, salt, and maybe some black pepper. But there's definitely a place for marinades in wild-game cookery. You just need to know when to break out your favorite marinade and when it's better just to make a nice sauce.

WHY MARINATE?

Marinades are acid-based (occasionally enzyme-based) liquids or loose pastes that are used to infuse meat (or vegetables) with flavor while tenderizing them at the same time. At least that's the theory.

Bathing a turkey breast or any other meat in an acidic sauce (or with certain enzyme-rich fruit juices like papaya or pineapple) will indeed break down some of the muscle tissues on the outer surface of the meat. The acid or fruit enzymes act to denature the proteins, making them a bit mushy, which we register as tenderness when we eat it. What's more, marinades can't penetrate meats the way salt-based brines do. According to most food scientists, a marinade can't penetrate a piece of meat much deeper than an eighth of an inch, even after several days.

The bottom line is that acidic marinades don't tenderize meat, and marinades with pineapple or papaya juice just make meat mushy. I can hear you saying, "But when I marinate venison roasts, they are absolutely more tender than when I don't!" And you're right. But it's not the marinade that's making your roast more tender.

According to the great French food scientist Hervé This, long marinades do have an effect: "The meat *is* more tender," This told the *Washington Post*. "But it is not the marinade that makes it

tender: It is time. If you use an acidic marinade, it will protect the surface from spoilage while the rest of the meat matures. And you know, when meat matures, it becomes tender." This is the secret behind the long marinades in German sauerbraten, which can marinate for a week in the fridge.

And marinades *do* impart flavor to the meat's surface. Even a few minutes of marinating will add flavor to the finished dish, because the flavorful liquid will soak into the crevices and cuts in a piece of meat.

Most importantly, marinating meat in an acidic sauce for at least forty minutes has been shown by the American Cancer Society to reduce by up to 99 percent the cancer-causing heterocyclic amines that are created when meat is cooked by a direct, open flame, as is the case when we grill. This means a marinade not only improves flavor but also makes that char-grilled piece of venison healthier.

WHEN TO MARINATE

Because marinades can penetrate into a piece of meat only a few millimeters at best, you'll want to use them when you're dealing with meats that aren't too thick. This means small birds, pheasant or grouse breasts, and cutlets from turkey breasts, that sort thing. Or go the sauerbraten route and marinate a whole bird for a week or more. Just remember that the acid in the marinade, usually from red wine, is just protecting the meat from spoilage, not actually tenderizing it. It's the wet-aging of the meat for a week that does the trick. Remember: don't do this with the enzyme-based marinades!

One thing a marinade will *not* do is tenderize connective tissue. Those sinews in your pheasant or turkey drumsticks will be just as gnarly after a marinade as before.

HOW TO MARINATE

You'll want to marinate your game in a sealable plastic bag or in a covered, non-reactive container, such as glass or plastic. Do this in the fridge to slow the growth of any bacteria. (A tip: if you like stir-fries and fajitas, marinate the slices of breast meat before you stir-fry them. You'll get more flavor that way.)

When you're ready to cook, take the meat out of the marinade, and pat it dry with paper towels. Wet meat won't brown.

If you want to use your marinade as a sauce, you can do one of two things: either boil your marinade for five minutes before using it; or, if boiling would destroy your marinade (as it would with chimichurri, for example, which relies on fresh raw herbs), make more than you need for the marinade and use the extra as the sauce. Please don't reuse the marinade you soaked a raw pheasant in; there's a chance, albeit a small one, that you might get food poisoning.

Mearns' quail country in Arizona's desert grasslands, just a few miles from Mexico.

PART TWO

LIGHT MEATS

CHAPTER 5

PHEASANTS, RUFFED GROUSE, AND BLUE GROUSE

The birds in this chapter are the chickens of the wild-game world. In many parts of the country, they're even *called* "chicken" in local parlance. Broadly speaking, you can use pheasants and ruffed and blue grouse with any of your favorite chicken recipes.

There are differences between store-bought birds and these "wildings," however. The most significant being the tough sinews in the legs of pheasants (grouse don't have such rough tendons). I've seen tricks for removing some of the tendons in a pheasant's leg, but in my experience, they don't work so well.

Pheasants and grouse will be smaller than most fryer chickens, and the meat will be denser, leaner, and more flavorful. They tend to be a little funkier than supermarket chickens, but I view this as a good thing, especially with ruffed grouse.

Ruffed grouse in Alberta, Canada's boreal forest.

ROAST PHEASANT OR GROUSE

When life gives you a beautiful pheasant, one that you haven't shot up, you should roast it whole like a chicken. But a pheasant isn't a chicken—it can get dry and ugly very fast if roasted poorly. This recipe relies on a few tricks to solve that problem. One is a brine, which will season the bird and help it retain moisture. Another is to start the bird in a searing-hot oven followed by a stint in a cooler oven. A third is resting the bird. Follow these general instructions, and you'll get a lovely, moist pheasant. This technique also works with ruffed or blue grouse and guinea hens.

It goes without saying that your birds need to be plucked for this recipe to work well.

Accompany this dish with some vegetables of your choice. A good option is to cut up some carrots, potatoes, parsnips, celery root, and turnips and roast them underneath the birds. Serve with a nice white wine or dry rosé.

Serves 4 | **Prep Time: 8 hours, if you brine the bird** | **Cook Time: 60 minutes**

2 whole, plucked pheasants

2 quarts water

½ cup kosher salt

2 tablespoons sugar

2 to 4 bay leaves (optional)

1 tablespoon crushed juniper berries (optional)

2 tablespoons olive oil or softened butter

Black pepper to taste

Make a brine by bringing the water, salt, bay leaves, juniper, and sugar to a boil. Cover and let cool to room temperature. When it cools, submerge your pheasants in the brine and keep it in the fridge for 4 to 8 hours. The longer you brine, the saltier the pheasant will become. I brine pen-raised birds for 4 hours and old roosters for 8 hours.

If you really want a crispy skin, take the birds out of the brine and set them uncovered in the fridge for 12 to 24 hours. This dries the skin and helps it crisp in the oven. This step is optional.

When you're ready to cook, take the pheasants out of the fridge, and let them sit at room temperature for at least 30 minutes and up to an hour. Heat your oven to 500°F if possible, but at least 400°F. Give yourself at least 15 minutes of preheating, and up to a half hour. Oil the birds with olive oil, or smear the entire birds with butter. Crack some black pepper over the birds.

Stuff with a piece of onion or apple and a few fresh herbs. Don't pack the cavities. I often truss the birds at this point to help the pheasants cook more evenly, though this step is optional.

Roast the pheasants for 15 minutes in the very hot oven. After 15 minutes, remove the pheasants from the oven and set them aside. Lower the temperature to 350°F, leaving your oven door open to speed the process.

Baste the birds with more butter or oil, and return them to the oven. Roast for 30 to 45 minutes. You want the internal temperature of the thigh meat to be between 155°F and 165°F and for the bird's juices to run pretty clear. You want a little pink in the juice and in the meat. The higher end of this cooking time will give you a well-done bird, which I try to avoid, though some prefer.

(continued)

Remove the pheasants, and let them rest for 10 to 15 minutes. This resting time is vital—it lets the juices redistribute within the pheasants and finishes off the cooking process through carry-over heating.

Variation: Glazed Roast Pheasant

There's always something special about a well-roasted, sweet-and-savory glazed bird. Be sure to brine the bird, and watch your glaze once it's on—you can go from caramelized loveliness to burnt hell in about two minutes.

I often use a prickly pear glaze, but you can use any fruit syrup, pomegranate molasses, honey, or maple syrup. All are good; they're just different. You'll need about ⅔ cup of whatever it is you're using.

Follow the directions for Roast Pheasant or Grouse on the previous page. For the glaze, if you want a bit of char or caramelization, you can paint the pheasant with your syrup at about 7 minutes into the 500°F roasting. Keep an eye on it, though.

After the pheasant comes out of the high-heat oven, paint the bird with the syrup mixed with 2 tablespoons of melted butter. Put the pheasant back into the oven for another 30 to 45 minutes, and paint it with the syrup every 10 to 15 minutes as it cooks.

Rest and carve the bird as normal.

SIMPLE SEARED PHEASANT OR GROUSE BREAST

This is a bedrock skill for the pheasant or grouse hunter. Once you master this one, you can play with any sauce you want. Basically, you'll be cooking the breast as if it were a piece of fish, which is to say *you're not flipping it*. Yes. You read that right.

This is how you get a fantastic, crispy crust on one side without overcooking the meat. The trick is to have enough oil or fat in the pan so you can ladle it over the exposed side of the breast with a spoon.

The fat matters. Given my choice, I'll use clarified butter because of its relatively high smoke point and good flavor. High-smoke-point oils are important; the pan gets hot and you don't want to burn the oil. Safflower, grapeseed, rice bran, peanut, or corn oil are all good choices. If you use one of these, put a pat of butter on the pheasant breast as it rests after you cook it. This steakhouse trick will do wonders for your kitchen reputation.

This is super easy once you get the hang of it, and it works with red-meat bird breasts, quail, or partridges, too.

You can use the tenders in another dish, or cook them up separately and eat as a cook's treat.

Serves 2 | Prep Time: 30 minutes, for the pheasant to come to room temperature | Cook Time: 8 minutes

2 skinless pheasant breasts, tenders removed

Salt

3 tablespoons high-smoke-point oil (see above)

2 tablespoons unsalted butter

Black pepper

Set the pheasant or grouse breasts on the counter, and salt both sides well. Let them come to room temperature. Note: if you are doing this with dark meat bird breasts, only let them rest 10 minutes.

Heat the oil in a pan that will just about fit two breasts; you can do as many as four per batch with this method, but be sure not to crowd the pan.

When the oil is hot, pat dry the pheasant breasts and place them in the pan, skin-side down. The skin side of these skinless breasts is the side that the skin *used* to be on—it's flatter, and it makes better contact with the pan, so you get a nicer, crispier crust.

Let the breasts sear over medium-high heat. Use a spoon to ladle fat over them every minute or so until the meat is opaque. Sear like this until the breasts are nicely browned on the bottom and come off the pan easily, anywhere from 4 to 8 minutes, depending on the size of the breasts. Cook dark meat bird breasts on the lower end of this range, which will keep the meat pink.

Move the breasts to a cutting board crust side up and top with the butter. Rest them for 5 minutes and serve.

GRILLED PHEASANT BREASTS

Grilling pheasant breasts can be challenging: you want to get enough exposure to the fire to make it all worth it, but you don't want to end up with a dry, unhappy pheasant or grouse breast. I find the best way to get there is to use whole crowns, not boneless breasts. Doing this gives you some protection against the harshness of an open fire, and it makes it much easier to keep the skin on. Grilled, crispy skin is a wonderful thing.

I also leave the drumettes, the first digit of the wings, on the breast crown. This helps anchor the skin on the bird, and the wings provide some protection for the side of the breast when you tip the crown on its side to crisp. To do this, use kitchen shears to clip away the breast crown and drumettes from the rest of the bird. I clip away the ribs, too. Once you have a gutted, whole bird, you hold the breast with one hand and the rest of the bird in another, and crack it backward; it's like opening a trunk. You can do this with either skin-on or skinless breasts. Pheasants, grouse, and partridges are ideal for this recipe.

Top the breasts with whatever BBQ sauce you like. You can try my South Carolina mustard-based sauce on page 73, or use the Maple-Bourbon BBQ sauce below.

Serve with cornbread and a side salad.

Serves 4 | **Prep Time: 30 minutes** | **Cook Time: 20 minutes**

---

1 or 2 pheasant breast crowns
    per person

Salt

Vegetable oil

MAPLE-BOURBON BBQ SAUCE

¼ cup butter

1 chopped chile, such as
    a serrano

1 medium onion, grated

1 cup bourbon or Tennessee whiskey

½ cup ketchup or tomato sauce

½ cup lemon juice

½ cup apple cider vinegar

⅓ cup dark molasses

⅓ cup Worcestershire sauce

2 or 3 tablespoons brown sugar

Oil and salt the pheasant breasts well, and let them rest while you get your grill going and make the barbecue sauce.

Melt the butter in a small pot and cook the chile pepper and onion over medium heat. Don't brown them. When the onion is translucent, about 3 minutes, add the remaining ingredients and mix well. Bring to a simmer, and adjust to your taste. Let this simmer slowly. (Note: you'll have more sauce than you need, but it will keep for a month or more in the fridge.)

Once your grill is hot, set the breasts on it, bone down. Paint them with the BBQ sauce. Let this cook with the grill cover closed for about 5 minutes, then paint again with the sauce. Repeat this.

Now, with the grill cover open, tip the breasts on their sides. I like to make sure that the drumette is between grill grates so it gets extra heat. Let this cook for a minute or three, then do the other side. You want a little char, but nothing too blackened.

Set the breast upright again and let them cook with the grill open, until the meat is done. How long? Normally it takes about 20 minutes total time for a rooster pheasant, a little less for grouse, maybe only 5 minutes for partridges. You want to reach about 150°F in the thickest part of the breast.

Paint the breasts one more time, then remove to a cutting board to rest 5 minutes. Carve the meat off the bone and serve.

BEER-CAN PHEASANT

Beer-can chicken is one of the best ways I know to roast a chicken, especially in summertime, when you can do this recipe on the grill. To make this technique work for pheasant, you need to make a few modifications. First off, while you can sometimes jam a regular beer can into a pheasant, the birds are generally too small. But a Red Bull can or a narrow jelly jar will fit. Fill it halfway with beer.

You also should consider brining your pheasant first, especially if it was a wild bird, and definitely if it was an old bird. You do not need to brine pen-raised pheasants.

This recipe would also work with large blue grouse.

Serves 2 | Prep Time: 30 minutes | Cook Time: 40 minutes

BRINE

¼ cup kosher salt

4 cups cold water

Brining seasonings (I like bay leaves, rosemary, and cracked black pepper)

PHEASANT

1 empty Red Bull can

Enough beer to fill half the can (any beer will do)

1 whole pheasant, plucked and gutted

2 tablespoons olive oil to coat the bird

Salt and black pepper

1 tablespoon dried thyme leaves

If you're brining your bird (see note above), mix the kosher salt and the water and add the seasonings. Submerge the pheasant in this brine for 4 to 8 hours, then drain and let sit in the fridge uncovered the next day; this helps you get a crispy skin.

Let the pheasant rest at room temperature for about 30 minutes. If you're using cold beer, let it come to room temperature, too.

Prepare your grill for indirect heat. If you're using charcoal, put the coals on one side of the grill, leaving another side free of coals. If you're using a gas grill, fire up only half of the burners.

Rub the pheasant all over with olive oil. Mix the salt, pepper, and thyme in a bowl, and sprinkle the mixture over the pheasant.

Fill the Red Bull can halfway with the beer. Drink the rest of the beer. Put the can inside the pheasant's cavity, and place the pheasant on the cool side of the grill. The legs and the can will act like a tripod to keep the pheasant upright.

Cover the grill, and come back in 40 minutes. After that time, check the pheasant, and add more coals if needed. Stick a thermometer into the thickest part of the pheasant's thigh—you want it to read 160°F. If it's not ready, close the grill lid and come back in 15 minutes. Keep checking this way until the pheasant is done. If you don't have a meat thermometer, poke the spot between the leg and breast with a knife and look for the juices to run pinkish-clear, not red.

Carefully move the bird to a pan. Let the pheasant rest for 10 minutes. Carefully lift it off the can and carve up into serving pieces.

BARBECUED PHEASANT THIGHS

Slow-cooked thighs are my favorite part of any upland bird, and barbecue is a perfect match for this. Take your time, keep the heat moderate, and you'll be good.

I'm a huge fan of South Carolina's mustard-based BBQ sauce, so I give you my recipe for that iconic sauce below. Feel free to use whatever barbecue sauce you prefer, though.

Serves 4 | **Prep Time: 15 minutes, not including optional brine** | **Cook Time: 2½ hours**

12 pheasant thighs or 4 turkey thighs

¼ cup kosher salt

1 quart water

A little vegetable oil

SOUTH CAROLINA BBQ SAUCE

¼ cup butter

½ cup white or yellow onion, grated on a box grater

½ cup yellow mustard

½ cup brown sugar

½ cup cider vinegar

1 tablespoon mustard powder

1 bay leaf

Cayenne pepper and salt to taste

Brining the pheasant helps it retain moisture. You don't have to do this, but it will make for a juicier thigh. Stir the salt and water together until the salt dissolves. Submerge the thighs in the brine and refrigerate for at least 4 hours, or up to overnight. If you don't have enough brine to cover, double it.

Set up your grill up for barbecuing, leaving one side of it clear of coals or otherwise off the heat. Remove the thighs from the brine and pat dry. Coat with a little vegetable oil and set them on the cooler side of the grill. Cover and barbecue no hotter than 230°F—I try to keep it slower, closer to 180°F—for 30 minutes; turkey thighs will need an hour.

Meanwhile, make the sauce. Add the butter and onion to a medium pot, and sauté the onion until it softens. Don't let it brown. Add the remaining ingredients and stir well. Let this simmer slowly while the thighs cook. If you want a smooth sauce, buzz it in the blender.

When the thighs have been on the grill for at least 30 minutes, paint them with the sauce and turn them over. Rearrange them if there are hot spots on the grill. Cover and keep cooking until the meat wants to fall off the bone, at least another hour and up to 3 more hours for old turkey thighs. Paint with more sauce every 30 minutes or so during this time.

If you want, finish the thighs on the hot side of the grill for a minute or two on each side to get some char. Paint one last time and serve.

AUSTRIAN WIENER SCHNITZEL

Wiener schnitzel is deceptively simple, but like most such dishes, there's a secret to preparing it properly. Bad Wiener schnitzel is cafeteria food, or worse. At its best, however, this is one of life's simple joys: the meat is tender and can be cut with a fork. The breading is crispy, not greasy, and the squirt of lemon adds just the zing that the dish needs.

At its core, Wiener schnitzel is just a breaded cutlet fried in fat and served simply with lemon. It's a blue-collar lunch, a slightly more refined rendition of that Southern icon, chicken-fried steak.

The trick is in the technique. The cutlet must be very thin, the flour light, the eggs beaten, the breadcrumbs applied with a light hand—and, most importantly, the schnitzel must swim in hot fat. Not oil. Fat. Lard is ideal, but clarified butter is fine, as is duck or goose fat. Wiener schnitzel is such a simple recipe that you really ought to use a flavorful fat or you will wonder what all the fuss is about.

In Vienna, Wiener schnitzel is made from veal. Period. But Wiener schnitzel is equally good with a pounded pheasant breast, as well as breasts from partridges or cutlets sliced from wild turkey breasts. It's less successful with dark meats like sharp-tailed or sage grouse; those are better candidates for the jägerschnitzel recipe on page 265.

If you've never pounded your cutlets before, read the directions below before you start. It helps to have a rubber mallet or a meat mallet, but you can use an empty wine bottle or a small pot. Lemons are a must here, and remember that real Wiener schnitzel does not have a sauce! Lots of other schnitzel recipes do, but not this one.

Serve this with a simple green salad, bread, potato salad, or boiled potatoes. And make lots: these cutlets are awesome eaten cold as a sandwich filling the next day.

Serves 4 | **Prep Time: 25 minutes** | **Cook Time: 10 minutes**

---

4 to 8 skinless pheasant breasts, tenders removed

Salt

1 cup flour

2 eggs, lightly beaten

1 cup fine breadcrumbs

Enough lard, butter, or duck fat to come ½ inch up the sides of your frying pan

Set out a work surface and lay a pheasant breast on a piece of plastic wrap. Lay another piece of plastic wrap over the breast and pat it down to seal. Pound the meat into a very flat cutlet, about ¼ to ⅛ inch thick. Take your time, hitting the meat with about the same force as you'd use knocking on a door. Work from the center of the meat outward. You'll need to pound the thick end of the breast more than the thin end. Do one breast at a time. When you're finished with one, remove the top layer of plastic wrap and set it aside. As you finish more, stack them. (Removing the one layer of plastic wrap will make them easier to get off the plastic later.)

Tip: if you're using turkey, use the thinner portion of the turkey breast—the part farthest from the wishbone. If you use the portion closer to the wishbone, you'll need to slice the breast in half (between top and bottom) to get a thin enough piece to start pounding.

Preheat the oven to 200°F. Line a baking sheet with paper towels, place it in the oven, and set a rack on top of it; this is for the schnitzels as they come out of the frying pan.

Set up a breading station. Put the flour into a large tray, plate, or shallow bowl. Do the same for the eggs and for the breadcrumbs. Put the

lard or butter into the frying pan and turn the heat to medium-high. You want to fry at a temperature between 325°F and 350°F.

When the fat is heated, dredge a cutlet in flour and shake off the excess. Then dredge it in the egg and then the breadcrumbs. Don't press the breadcrumbs into the meat. Immediately put the breaded cutlet into the hot fat. Shake the pan a little to make sure the schnitzel doesn't stick to the bottom. The cutlet should float in the hot fat. Repeat quickly with as many cutlets as will fit in your pan.

Fry the schnitzels until they're golden brown, about 4 minutes total. As the first side is cooking, spoon some hot fat over the upper side. This will speed up the cooking process. Flip only once. When the schnitzels are done, put them in the oven on the rack over the baking sheet and repeat until you're done.

A NOTE ON LARD

Most people recoil in horror at the thought of cooking with lard, yet have no problems about cooking with butter. Truth is, fresh rendered lard is better for you than butter. Really, it is. But it must be freshly rendered—the kind you get in the refrigerator section or that's made daily in Latin markets. You do not want to use hydrogenated lard, which is indeed as bad for you as it sounds.

"See! from the brake the whirring pheasant springs,
And mounts exulting on triumphant wings:
Short is his joy; he feels the fiery wound,
Flutters in blood, and panting beats the ground."

—ALEXANDER POPE, WINDSOR FOREST, 1736

Variation: IOWA PHEASANT "TENDERLOIN" SANDWICH

This is *the* iconic Iowa sandwich, normally done with pork. But since I first ate one while attending Pheasants Forever's annual Pheasant Fest in Des Moines, I decided this would be every bit as good with a pheasant breast. I was right.

Many recipes substitute crushed saltine crackers for the breadcrumbs, but I prefer it with fine breadcrumbs. Either way works.

Simply make a batch of schnitzels as in the previous recipe, then get your fixins'. You'll need cheap burger buns, ketchup and mustard, sliced pickles, and chopped raw onions if you want them.

One nontraditional touch I'd suggest is to caramelize a big batch of onions and put some on top. Much better than raw onions, in my humble opinion. Here's how I make my caramelized onions:

CARAMELIZED ONIONS

Take your time when you make these. Rushed caramelized onions are not good. If you are forced to rush, you can add a pinch of baking soda to the cooking onions, which will speed the process. Don't add too much, or you'll make onion mush.

Make a big batch of these onions and store them in the fridge. They'll keep a week or so, and are good on pretty much everything.

---

4 large yellow or white onions

2 tablespoons butter or oil

A pinch of salt

2 teaspoons dried thyme (optional)

1 tablespoon honey (optional)

Slice the onions from root to tip; this helps them keep their shape as they cook. If you want an almost jam-like consistency, chop as normal.

Cook the onions over medium-high heat in the butter, tossing to coat, until you get the first signs of browning on the edges. Sprinkle them with salt.

Turn the heat to low, cover the pan, and cook for 20 minutes, stirring from time to time. Add the optional thyme and honey, and keep cooking like this until the onions are a rich brown, about 20 minutes more.

GROUSE NORTHWOODS

I designed this dish to evoke the forest of the Minnesota Northwoods—deep "brown" flavors from the mushrooms and wild rice punctuated by the bracing tartness of the cranberries and vinegar-fruit syrup. And the grouse! Those of you who have eaten ruffed grouse know. There's no flavor like it in the world. It looks like chicken, but smells and tastes gamy in the best possible way. Grouse is not for timid eaters, but nor is it challenging in the way that, say, stinky French cheeses are. Even the texture hints at a walk in the woods. You get the soft "give" of treading on wet leaves, but then there are the popping cranberries, the chewy wild rice, and the surprising crunch of the ground-wild-rice coating on the grouse; it's just enough crunch to be interesting without being off-putting.

I urge you to make this recipe with grouse if you have them. If you can't get your hands on grouse, any white-meat bird will do: pheasant, partridge, chicken, or turkey. I bet this would even be good with walleye fillets.

And I prefer true wild rice, which is not cultivated, but any wild rice will work. The choice of mushrooms—store-bought or wild—is up to you. Just don't skimp on them. As for the fruit syrup, I prefer something that lives in the Northwoods, like gooseberry or highbush cranberry or blueberry. I also use homemade gooseberry vinegar here, but cider vinegar is perfectly fine.

Serve this with a light red wine or a white like a viognier or albariño. Beer is also a good choice. A simple green salad rounds it all out.

Serves 4 | **Prep Time: 20 minutes** | **Cook Time: 30 minutes**

1½ cups wild rice (divided—1 cup for the dish, ½ cup for the breading)

3 cups stock (grouse or chicken)

Breasts from 4 grouse, skinned and with tenders removed

Salt

4 tablespoons butter (divided—3 tablespoons to sauté the breasts, 1 tablespoon to sauté the mushrooms)

½ cup rye, barley, or whole wheat flour

1 to 2 pounds fresh mushrooms (any kind)

2 cloves garlic, minced

1 teaspoon dried thyme

1 cup cranberries

¼ cup fruit syrup (see above for preferences)

⅓ cup cider vinegar

Salt the grouse breasts well and set aside at room temperature.

Simmer 1 cup of the wild rice in the grouse or chicken broth until tender, anywhere from 20 minutes to 50 minutes depending on whether you have truly *wild* wild rice or the cultivated variety. When the rice is done, drain and set aside in a covered bowl.

Grind the remaining ½ cup of wild rice in a spice grinder into a powder. There will still be some larger bits; this is fine—it adds some texture. Mix this with the rye flour and dredge the grouse breasts in it.

Heat 3 tablespoons of the butter in a large sauté pan and sauté the grouse breasts until they're just barely done, about 4 to 5 minutes per side. Remove the breasts and set them aside.

Put the remaining tablespoon of butter in the pan and turn the heat to high. Add all the mushrooms, shaking the pan as you add them so they don't stick to the bottom (it's OK if some do stick). Keep searing and shaking the pan until the mushrooms give up their water. Sprinkle the mushrooms with salt, and add the garlic and thyme. Let the mushrooms sear, without moving the pan, for 1 to 2 minutes. Stir the mushrooms and repeat until you get them as browned as you want. I like them to be about halfway browned, which takes about 8 minutes.

Add the cranberries and toss to combine. Cook until the cranberries just start popping, then add the wild rice, vinegar, and fruit syrup. Toss to combine and serve with the grouse.

PHEASANT PICCATA

I didn't enjoy an especially lavish childhood—times were downright hard in some of those early years—but the one luxury my mother and stepfather allowed themselves was eating out at restaurants. In fact, it'd be fair to say that I grew up in restaurants. And in one restaurant in particular: the Sleepy Hollow, in Scotch Plains, New Jersey.

I am pretty sure it closed years ago, alas, but you know what it looked like. Every town had a place like this in the 1970s and early 1980s—big, dark, wood panels, a great bar with sports on the TV, a fireplace that was never lit, and a white-linen dining area where all the hoary greats of the age were served: duchess potatoes, asparagus with hollandaise, shrimp scampi, a prime rib so good it remains the standard by which I measure all others—and, if you're feeling like a lighter dinner, chicken piccata.

Piccata is one of a triumvirate of similar classical preparations, the others being saltimbocca and marsala. They were always done with either veal or chicken, and when I wasn't allowed to order the prime rib (it being reserved for special dinners), I would cycle through these dishes one after the other.

My stepfather, Frank, used to hold court at the bar after work, and for a time we ate dinner there several times a week. I became an expert at whichever video game the restaurant had tucked into its one quiet corner; I remember being a god in an odd game that involved a mouse called Mappy.

I drank gallons of some sort of virgin cocktail variant of a Tom Collins, then had my way with Shirley Temple before settling on ginger ale, straight up. I liked ginger ale. It made me feel like an adult, and it was the same color as Frank's J&B. I ordered my ginger ale in exactly the same glass with exactly the same amount of ice as he did. I still wonder why I never developed a taste for J&B.

I loved the Hollow. It's where I developed my Monday night football habit, hit on my first waitress, and snuck my first drink. In no small way, I grew from a boy into a man at the Hollow. I grew so comfortable in that place, and that place with me, that I was practically the restaurant's mascot. It's probably why I became a cook. And it's probably why I love being in restaurants so much today. I miss it.

And I miss those old dishes. They're like that special blanket you had as a kid that mom would throw on the bed when it was extra cold. You may not cook the classics for years—decades, even—but you know that they're in the closet of your mind, waiting to warm you when you need a little comfort.

I don't cook with chicken much anymore, but pheasant is a perfect bird for piccata; any white-meat bird is, actually. Classic piccata starts with a cutlet, the thinner the better, which is lightly floured (not breaded) and sautéed in olive oil and butter. You want both fats in there, not because of a smoke-point issue, but for flavor. Once the cutlets are done, you add lemon juice and white wine to the pan, deglaze it, add capers, boil it down, turn off the heat, and swirl in some more butter. Garnish with parsley—curly parsley, if you want to be very 1978.

Piccata is a very easy dish to make, except for one point: to make the sauce properly, it must be finished with sweet (unsalted) butter *off the heat*. Skip this and the sauce will break. Because this dish comes together quickly, be sure to have everything ready before you start cooking .

Pound your pheasant, grouse, or partridge breasts—or turkey cutlets—as you would for Wiener Schnitzel (page 74).

Serve with mashed potatoes or just a really good piece of bread. An austere white wine, like a Chenin blanc or a pinot grigio, would be typical, but I ate most of my piccata with ginger ale. Of course, I was ten years old at the time.

Serves 4 | **Prep Time: 10 minutes** | **Cook Time: 8 minutes**

- 4 to 6 pheasant breasts, skinless and boneless
- Salt
- Black pepper
- ½ cup flour
- 2 tablespoons olive oil
- 6 tablespoons unsalted butter (divided—2 tablespoons to sauté the breasts, the rest for the sauce)
- 1 cup white wine
- 3 tablespoons lemon juice
- 2 tablespoons small capers
- 2 tablespoons chopped parsley, for garnish

Pound each breast as you would for Wiener Schnitzel (page 74). Salt and pepper the cutlets well, and dust with the flour. White flour is traditional here, but I like to pair darker flours with game, so I add a few tablespoons of whole wheat, rye, or spelt flour.

Heat the oil and 2 tablespoons of the butter over medium-high heat, and sauté the floured breasts for 3 minutes on one side, then 2 minutes on the other. You may need to do this in batches. Move the sautéed breasts to a plate for now.

Add the lemon juice and white wine to the pan, and scrape any brown bits off the bottom of the pan with a wooden spoon. Add the capers, and boil this down by half over high heat, about 2 minutes.

Turn off the heat, and remove the pheasant breasts to serving plates. Put the remaining butter in the sauté pan one tablespoon at a time, swirling each tablespoon around until it melts before adding the next. The sauce should be emulsified and smooth. Pour the sauce over the pheasant and garnish with the parsley. Eat at once.

"The last partridge to rise will take the most arrows."

—AFRICAN PROVERB

GENERAL TSO'S PHEASANT

Many of us have eaten The General's chicken at cheap, steam-table Chinese restaurants—gloppy, over-breaded, and so sweet that you fall into glycemic shock afterward. It's just not good, and you know this is so if you've been lucky enough to eat General Tso's chicken at a top-notch Chinese restaurant.

Done correctly, General Tso's chicken is irresistible. Tender meat with a light, crunchy batter reminiscent of tempura, tossed in a sauce perfectly balanced between sweet and spicy, studded with green onion and Chinese tien tsin chiles. It is the crack cocaine of Chinese food. You want it. No, you must have it. At any cost. I know people who will do shameful things for a plate of perfect General Tso.

This is that perfect plate. And it has a history.

General Tso was an actual historic figure, a Qing dynasty statesman and general in Hunan Province, China. But the general did not make this dish, nor would he really have recognized it. A Taiwanese refugee from Hunan, one Peng Chang-Kuei, invented this in the 1950s. Peng's version was not nearly as sweet or crunchy as what we're all used to today; that version has its origin in the early 1970s, when a chef named T. T. Wang, who had eaten Peng's original in Taiwan, opened a Hunan restaurant in New York City.

By all accounts, Peng loathed the American version of his recipe. Too sweet. And he apparently rolled his eyes at the notion that extraneous vegetables such as water chestnuts or baby corn should appear in the dish, which is supposed to be meaty through and through. Fuchsia Dunlop has more details on the story in her excellent *Revolutionary Chinese Cookbook: Recipes from Hunan Province*, where my version originates.

My take on General Tso's is slightly more powerful and hearty than most "authentic" versions. It is definitely less sweet than the cheapy Chinese style, and definitely spicier. I also make a little more sauce than Dunlop's rendition because, well, I like the sauce. And I use pheasant breast. Pheasants happen to be indigenous to Manchuria in Northern China, so it seems right. Any white meat works, though.

There are a few unusual ingredients in an authentic General Tso's that you will want on hand, notably the black vinegar and the tien tsin chiles. Both are readily available in larger supermarkets or in Asian markets. That said, if you live in an area without a large supermarket or an Asian community, you can use malt vinegar and any small, hot, dried chile.

Note that although you need a lot of oil to fry the pheasant in, you can reuse the oil several times. Just let it cool a bit and strain it through a paper towel back into the bottle.

Serves 4 | Prep Time: 15 minutes | Cook Time: 15 minutes, including pre-frying step

---

MARINADE

4 tablespoons potato starch
  or cornstarch

2 egg yolks

1 tablespoon soy sauce

In a small bowl, mix the egg yolks, soy sauce, and potato starch together with the pheasant pieces. Set aside at room temperature while you chop everything else.

Mix the sauce ingredients in a small bowl and set aside.

Pour the peanut oil into a wok or a large, heavy pot and heat it to about 350°F. If you don't have a thermometer, you can test by putting a little flour or the end of a wooden chopstick into the oil—if it sizzles immediately, the oil is hot enough. Get a chopstick or something similar ready; you'll need this to quickly separate the pieces of pheasant when they hit the hot oil. Lay out a baking sheet with a paper towel on it for the finished pheasant pieces.

(continued)

½ cup stock (pheasant or chicken)

1 tablespoon soy sauce

1 tablespoon sugar (or more if you
    want it sweet)

1 tablespoon Chinese black vinegar
    or malt vinegar

2 tablespoons tomato paste mixed
    with 2 tablespoons water

1 teaspoon potato starch
    or cornstarch

STIR-FRY

1 pound pheasant breast meat,
    cut into bite-sized pieces

3 cups peanut oil or vegetable oil
    (for frying the meat)

3 tablespoons peanut oil, lard, or
    vegetable oil (for frying the
    chiles, ginger, and garlic)

8 dried hot chiles, broken in half
    and seeds shaken out (use less
    if you don't want it spicy)

A 2-inch piece of ginger, peeled and
    minced

3 cloves garlic, thinly sliced

6 green onions, chopped

2 teaspoons sesame oil

When the oil is ready, add about a third of the pheasant pieces and immediately use the chopstick to separate them. Fry until they're golden brown, about 2 to 3 minutes. Remove the pheasant from the hot oil with a slotted spoon and set on the baking sheet. Repeat twice more with the remaining pheasant pieces, frying a third of them at a time. Doing it this way keeps the oil hot.

Turn off the heat and let the oil cool a bit. Pour the cooled oil into a heatproof container (I use a large Pyrex measuring cup) and deal with it later. Wipe out the inside of the wok. If you're not using a wok, get out a large sauté pan.

Heat the 3 tablespoons of peanut oil in the wok or sauté pan over high heat for 1 minute. Add the dried chiles and cook until they almost turn black, another minute or so. Add the ginger and stir-fry 20 seconds, then add the garlic and stir-fry another 20 seconds.

Add all the pheasant pieces and the green onions. Stir the sauce in the bowl and add that to the wok, making sure you get all the potato starch, which will have sunk to the bottom. Stir-fry 1 minute. Turn off the heat and mix in the sesame oil. Serve at once with steamed rice.

CHINESE ORANGE PHEASANT

"Hi, my name is Hank, and I am addicted to Sad Panda's orange chicken."

"Hi, Hank."

I admit it: I'm a sucker for this addictive approximation of Chinese food sold at Panda Express all over the country. I have no idea whether so-called orange chicken actually exists in China, although there is a vaguely similar dish called tangerine beef that I like quite a lot. Orange chicken consists of pieces of chicken—usually thigh—marinated and coated in a batter, fried crisp, then tossed in a zippy, citrusy sauce that ranges from pleasantly sweet to cloying, depending on who makes it.

Some varieties also add chiles to balance things out. If Panda does this, I can't tell, so when I'm there, I always order it with some other entrée that has those little dried chiles in it. I then bite off a piece of the chile and take a bite from a piece of orange chicken. The sweet-hot-sour is an addictive combination.

I didn't set out to mimic Panda's recipe when I designed this rendition. This is basically an adult version of orange chicken. The crust isn't as thick, but it's crispier. The sauce isn't as sweet, there's significant heat from the chiles, and there's a bigger orange flavor from the juice, marmalade, and slivered peel, which also adds a touch of bitterness that deepens the flavor of it all. If you loathe any sort of bitter, leave out the peel or just don't eat it—treat it like a bay leaf.

Once you get the hang of this, which takes maybe twice, you'll want it more and more and more. It's almost as addictive as my General Tso's Pheasant (page 81). Almost.

This recipe can be done with any white meat, not just pheasant. The optional ingredients—white pepper, tangerine peel, and green onions—give the dish a more Chinese feel, but are not often seen in American Chinese restaurants. As for the tangerine peel, in China they dry the peel and store it for a very long time, years even. They then soak the peel in water to soften, then slice it thin. I like it a lot. What's more, using the water you soaked the peel in to make up some of the orange juice or starch slurry adds even more flavor.

I personally like this dish sweet and hot. But some people just like sweet, and that's OK. You should know that this is not as sweet as Panda Express. To get there, you'll need another tablespoon or even two of honey or marmalade. And if you like a thicker crust, add a couple of tablespoons of flour to the cornstarch you toss the pheasant in.

Serves 4 | **Prep Time: 30 minutes** | **Cook Time: 15 minutes**

MARINADE

2 tablespoons soy sauce

2 tablespoons rice wine, vermouth, or dry sherry

2 teaspoons minced ginger

1 garlic clove, minced

¼ teaspoon white pepper (optional)

2 eggs, lightly beaten

Mix together all the marinade ingredients. Add the pheasant pieces, making sure each piece is well coated. Set aside while you prep everything else, about 20 minutes.

For the sauce, mix together the soy, orange juice, marmalade, honey, and vinegar and set aside.

Make a cornstarch slurry by mixing the 1 tablespoon of cornstarch with about 2 tablespoons water in a small bowl, and set aside.

Heat the oil in a wok or a small, heavy pot to 350°F to 360°F. Line a baking sheet with paper towels and set aside. While the oil is heating, add the ¼ cup of cornstarch to the marinating pheasant pieces and toss to coat (this is a messy process, so you'll need to wash your hands at some point). When the oil is hot, fry the pheasant in 3 or 4 batches

SAUCE

1 tablespoon soy sauce

⅔ cup orange juice, ideally fresh squeezed

1 tablespoon honey

1 tablespoon marmalade

1 tablespoon rice vinegar

TO FINISH

1 to 1½ pounds pheasant (or other white meat), cubed

¼ cup, plus another tablespoon, cornstarch, tapioca, or potato starch

2 cups cooking oil

Chopped green onions (optional)

Drizzle of sesame oil

1 to 5 small dried hot chiles, broken up and seeds discarded

1 tablespoon tangerine peel, thinly sliced (optional)

until golden brown, about 2 to 3 minutes per batch. As each batch finishes, set it in the baking sheet to drain.

After you've fried all the pheasant, pour out the oil into a glass or metal container; you can strain and reuse it later. Rinse the wok and wipe it out with paper towels, then set it back on very high heat. Add about 2 tablespoons of oil from the container you just used. When it's hot, add the chiles and tangerine peel and stir-fry for 30 seconds. Add the pheasant back to the wok and the ingredients for the sauce you mixed together earlier. Stir-fry this for a few seconds.

Now, start stirring the cornstarch-water slurry, and, while still stirring, pour it over the meat. Stir-fry until it gets thick, a couple of seconds.

Drizzle the sesame oil over everything, give it one more toss, and serve immediately with steamed rice.

"Pheasants are fools if they invite the hawk to dinner."

—DANISH PROVERB

KUNG PAO PHEASANT

Kung Pao chicken is one of my absolute favorite dishes whenever I eat Chinese food, even at the cheapy Chinese steam-table places. I think it's the combination of texture and flavor: hot, fried chiles, silky chicken, crunchy peanuts. What's not to love?

Kung Pao chicken is originally from Sichuan and is supposed to be loaded with chiles and that crazy spice, Sichuan peppercorns, which make your mouth a little numb.

When you make this recipe, try to find the authentic ingredients: Chinese black vinegar, Shaoxing wine, potato starch, and Sichuan peppercorns. If you can't find them, it's fine to substitute, but the recipe won't be quite as good.

This recipe was designed for pheasant, but it will work with any boneless white meat.

Serves 4 | Prep Time: 25 minutes | Cook Time: 10 minutes, including the pre-frying step

SAUCE

1 tablespoon sugar

1 tablespoon soy sauce

1 tablespoon Chinese black vinegar
or rice vinegar

1 teaspoon potato starch
or 1½ teaspoons cornstarch

2 teaspoons sesame oil

¼ cup chicken stock

MARINADE

½ teaspoon salt

1 tablespoon soy sauce

1 tablespoon Shaoxing wine
or dry sherry

2 teaspoons potato starch
or 2½ teaspoons cornstarch

1 tablespoon water

PHEASANT

Skinless breasts from 2 pheasants

5 cloves garlic, slivered

A 2-inch piece of ginger, peeled and
minced (about 2 tablespoons)

5 or 6 green onions, chopped

10 dried hot chiles (such as Sichuan
or cayenne)

1 teaspoon Sichuan peppercorns

2 tablespoons chicken fat, pheasant
fat, lard, or peanut oil

¾ cup roasted, unsalted peanuts

Whisk together all the ingredients for the sauce and set aside.

Whisk together all the ingredients for the marinade in a medium bowl.

Cut the pheasant breasts into small chunks about ½ inch across and mix with the marinade ingredients. Set aside for 20 to 30 minutes.

Meanwhile, slice the garlic cloves into slivers, mince the ginger as fine as you can, and cut the green onions into ½-inch pieces. Break the dried chiles into ½-inch pieces and shake out as many seeds as you can.

Set a wok over high heat for 1 minute. Add the fat, and heat this for another 30 seconds. Add the Sichuan peppercorns and the dried chiles, and stir-fry 30 seconds.

Add the pheasant, and stir-fry for 30 seconds. Then add the garlic, ginger, and green onions and stir-fry another 20 seconds.

Stir the sauce well and pour it into the wok. Add the peanuts and toss to combine. Bring to a rapid boil and cook, stirring constantly, for 30 seconds. Serve immediately over white rice.

GROUSE MOO GOO GAI PAN

This is another of those classic Chinese dishes that has made its way into the American consciousness. But the Americanized version of this dish only barely resembles the real deal. As my friend Kian Lam Kho wrote in his excellent book *Phoenix Claws and Jade Trees: Essential Techniques of Authentic Chinese Cooking*, "In many American Chinese restaurants moo goo gai pan is made with a psychedelic array of colorful vegetables. Yet the name simply means 'stir fried chicken slices with mushrooms.'" And that's what this dish is, but with grouse or pheasant in place of the chicken. This recipe is pretty close to Kian's and is, more or less, what you'd get if you ordered this dish in China. Note that I use wild chicken-of-the-woods mushrooms in the picture, but any fresh mushroom will do.

Serves 4 | **Prep Time: 20 minutes** | **Cook Time: 15 minutes**

1 pound boneless, skinless white meat, cut into small chunks

MARINADE

2 egg whites, lightly beaten

3 teaspoons potato starch, cornstarch, or tapioca

A healthy pinch of salt

½ teaspoon white pepper

SAUCE

½ cup stock (grouse, pheasant, or chicken)

½ cup Shaoxing wine or white wine

2 tablespoons oyster sauce

2 tablespoons soy sauce

1 tablespoon potato starch, cornstarch, or tapioca

TO FINISH

2 cups peanut or other vegetable oil

4 cloves garlic, thinly sliced

4 thin slices of fresh ginger

½ pound various fresh mushrooms, cut into chunks

¼ cup stock (grouse, pheasant, or chicken)

¼ pound bamboo shoots, cut into matchsticks (optional)

Sesame oil, for garnish

Chopped green onions, for garnish

Chopped cilantro, for garnish

Mix the marinade ingredients in a small bowl. Add the grouse chunks and mix with your clean hands. Let this sit while you chop the other vegetables, or up to 30 minutes.

Whisk together all the sauce ingredients and set aside.

Heat the peanut oil in a wok or pot to about 350°F. If you don't have a thermometer, you want the end of a chopstick to sizzle immediately when you put it into the oil. Fry the grouse chunks in the oil a third at a time, using the chopstick or some other implement to separate the pieces as they hit the hot oil. Cook them so they're mostly cooked but not cooked all the way, about 2 minutes.

Turn off the heat, drain the oil (you can use it several times) and wipe out the wok. Add back a tablespoon or two of the oil and heat it over the highest heat you can generate on your strongest burner.

When the oil starts to smoke, add the sliced garlic and ginger, and stir-fry for 20 seconds or so. Add the mushrooms and the stock and stir-fry for about 30 seconds. Cover the wok and let it all cook another minute.

Return the grouse to the wok along with the bamboo shoots (if using) and stir-fry 30 seconds. Stir the sauce well, then pour it into the wok. Stir-fry this for 1 minute, turn off the heat, and add the sesame oil, green onions, and cilantro. Serve with steamed rice.

PHEASANT SATAY WITH PEANUT SAUCE

If you've never had satay, you're missing out. It's a Southeast Asian appetizer of skewered meat grilled over charcoal. It's usually spicy and curried, and it can be done with more or less anything you can put on a skewer. Make sure the meat is tender, however, because you're eating it off a stick—and you don't want to be chewing endlessly.

Don't skimp on the marinating time with this recipe; the aromatic buttermilk soak goes a long way toward tenderizing the pheasant. If you happen to be working with pen-raised birds, you should only need two hours of marinating time, but if you have old, wild roosters, lean more toward the four-hour soak time. Don't let the pheasant soak more than 8 hours, though, or they'll get mushy.

Serves 4 to 6 as an appetizer | **Prep Time: 2 to 4 hours marinating time** | **Cook Time: 10 minutes**

1½ pounds skinless pheasant breasts (about 2 to 3 birds' worth)

Bamboo or metal skewers

Oil for coating the pheasant

MARINADE

1 cup buttermilk

1 tablespoon minced fresh ginger (or 1 teaspoon ground ginger)

1 large garlic clove, minced (or ½ teaspoon garlic powder)

2 tablespoons yellow curry powder

1 teaspoon cayenne (optional)

3 tablespoons Asian fish sauce or soy sauce

Juice of 2 limes

PEANUT SAUCE

½ cup smooth peanut butter

2 tablespoons soy sauce

1 to 3 teaspoons chile bean paste or Sriracha

1 tablespoon brown sugar (or to taste)

Juice of a lime

½ teaspoon garlic powder

¼ cup coconut water (regular water is fine)

1 teaspoon sesame oil (optional)

Lime wedges, for garnish

Cut the pheasant breasts lengthwise into long strips. You'll be threading them onto skewers, so cut them as long as you can. You can cut the pheasant into chunks, but chunks won't cook quite as evenly as strips.

Put the skewers in water to soak.

Mix together the marinade ingredients in a bowl or small container, add the pheasant strips, and coat the strips well. Cover the container and marinate in the fridge for 2 to 4 hours, depending on how old your birds were (see note above).

Meanwhile, mix together all the peanut sauce ingredients and set aside, covered, at room temperature while the pheasant marinates. You might need a little more water than is called for here, depending on how thick your peanut butter is; you want the sauce to be a little thicker than melted ice cream, a little thinner than pancake batter.

To grill: Take the pheasant out of the marinade and thread one strip per skewer. Shake off any excess marinade and set on a tray. Get your grill hot and scrape it down with a grill brush. Soak a paper towel in some vegetable oil and grab it with tongs to wipe down the grates. Brush the pheasant skewers with a little more vegetable oil and grill over high heat (with the lid open) until the pheasant is done, about 2 to 4 minutes per side, depending on how hot your grill is.

To broil: Take the pheasant out of the marinade and thread one strip per skewer. Shake off any excess marinade and set on a broiling pan. Set an oven rack about 4 inches from the broiler. Get your broiler hot for 10 minutes or so. Brush the pheasant skewers with a little vegetable oil and broil about 5 minutes per side, until the pheasant is fully cooked and has a little char on it.

Serve on a platter with the dipping sauce and lime wedges.

SOUTH DAKOTA PHEASANT SALAD SANDWICH

I first learned about this venerable sandwich during a pheasant hunting trip to Aberdeen, South Dakota, arguably the epicenter of pheasant hunting in America. As the story goes, these sandwiches were made by the thousands during World War II for the troops stopping briefly in Aberdeen as their trains took them east or west.

It's not a particularly glamorous sandwich, but it is a piece of history. I include this recipe here largely because of the method I use to cook the pheasant, which is the absolute best way to cook a white meat prone to drying out—pheasant, grouse, partridge or turkey breast, or rabbit saddles.

Use this method for any sort of pheasant salad, not just this sandwich. Trust me: do this and it will change the way you think about pheasant.

I like these sandwiches like a BLT: bacon, lettuce, tomato, and the salad. It's a damned good lunch.

Serves 4 | **Prep Time: 20 minutes** | **Cook Time: 25 minutes**

1 pound white, tender meat,
   such as pheasant breasts

1 quart stock (pheasant, grouse,
   or chicken)

2 or 3 hard-boiled eggs, chopped

¼ cup minced sweet onion

½ cup minced celery

1 tablespoon relish, either sweet
   or hot

½ cup mayonnaise, or to taste

1 tablespoon mustard, or to taste

1 teaspoon paprika

Salt and black pepper to taste

Bread and accompaniments of
   your choice

To cook the pheasant, take the breasts out and salt them well. Let them sit out about 20 minutes or so while you cook the eggs and chop the vegetables.

Bring the stock to a boil and drop the pheasant in. Turn off the heat, and cover the pot. Let the pheasant cook in the cooling stock for 25 minutes. Remove the pheasant, and shred or chop finely; remember, this is going in a sandwich.

Mix all the other ingredients together and chill. Serve on the bread or roll of your choice; I prefer lettuce, tomato, and bacon on a Kaiser roll.

PHEASANT KAESESPÄTZLE

This is basically a German mac-n-cheese with some pheasant bits tossed in. It's easy, homey, and kids will love it. You can serve this in a big casserole or, for a dinner party, in individual ramekins. It reheats well, so you might want to make a big batch on the weekend and eat it for weeknight meals.

Obviously, any boneless light meat works here, not just pheasant breast. Chunks of wild turkey breast or rabbit are especially good here.

Feel free to substitute flours here. With game, I like using old wheats like emmer, einkorn, or spelt. Rye, barley, or whole wheat flour are also fun.

Serves 4 to 6 | **Prep Time: 45 minutes** | **Cook Time: 15 minutes**

¾ pound boneless meat, such as pheasant breast

4 cups onions (about 2 large), sliced root to tip

3 tablespoons butter

½ teaspoon dried thyme

2 to 4 teaspoons honey

SPÄTZLE

2 cups flour (see above)

A few gratings of nutmeg, about ¼ teaspoon

2 eggs, lightly beaten

¼ cup heavy cream

1 cup buttermilk

A healthy pinch of salt

TO FINISH

5 ounces Gruyère or Swiss cheese, shredded

¼ cup chopped chives or parsley

Preheat the oven to 400°F, and grease a casserole dish or several ramekins.

Start by poaching the pheasant meat using the method for South Dakota Pheasant Salad Sandwiches on page 91. Once the meat is cooked, cool and shred or chop.

While you're poaching the meat, caramelize the onions. Heat the butter in a large frying pan over medium-high heat and sauté the onions until they begin to brown on the edges. Then turn the heat to low, cover the pan, and cook, stirring occasionally, for about 30 minutes. Toward the end of this time, stir in the thyme and honey. When the onions are pretty and brown, turn off the heat and set aside.

You can make the spätzle while the onions are cooking. Mix all the spätzle ingredients together into a batter that should be a bit thicker than pancake batter. Bring to a boil a large pot of water and salt it well.

To make the spätzle, use a spätzle hopper—easy to get on Amazon.com for less than $10—or use a colander with wide holes. Add the batter to the hopper or the colander, hold it over the simmering water, and drip the batter into the water (if you're using a colander, a rubber spatula will help move the batter through the holes). You'll be making lots of little dumplings. Let them boil on the surface for a minute or two, then scoop the dumplings out with a slotted spoon and arrange them on a baking sheet to cool. Coat them with a little butter or oil to keep them from sticking together.

Make the dish by layering some spätzle, then pheasant meat, then caramelized onions, then a bit of the chopped herbs, then cheese into the casserole dish or ramekins. Shoot for at least two layers—three is better—and be sure that shredded cheese is on top.

Bake for 15 to 20 minutes, until the cheese melts and begins to brown.

PHEASANT BURGERS

Pheasant burgers? You betchya. When you have a great trip and bring home lots of pheasants, or if you have a few birds that have been a bit mauled by the dog—or you've hit them a little too squarely—this is a great recipe for less-than-perfect roosters. It's even better with wild turkeys.

You can grind the meat in advance and freeze it, or you can grind fresh. Either works. If you use bacon (see below), it's better to grind and serve rather than grinding and freezing later; the salt in the bacon changes the texture of the burger, making it more like sausage than a traditional burger.

Of course, you can top your bird burgers any way you want, but I like this Asian take on the American classic.

If you can't find fatty pork shoulder, substitute bacon. It's a bit different, but still good.

Serves 4, and can be scaled up | Prep Time: 45 minutes, if you're grinding | Cook Time: 20 minutes

---

1½ pounds skinless pheasant meat

¼ pound fatty pork shoulder
or bacon

Salt

½ cup mayonnaise

¼ cup Sriracha (or more to taste)

Fresh cilantro, chopped, for burger
topping

½ cup lime juice or rice vinegar

1 medium red onion, sliced root to tip

Burger buns

Submerge the red onion slices in the lime juice or vinegar and set aside for at least 30 minutes, and up to two days ahead of time. This takes the sulfur sting out of raw onions.

Grind the pheasant meat with the fatty pork shoulder through a medium die, about 6.5 mm. If you don't have a meat grinder, get one. But in the meantime, you can chop the pheasant and pork and pulse it in the food processor. This isn't nearly as good, but it'll get you close. Shape into 4 patties and set aside.

Mix the Sriracha and the mayo in a small bowl. Start with a couple of tablespoons of the hot sauce at first, and add to taste.

Salt the burgers well on both sides; if you use bacon, you don't need to do this. Set the burgers in a room-temperature frying pan and turn the heat to high. As soon as the burgers start to sizzle, drop the heat to medium and cook until the interior hits about 155°F, normally about 8 minutes total. Flip the burgers after 4 minutes.

Set the burgers on a cutting board to rest and set the burger buns, cut-side down, onto the frying pan to brown for a minute or three. If there isn't enough fat in the pan, add some butter.

Spread the Sriracha mayo on the buns, add the patties and top with pickled onions and cilantro. Serve with beer.

PHEASANT CACCIATORE

Cacciatore is shorthand for *alla cacciatore*, which means "hunter's style" in Italian. The French call it *chasseur*, the Spanish *cazadores*. This dish in its variations is usually done with chicken, which makes me wonder: is this the meal that the failed hunter gets from his wife when he returns empty handed? A meal eaten in sullen reflection of missed shots, sore feet, birds flushed just a little too far away?

Probably not. I don't know the actual history of hunter's style chicken, but I'm guessing it's an outgrowth of the seventeenth century and was initially done with pheasants, quail, or partridges. Another possibility is that this is what the housewife (or servant, more likely, given the European hunting tradition), stewed for several hours while the hunters were out chasing pheasants or deer, making this chicken stew a welcome-home meal. Who knows. Five items connect all versions of this dish: a white meat, such as partridge, pheasant, or rabbit; white wine; tomatoes; mushrooms, usually wild; "woodsy" herbs such as sage and rosemary.

This dish is so satisfying, as only the combination of tomatoes, wine, mushrooms, and meat can be.

Serves 4, and can be doubled | **Prep Time: 20 minutes** | **Cook Time: 2 hours**

2 pheasants, cut into serving pieces

¼ pound pancetta, or 4 strips bacon

4 tablespoons olive oil (or pheasant fat or chicken fat)

1 chopped celery stalk

1 chopped carrot

5 cloves chopped garlic

1 onion, sliced in half-moons

½ pound cremini or button mushrooms

2 cups white wine

2 tablespoons chopped fresh sage

1 tablespoon chopped fresh rosemary

1 teaspoon crushed juniper berries

4 bay leaves

½ ounce package dried wild mushrooms (about a handful)

1 quart crushed tomatoes

Salt and pepper to taste

4 tablespoons minced parsley

Preheat the oven to 350°F. If using pancetta, cut it into little batons about ¼ inch thick. Chop bacon. In a large braising pan or Dutch oven, heat 2 tablespoons of the olive oil or fat over medium heat and cook the pancetta or bacon. Remove and reserve.

Add the pheasant pieces to the pan, and brown them well. Take your time, and do it in batches. Remove the pheasant pieces as they brown.

Add the carrot, celery, onions, and fresh mushrooms to the pan. Turn the heat to high. Sauté until the onions begin to brown. Add more oil if needed. When the onions begin to brown, add the garlic and cook for another minute, stirring occasionally.

Add the herbs, the dried mushrooms, and the white wine, and turn up the heat to maximum. Stir well. Let the wine cook down by half. Add the tomatoes and mix well. Add some salt if needed. Add the bacon and the pheasant pieces, skin side up. Do not submerge the pheasant; just nestle the pieces into the sauce so the skin stays out of the liquid.

Cover the pan and place it in the oven. After 1 hour, check to see if the meat is thinking about falling off the bone. It'll likely take more like 2 hours, but it's worth checking early. When the meat is as tender as you want, remove the cover from the pan and cook until the skin crisps, about 30 to 45 more minutes.

Move the pheasant pieces to a plate. Add the parsley to the pan and mix to combine. To serve, ladle out some of the sauce, top with a pheasant piece, and serve with either polenta or a good crusty bread. I like a dry rosé or a light red like a Sangiovese for this dish.

SATURDAY PHEASANT

This is a retro 1970s dish my mom used to make, on, well, Saturdays—only she used chicken. But even in the 70s, she knew to use a high-quality chicken. We got ours from Gage's Chicken Farm in New Jersey. "The quality of the chicken really makes or breaks this recipe," Mum says. The recipe translates beautifully for pheasant—it requires only thirty minutes longer than the original chicken recipe to get the meat on the pheasant legs to begin to fall off the bone.

If you want to make this dish so it eats a bit more easily, use just thighs of pheasants or turkeys. Otherwise, you'll need to pick through the tendons. Rabbits are a good choice, too.

Serves 4 | **Prep Time: 5 minutes** | **Cook Time: 2 hours, or more if using turkeys**

2 to 3 pounds pheasant legs

Salt

2 teaspoons garlic powder

¼ cup sweet paprika

1 can condensed Campbell's
  cream of mushroom soup

1 cup cream

1 cup chopped fresh parsley,
  loosely packed

Preheat the oven to 350°F.

Salt the pheasant or chicken legs well and dust with garlic powder and paprika.

Mix the condensed soup with the cream and add any remaining paprika and a hit of garlic powder. Pour half of this into a casserole dish. Put the pheasant legs down, skin side up, and then pour the rest of the cream-soup mixture over the legs. Cover the casserole with foil and bake for 1 hour.

Take the casserole out and remove the foil cover. Put it back in the oven and bake, uncovered, for about another hour, or until the meat begins to fall from the bone.

When the meat is done, take the casserole out of the oven and mix in the parsley. Serve over mashed potatoes, polenta, or a split and opened baked potato.

A TASTE OF BOYHOOD

IT'S AMAZING TO what lengths we'll go to recapture a sliver of our childhood, especially as we approach middle age. With the passage of so many years, early memories are always in soft focus, the music of the period wafting in and out of hazy scenes we can only imperfectly recall. Food becomes the anchor, the one vivid thing within the clouds.

Shining through is this recipe, a rich, ruddy chicken casserole my mom called "Saturday Chicken." I remember loving this dish, which we would often have on days other than Saturday—a fact that confused my little brain. Should it be called Tuesday Chicken, then? "No," Mum said, "It's always called Saturday Chicken." But why? "It just is."

Even thirty years later, I can instantly recall the flavor of this dish—mushroomy, creamy, "red," and a little burnt-crispy. We always savored the caramelized skin of the chicken pieces that rose from the simmering sauce like islands in a lava flow. And we always ate it with baked potatoes.

Mum grew busier as I grew older, as did I. I can't remember the last time she made Saturday Chicken for me, but it was some time before 1988. Over the years, the dish faded from my culinary memory. But it never quite flickered out.

Re-creating Saturday Chicken confounded me. I had no idea how it was made. So I called Mum to ask. "You're not going to like it," she said. Why? How bad could it be? I mean, it didn't have globs of mayonnaise in it or those broken-up potato chips all over like her tuna casserole, which is a war crime of a recipe.

Then I heard the words: "It has canned, condensed cream of mushroom soup."

Nooooo! Seriously? "Yes," she said. "And Saturday Chicken cannot be made any other way." I hung up the phone, crushed. Cream of mushroom soup is everything I despise about 1970s cooking, everything I despise about the many modern wild-game recipes that rely heavily upon it. Cream of mushroom soup is That Which Shall Not Be Named in my cooking world.

After a bit of soul searching, I emailed Mum for the recipe, promising to use That Which Shall Not Be Named. She sent it, word for word, from her favorite cookbook during that time, *The I Hate to Cook Book* by Peg Bracken. She also sent a commentary about how she, too, over the years, had tried to improve the recipe by using fresh and natural ingredients. To no avail.

Sigh. So I went to the supermarket to buy Campbell's condensed cream of mushroom soup. My hand actually shook as I reached for it. It felt like grabbing a Playboy at the 7-Eleven back when I was twelve. Dirty. Forbidden.

Back in the kitchen, I decided to make the recipe mostly as written, with two changes: first, I was going to put the parsley in at the end, not at the beginning; I'm not a fan of parsley cooked for ninety minutes. Second, I had no chicken. So I would use pheasant legs instead. Saturday Pheasant.

When the dish came out, it looked pretty much as I remembered, although I think Mum let the sauce cook down even more, to the point where some parts of the chicken burned. It definitely smelled right—like paprika, roasted bird, and mushroom.

I served it over smashed potatoes and took a bite. There it was! That thick, ultra-rich, and tangy sauce, a little sweet with paprika, a little meaty from the mushroom soup. I took another bite. And another. Soon all that was left were bones.

And then I felt my age. This, my friends, is a gut bomb. Cream + condensed cream of mushroom soup = lots and lots of calories and fat. I felt like you do after Thanksgiving dinner, tryptophan seeping into my veins. Mussst . . . sleeep . . .

I know you're asking yourself, "So, Mr. Fresh-Local-Wild-Food-Smarty-Pants, bet you liked that cream of mushroom soup, eh?" Well, yes. I did. In that recipe. But I still won't be buying canned soup anytime soon.

Saturday Chicken is a wonderful blast from my past, a brief flirtation with being an eight-year-old in 1970s New Jersey, a savory slice of memory. But it's not who I am anymore. I possess neither the metabolism to eat the dish on a regular basis nor the desire to cook with any products that come in a package—no matter how time honored, or sustainable, or earthy-crunchy, or whatever. It ain't me, babe. No, no, no it ain't me. What they say is true: you really can't ever go home again. And I'm OK with that.

BRAISED PHEASANT WITH ROOT VEGETABLES

Pheasant and parsley root are a natural match. I love using parsley root, but it can be tough to find. Parsnips are an excellent substitute, but so are carrots (of any color), turnips, rutabagas, or celery root. Any root vegetable will do.

I also add a ton of garlic, but it's roasted first, which mellows it out and adds a needed jolt of umami to an otherwise subtle and delicate dish. The lemon goes in at the end to brighten everything.

A word on the pheasant thighs. Note that there are no drumsticks here. This is because you really can't just sit and eat a pheasant drumstick—there are just too many tendons that will not break down. If all you have are whole legs, separate the thighs and drumsticks before you cook them, and, when everything's tender, fish out the drumsticks, pull off all the meat, and put the meat back in the braise. Keep the thighs whole; they're easy to deal with at the table.

The one thing not to skimp on is the roasted garlic. Yes, you really do want two whole heads.

Serve this dish with a full-bodied white wine such as a Côtes du Rhône, chardonnay, viognier, or an off-dry Riesling. For beer, go with a crisp lager or a pale ale.

Once made, this will keep in the fridge for a week.

Serves 4 | **Prep Time: 45 minutes, to roast the garlic** | **Cook Time: 2 hours**

---

2 heads garlic

1 tablespoon olive oil

1 to 2 pounds pheasant or turkey thighs

Salt

2 tablespoons pheasant fat, chicken fat, or butter

1 large onion, sliced thinly root to tip

1 pound parsley roots (or other roots), peeled and cut into large chunks

¼ cup minced parsley, for garnish

Zest and juice of a lemon

Black pepper to taste

Start by roasting the garlic. Preheat the oven to 375°F. Slice the top quarter off the heads. Nestle them into some foil and drizzle the olive oil into the cut ends. Close the foil and roast until browned and soft, about 50 minutes. When the garlic is done, drop the heat to 325°F.

While the garlic is roasting, make a quick stock from the greens and peelings from the root vegetables and parsley. Chop the stems of the parsley you're using to garnish, and add them to the peelings of the roots along with the tops, if you have them. I like to add the fronds from a fennel bulb, too. Cover everything with 3 cups of water and bring to a boil. Drop the heat to a simmer and cook gently while the garlic is roasting.

While all this is going on, brown the pheasant thighs in the pheasant fat (or butter) in a large Dutch oven or other heavy, lidded pot. Salt them as they cook. Once the pheasant has browned, set it aside for the moment and sauté the onion over medium-high heat until the edges brown. Salt the onion as it cooks, too.

When the garlic is ready, remove it from the oven and let it cool. Put the root vegetables into the Dutch oven with the onions and squeeze the garlic into the pot. Set the pheasant, skin-side up, on top of everything. Strain the stock and pour enough into the Dutch oven to come up to the level of the skin on the pheasant. Salt everything well.

Cover the pot, put it into the oven, and simmer gently for 90 minutes. Uncover the pot and raise the heat to 425°F to crisp the pheasant skin. This should take about 20 minutes.

When you're ready to serve, add the minced parsley, lemon zest and juice, and grind some pepper over everything. Serve with bread or rice.

PHEASANT PAPRIKASH

Making Hungarian food is an adventure fraught with danger; the Magyars take their food very, very seriously, and they will let you know if you screw it up. Problem is, most of these dishes—goulash is the classic case—have as many variations as it has cooks. Paprikash is another example. Hopefully, this version will pass muster with the Hungarians among us. At the very least, it tastes great and is easy to make.

Paprikash is often served over *nokedli*, Hungary's version of German spätzle. You can, of course, use store-bought spätzle, but these are easy to make.

Serves 4 to 6 | Prep Time: 30 minutes | Cook Time: 90 minutes

PAPRIKASH

2 whole pheasants, cut into
    serving pieces

3 tablespoons bacon fat, lard,
    or butter

Salt

2 very large yellow onions,
    sliced root to tip

¼ cup paprika, Hungarian if possible

2 bay leaves

2 jarred roasted red peppers, chopped

Stock to cover, up to 3 cups
    (pheasant, grouse, or chicken
    stock—see below)

½ cup sour cream, at room
    temperature

1 tablespoon flour

¼ cup chopped parsley

DUMPLINGS

3 eggs, lightly beaten

A healthy pinch of salt

1½ cups warm water

3 cups flour

Heat the bacon fat over medium-high heat in a large Dutch oven or other heavy, lidded pot. Brown the pheasant pieces well, taking your time. Chances are you'll need to do this in batches.

When the pheasant has been nicely browned, remove the meat. Add the onions to the pot and cook over medium heat until they brown at the edges, about 8 to 10 minutes. You might need to add another tablespoon of fat. Salt them as they cook.

Mix in the paprika, bay leaves, and roasted red peppers, followed by about 1 cup of stock. Return the pheasant to the pot. You want the liquid to come up to the sides of the pheasant, but not submerge it. You'll likely need another cup or two of stock. Cover the pot and cook on low heat until the pheasant is tender, about 90 minutes to 2 hours.

While the paprikash is cooking, make the dumplings by mixing all the ingredients together. You want it the consistency of pancake batter—not a dough—so add enough water to get there. Bring a large pot of water to a boil, and salt it well. Put the batter into a spätzle hopper (easily available on Amazon.com), a colander with wide holes, or a perforated pan and set this over the hot water. Let the batter drip through the holes, making little dumplings (if you're using a colander or a perforated pan, a rubber spatula will help move the batter through the holes).

Let the dumplings boil on the surface for a minute or two, then scoop them out with a slotted spoon and put them on a baking sheet. Coat with some butter so they don't stick, and set aside.

When the pheasant is tender, whisk the sour cream and the flour in a bowl, and then add a little of the cooking liquid to this. Stir well and repeat several times, then pour the contents of the bowl into the pot and stir. Turn off the heat and add the chopped parsley.

Serve the paprikash over the *nokedli*.

PHEASANT WITH APPLES

There's something about the combination of poultry and apples that just sings. This dish is a wild game variation on a French classic done with chicken. I first learned about chicken Normandy, as it's called, while watching Emeril Lagasse, of all things; he made it on his stand-and-stir show decades ago.

It's a simple mix of sweet onions, gently cooked apples, cider, cream, brandy, and pheasant. There's no special technique involved here, no great difficulty or esoteric ingredients. This is comfort food, and all it asks of you is a little time.

I designed this recipe for skinless pheasant legs, which can be cooked entirely on the stovetop. If you have skin-on legs, you can crisp the skin in a 375°F oven at the end.

Serves 4 | **Prep Time: 15 minutes** | **Cook Time: 2 hours**

4 tablespoons unsalted butter

2 cooking apples, peeled, cored, and sliced into wedges

Flour for dredging

1½ to 2 pounds pheasant legs (with thighs)

Salt

1 large yellow onion, sliced root to tip

½ cup Calvados or other apple brandy

2 cups apple cider (non-alcoholic)

1 teaspoon dried thyme

¼ cup heavy cream

¼ cup chopped parsley, for garnish

Salt the pheasant legs and let sit at room temperature for 30 minutes.

Heat 2 tablespoons of the butter in a Dutch oven or other large, oven-proof pan over medium heat. Add the apple slices and sauté, turning occasionally, until they turn a little brown around the edges. This should take about 5 minutes. Sprinkle the apple slices with a little salt. Set aside on paper towels.

Dust the pheasant in flour and add the remaining 2 tablespoons of butter to the pan. Brown the pheasant well, then remove and set aside.

Add the onion and increase the heat to medium-high. Sauté, stirring occasionally, until it just begins to brown, about 6 to 8 minutes.

Take the pan off the heat, and pour in the brandy (don't add the brandy while the pan is still over a flame; you want to avoid an unintentional flambé). Put the pan back on the heat, and using a wooden spoon, scrape any browned bits off the bottom of the pan. Let the brandy boil until it has reduced by about half. Add the cider and bring it to a boil. Add the thyme. Lay the pheasant legs in the pan, cover, and simmer gently until tender, anywhere from 1½ to 2½ hours.

Fish out the pheasant legs. If you prefer to serve this dish off the bone, strip the meat off the bones; otherwise, leave the legs and thighs intact. Turn the heat to high, add the apples, and boil down the sauce by half. When the sauce gets a little syrupy, turn off the heat and add the cream. Add salt to taste. Serve by spooning some apples and onions onto everyone's plate and topping it with the pheasant. Garnish with parsley.

HONEY-MUSTARD PHEASANT WINGS

One of my great crusades in wild-game cookery is to convince people to keep more of the animals they bring home. In the case of bird hunting, this often means the wings. Wings are a staple at sports bars, but eating wings made with wild birds can be like chewing on flavored leather.

The trick here is to braise the wings until they're tender. And if you are using wild birds, not all wings will get tender at the same time. So you can do one of two things: pick out the wings as they become ready, or just braise them all until the last one wants to fall off the bone. I prefer the second method. You might have a couple of wings fall apart if you do this, but in the end, it's easier.

Once the wings are tender, coat them in the sauce and let them sit an hour or more, up to overnight, really. Then roast them in a hot oven until crispified. Coat with a bit more sauce, and hammer 'em!

This method works great with all kinds of wings, from giant turkey wings to grouse wings. It's also fun with the front legs of rabbits and squirrels. But it's best with the wing sections of pheasants or the back legs of squirrels.

To make this recipe, save the drumettes from all your birds, the second digits (the "forearms") of pheasants, or the legs from squirrels. As you collect them, vacuum-seal them in packages or just wrap them in plastic wrap until you get at least twenty wing pieces. Then make wings for Football Day or whenever.

Serves 4 to 6 | **Prep Time: 10 minutes** | **Cook Time: 3 hours, mostly braising time**

---

3 to 4 pounds pheasant wings

1 quart chicken broth

Salt

½ cup yellow mustard

2 tablespoons water

3 tablespoons honey

1 tablespoon cider vinegar

Splash of Worcestershire sauce

Cayenne and black pepper to taste

Put the wings and the broth in a heavy, lidded pot. If they are not totally covered by the broth, add water until the wings are just barely covered. Bring to a bare simmer and cook gently, with the lid on, until all the wings are tender. You want the meat to be thinking about falling off the bone. Normally this takes 2 hours, but 3 hours isn't unreasonable. If you need to add water during cooking, sprinkle a little salt in there, too. This can be done ahead of time.

While the wings are cooking, make the sauce by mixing all the other ingredients in a small pot and bringing it to a simmer. Turn off the heat and tinker with the flavors by adding more salt, honey, cayenne, or black pepper.

When the wings are ready, put them in a bowl and add the sauce. Toss to coat. At this point, you can refridgerate them for up to a day.

When you're ready to cook your wings, preheat the oven to 425°F. Set the wings on a baking sheet (saving the excess sauce) so they don't touch each other and bake until they begin to brown on top, about 15 minutes or so. Turn and repeat. Toss with the remaining sauce and eat.

YASSA PHEASANT

This is one of the iconic dishes of Senegal, in West Africa. It's an easy dish to wow a crowd with, and the flavors are bright and strong like the tropical sun. You can definitely pick up the French influence here (Senegal was once a French colony) in the Dijon mustard and caramelized onions. Pretty much any light meat works here, and it's commonly done with fish, too.

Serves 4 | **Prep Time: 8 hours, mostly marinating time** | **Cook Time: 90 minutes**

2 pheasants, grouse, or cottontails;
   or 4 squirrels; or 8 quail; or
   2 turkey thighs

4 cups sliced onions

1 cup lemon or lime juice

Salt (smoked, if you have it)

¼ cup peanut or palm oil

2 to 3 tablespoons Dijon mustard

1 cup stock (pheasant or chicken)

½ teaspoon dried thyme

Chopped hot chiles, to taste

Cut the pheasants into serving pieces, leaving the breast meat on the bone; this will keep it from drying out too much. Chop each breast half into 2 or 3 pieces. Salt the meat well.

Combine the lime juice and onions in a bowl, add the pheasant, and soak for at least an hour and up to a day. Shake the container from time to time to make sure everything had good contact with the lime juice.

When you're ready to cook, remove the pheasant and reserve the onion marinade.

Heat the palm or peanut oil in a large pan and add the onions from the marinade. Cook the onions over medium heat. You want them to get soft and sweeten, but it'll be hard to brown them because they've been pickled. Keep these cooking while you cook the pheasant.

You can brown the pheasant in a number of ways. You can broil the pieces, sauté them in some more oil, or you can do what I do (and which is traditional): you can grill them. Get your grill hot, and make sure the grates are clean. Dip a paper towel into some oil and wipe the grates down, then place the pheasant pieces, skin-side down, on the grill. However you cook the pheasant, make sure it's well browned; if grilling, you want a bit of char on it.

Once the pheasant is ready, mix the mustard and thyme into the onions, and add the stock and the reserved marinade. Nestle the pheasant pieces in this, cover, and simmer until the meat is tender, about an hour or so.

Add the chiles to taste and serve with white rice.

PHEASANTS, RUFFED GROUSE, AND BLUE GROUSE |

GROUSE DORO WAT

From West Africa to East Africa we go! This is doro wat, arguably the national dish of Ethiopia and a dish close to my heart. I once worked in an Ethiopian restaurant called the Horn of Africa in Madison, Wisconsin. This was by far their most popular dish. It's normally done with old chickens, and pheasants or grouse are great alternatives.

There are a few esoteric ingredients in this recipe that you really must have; these are what make Ethiopian food special. The good news is that some ingredients, like the berbere spice mix, can be found in some fancy supermarkets, online, or can be made by hand. The *niter kebbeh* butter is easily made and lasts for many months in the fridge and forever in the freezer.

So once you get yourself set up, making this recipe is much easier. Traditional doro wat is made with *t'ej*, an Ethiopian mead. If you have some mead lying around, use it. Red wine is another traditional alternative.

Note that most recipes for doro wat will add even more berbere than I do, but be warned: it's hot stuff!

Serves 4 to 6 | **Prep Time: 1 hour** | **Cook Time: 3 hours**

2 whole grouse or pheasants, cut into serving pieces

¼ cup lime juice

6 cups red onions, about 4 medium onions, sliced root to tip

½ cup spiced butter (see next page)

4 garlic gloves, minced

1 tablespoon minced fresh ginger

3 tablespoons tomato paste

¼ cup berbere (see next page)

½ teaspoon black pepper

½ teaspoon ground cardamom

½ teaspoon ground fenugreek (optional)

1 cup mead or red wine

2 cups stock (game or chicken)

Salt to taste

6 hard-boiled eggs, peeled

Soak the grouse in the lime juice for an hour, and up to overnight.

In a large, heavy pot, add the sliced onions, and turn the heat to medium. Cook the onions dry, stirring frequently. They will give up their water, wilt, and eventually brown.

When the onions are close to browning, add the spiced butter, the garlic, and the ginger. Cook another minute or three. Add the tomato paste, berbere, black pepper, cardamom, and fenugreek. Mix well.

Add the grouse pieces, and turn to coat. Cook another few minutes, until the meat turns opaque.

Add the stock and mead or wine. You want all the meat to be covered by about an inch; add water if you need to. Bring to a simmer, taste for salt, cover the pot, and cook gently until the meat is tender, typically about 2 hours. The sauce should have cooked down a lot by now; add a little water if it gets thicker than gravy.

When you're about 15 minutes from serving time, add the hard-boiled eggs to the pot. You can either strip all the meat from the bones or leave it as-is. Serve with rice, bread, or the Ethiopian crepes called *injera*.

(continued)

ETHIOPIAN SPICED BUTTER

I love this butter so much that I use it far beyond Ethiopian dishes. If you use it in any of the curries in this book (see African Rabbit Curry on page 199) it will add another layer of awesome. And as I mentioned, it will keep for months in the fridge and for years in the freezer.

1 pound unsalted butter

¼ cup minced shallot

2 cloves garlic, minced

2 tablespoons minced fresh ginger

12 to 15 cardamom pods, crushed

5 cloves

1 cinnamon stick, about 1 inch long

1 tablespoon dried oregano

½ teaspoon turmeric

1 teaspoon fenugreek

Toast the cardamom, cloves, and cinnamon in a dry pan over medium heat until they're aromatic, about a minute. Cut the butter into cubes.

Toss everything into a heavy pot, and turn the heat on low. Let this come to a bare simmer, and cook gently for at least 30 minutes. We cooked ours at least an hour at the restaurant. It's vital that the milk solids don't burn. If they do, you will have ruined the butter. Watch for browning, and when you see it, turn off the heat.

Strain through cheesecloth, and store in a clean glass jar. It'll last six months in the fridge, at least a week on the counter, and forever in the freezer.

BERBERE (ETHIOPIAN SPICE MIX)

This is some serious stuff. Complex, fragrant, and hotter than hell. It's to Ethiopian food what masala is to Indian: indispensable. Once made, it will keep a year in the cupboard.

1 cup cayenne

¼ cup sweet paprika

1 tablespoon onion powder

1 tablespoon salt

2 teaspoons garlic powder

1 tablespoon ground ginger

1 tablespoon ground rue seed (optional)

1 tablespoon ajwain seed (optional)

2 teaspoons ground cardamom

2 teaspoons ground cumin

2 teaspoons ground fenugreek

1 teaspoon ground turmeric

1 teaspoon ground clove

Mix all the ingredients together and store in a cool, dark place. Note that rue seed and ajwain are very hard to find. I include them here for authenticity's sake.

PHEASANT AND DUMPLINGS

Pheasant and dumplings is a dish of love, of time and patience. First you simmer the bird to make a stock, then you pull the meat from the bones to return to the soup later. You strain the stock and rebuild the soup with what is essentially a French velouté, a combination of a flour-and-butter roux and the hot stock. New vegetables go in, as well as the pulled meat. You finish it off with the dumplings, which need to be as light as possible.

In many parts of the country, chicken and dumplings is the ultimate comfort food. Making it with wild birds is only a matter of increasing the cooking time. Wild birds work for a living, so some can take hours before the meat falls off the bone. But have faith—fall off it will, in time.

If you save the giblets, use the heart, gizzard, and neck in the broth; don't use the liver, as it will make the broth cloudy and give it an off taste.

You might find yourself wondering about the cake flour in the dumplings. Don't. Cake flour makes the dumplings much lighter and fluffier (it's the lower protein content that does it). If you can't find cake flour, you can use all-purpose. Just don't use bread flour.

Serves 6 to 8 | **Prep Time: 15 minutes** | **Cook Time: 2 hours**

BROTH

1 pheasant; wings and carcass of a turkey; 8 quail; 2 rabbits; or 4 squirrels

Salt

2 carrots, chopped

2 celery stalks, chopped

1 large onion, chopped

½ a parsnip, or 1 small parsnip

2 bay leaves

2 teaspoons dried thyme

1 ounce dried mushrooms (any kind)

Start with the broth. Toss all the broth ingredients into a large stockpot, cover with at least 2 quarts of water (you can save any extra broth for later) and bring to a strong simmer, about 200°F if you're checking. Drop the heat to below a simmer—look for lots of steaming and just a few bubbles on the surface—and let everything cook for 20 minutes. Fish out the pheasant and remove the breast meat. Shred it, then set it aside in the refrigerator and return the rest of the pheasant to the pot. Cook for as long as it takes for the meat to want to fall off the leg bones, from 45 minutes for a pen-raised bird to 2½ hours for an old rooster.

When the pheasant is done, gently remove it from the broth and let it cool enough to handle. Pick all the meat off the bones, being sure to remove all those nasty tendons in the pheasant's legs. Put the meat into the bowl with the breast meat.

Strain the broth. Put a fine-meshed strainer that has a paper towel set inside it over a large bowl or pot. Pour the stock through this. You might need to change paper towels halfway through if it gets too gunked up. Pour the broth into a pot, and set it on low heat.

To make the stew, heat the butter in a large pot or Dutch oven set over medium-high heat. Sauté the carrot, celery, and parsnip for 3 to 4 minutes, stirring often. You don't want the veggies to brown. Add the flour and stir to combine. Everything in the pot will seize up, but that's OK. Drop the heat to medium-low and cook, stirring often, until the flour turns the color of coffee with cream. Add the vermouth and stir well,

(continued)

4 tablespoons unsalted butter

2 carrots, sliced into rounds

2 celery stalks, sliced about
    ¼ inch thick

½ a parsnip, or 1 small parsnip,
    chopped

4 tablespoons flour

½ cup vermouth or dry sherry

1 cup fresh or frozen peas

1 cup chopped parsley

¼ cup heavy cream

Salt and black pepper

DUMPLINGS

2 cups cake flour

2 teaspoons baking powder

1 teaspoon salt

2 tablespoons melted butter,
    slightly cooled

¾ cup milk

then start adding the broth, 1 cup at a time, stirring constantly, until it looks silky. It should take 6 to 8 cups.

Add the pheasant meat and bring this to a simmer. Cook gently until the veggies are soft, about 30 minutes.

While the stew is simmering, make the dumpling dough. Mix together all the dry ingredients, then add the melted butter and the milk. Stir just to combine—do not overwork the dough.

Drop the dough by the teaspoonful into the simmering stew. When all the dough is in, cover the pot and cook over low heat for 15 minutes. It is very important that the stew not boil during this time, or your dumplings will get tough.

At 15 minutes, uncover the pot and add the peas and parsley, stirring gently to combine. Let this cook a minute or two, then turn off the heat. Add salt and freshly ground black pepper to taste, then the heavy cream. Serve at once.

PHEASANT WHITE CHILI

White chili is one of those Tex-Mex hybrids that you won't find in Mexico, or even very often in Texas. It seems to be a Northern adaptation of traditional chili, with white beans and chicken as its base. It's good with pheasant or any other white meat. White chili is basically the same as regular chili except that it's made with white beans, no tomato, and green chiles instead of red. It's a great change of pace, especially in spring.

You can make your white chili in one of two ways: you can use a whole pheasant, simmer it gently to make a pheasant broth, pick off all the meat, and then use the broth and the meat in the chili; or you can do this the quick and easy way by using premade broth and whatever pheasant you have lying around. I'll go through each option in the recipe below.

Serves 6 to 8 | Prep Time: 20 minutes | Cook Time: 3 hours, less if you use canned broth

BROTH

1 pheasant; 2 turkey drumsticks;
    3 partridges; 6 quail; 2 rabbits; or
    3 squirrels

10 cups water

2 bay leaves

6 to 10 cracked black peppercorns

1 teaspoon dried thyme, or
    a fresh thyme sprig

1 teaspoon dried rosemary, or
    a fresh sprig (optional)

6 to 10 crushed juniper berries
    (optional)

Salt

CHILI

3 tablespoons olive oil

1 large onion, chopped

3 cloves garlic, minced

2 poblano or green bell peppers, diced

One 28- to 30-ounce can white beans,
    drained and rinsed

One 28- to 30-ounce can white
    hominy corn, drained and rinsed
    (optional)

2 teaspoons ground cumin

1 teaspoon ground coriander

1 teaspoon dried oregano

1 small can of green Hatch chiles or
    jalapeños

Chopped cilantro and limes to garnish

If you are making the broth yourself, put the pheasant in the water and bring it to a boil over high heat. As soon as it boils, drop the heat to a simmer and skim any scum that floats to the top. Add the herbs and spices, and simmer for 30 minutes. Pull out the pheasant and pick off all the breast meat. Return the pheasant to the broth and simmer gently another hour or two. Take the pheasant out again and pick off all the rest of the meat from the bird. Reserve all this meat for the chili. Strain the broth and reserve it.

To make the chili, heat the olive oil in a large pot or Dutch oven over medium-high heat. Sauté the onions and poblano or bell peppers until they just barely begin to brown on the edges, about 5 to 7 minutes. Add the garlic and sauté another minute.

Pour in 1 quart of chicken stock or the broth you just made. Add the beans, hominy (if using), and the spices. Bring to a simmer. You want a dense stew, not a soup, so you might not need all the broth you made; use it for something else (it'll keep for a week in the fridge).

Add the reserved pheasant meat—or coarsely chopped pheasant meat if you didn't make your own broth—and the canned green chiles. Add salt to taste. Simmer 10 to 15 minutes. Finish the chili with fresh cilantro and lime juice and maybe a little green hot sauce if you like.

PHEASANT NOODLE SOUP

Pheasant soup is satisfying to body and soul, a tonic for your down days or those days when the icy chill of the world has cut a bit too deep. My recipe is hardwired in me, a soup I've enjoyed virtually unchanged since I can remember being me. I make it without conscious thought. Roast the carcasses of the pheasants with a little oil and salt. Make a broth from them. Pick off the meat, strain the broth, and add new vegetables, a little wine, and the obligatory egg noodles. In my world, chicken noodle soup always has egg noodles. I've eaten it this way for more than forty years, and I'm not about to change now. You might prefer rice, or orzo, or something else—and that's OK by me.

Next time you have a shot-up pheasant, or grouse, or rabbit, make this soup. Make it for your down days. Make it for your children. Watch them wrap their hands around the bowl and inhale the gift you've given them. Watch them eat one bowl, then another, then another. Watch them file away this moment forever. Watch them smile.

Once made, the broth will keep a week in the fridge. If you want to have leftover soup ready to go, undercook the noodles so they're al dente when you first eat the soup. They'll absorb more broth in the fridge and still be nice a few days later.

BROTH

2 pheasants, breast meat removed

A little oil to coat the carcasses

Salt

3 bay leaves

2 celery stalks, chopped

4 leek greens, chopped, or 1 onion, chopped (save the white parts of the leeks)

2 carrots, chopped

1 garlic clove, mashed

1 sprig rosemary

2 star anise pods (optional)

SOUP

3 tablespoons butter

White parts from the leeks, chopped, or 1 chopped onion

2 celery stalks, chopped

2 carrots, peeled and sliced into discs

1 bay leaf

½ to 1 cup white vermouth or white wine

Salt and black pepper

1 pound egg noodles, orzo, or other soup pasta

¼ cup chopped parsley

Make the broth first. Coat the pheasants with some oil and salt well. Put them in a roasting pan and roast in the oven at 400°F for about 1 hour. Remove the pheasants and put into a stockpot and just barely cover with water. Set the heat to medium-high. Pour some water into the roasting pan and let that sit for a few minutes to loosen things up. Scrape any browned bits off the bottom of the roasting pan with a wooden spoon and pour that into the stock pot. As soon as the stock begins to simmer, drop the heat to low and let this cook very gently for 2 hours.

Fish out the pheasants and pick off all the meat from the legs, thighs, wings, and carcass. Set this aside and return the bones to the stockpot. Add the celery, carrots, garlic, rosemary, bay leaves and star anise if using. Separate the light from dark parts of the leeks. Add the dark-green leek parts to the broth, saving the white and light-green parts for the soup. If you're using onions, add 1 chopped onion now. Let the stock cook another 90 minutes.

When you're ready to make the soup, you can do one of two things: you can simply set up a fine mesh strainer over the pot you're going to make the soup in, or you can properly strain your broth and use that. To properly strain the broth, put a piece of paper towel in the strainer and set that over a big bowl or other large container. Ladle the broth from the stockpot through the strainer setup into the big bowl. This will give you a nicer, clearer broth.

To finish the soup, heat the butter in a Dutch oven or other soup pot set over medium heat. Add the white parts of the leeks (or the onion), the remaining 2 celery stalks, and the carrots, and sauté until soft and translucent, but not browned. This should take about 5 to 8 minutes. Add the vermouth, and let this boil a minute or two. Then add the bay leaf and about 4 to 8 cups of the broth you just made. Let this simmer very gently.

To cook the noodles, you can do one of two things: you can just drop them into your soup, which is fine but it will make the broth cloudy; or you can boil your noodles in some salty water and add them later. I boil mine separately because I like clear broth.

While the noodles are cooking, return the picked-over pheasant meat to the soup. Add salt and freshly ground black pepper to taste. When the noodles are ready, add the parsley and serve.

THAI GREEN CURRY WITH PHEASANT

Thai curries are in many ways the ultimate thirty-minute meal. Add coconut milk, a little water or stock, meat or fish of your choice, curry paste of your choice, whatever veggies you have around, some fresh herbs, and bang! Done.

Thai curries are lighter, brighter, and to my mind, more approachable than Indian curries. There are lots of different kinds, but the basic categories are red, green, and massaman, which is yellow. I tend to do green curry with fish, or with light-colored meats—in this case, skinless pheasant breasts.

I can hear some wondering why I'd rely on a store-bought curry paste. Well, for whatever reason, the premade curry pastes stand up very well compared to the homemade stuff. I've done it by hand, and it's great, but not so much better that I feel the need to start from scratch every time.

My advice: buy a selection of these curry pastes, a bottle of fish sauce, and a few cans of coconut milk to keep around the house. They'll all last for months (years, even) and, armed with them, you can whip up something addicting and exotic in the time it takes to cook the rice you eat it with.

I have snow peas in this curry, but use whatever you want, as long as it's green. Asparagus, regular peas, sugar snap peas, more herbs, bok choy, green beans—you get the point. Serve the curry with jasmine rice and a lager beer.

Serves 4 | **Prep Time: 10 minutes** | **Cook Time: 25 minutes**

1 small yellow onion, sliced thinly from root to tip

½ pound mushrooms, such as oyster or shiitake

1 tablespoon peanut or other vegetable oil

Salt

One 15-ounce can of coconut milk

¼ cup chicken stock (optional)

3 citrus leaves (optional)

2 tablespoons fish sauce or 1 tablespoon soy sauce

3 to 4 tablespoons green curry paste

1 pound tender white meat, cut into bite-sized pieces

1 to 4 serrano or jalapeño chiles, sliced thin

½ pound snow peas

⅓ cup chopped Thai basil or cilantro

Heat the oil over high heat in a wok or large frying pan. Sear the onion and mushrooms over high heat, stirring often, until the onion browns on the edges, about 5 minutes. Salt everything as it cooks.

Pour in the coconut milk and the stock, if using. Fill the coconut milk can halfway with water and pour that in, too. If you're not using stock, fill the entire can with water and pour the whole can into the pan. Add the citrus leaves if you're using them, as well as the fish sauce or soy sauce and the curry paste. Bring this to a boil, then simmer it for 15 minutes.

Add the pheasant breast and simmer gently for 5 minutes, then add the chiles and snow peas and simmer for another 5 to 8 minutes. Stir in the basil or cilantro and serve.

GROUSE AU VIN

Winter is a perfect time for this dish, which, used with an old rooster, is said to have been cooked in France since Roman times. I used a big blue grouse rooster for this one. Honestly, any of the meats in this book will work with this classic of a dish.

It's best with crusty bread, but polenta or mashed potatoes would also be nice.

Serves 4 | **Prep Time: 20 minutes, not including marinating time (see below)** | **Cook Time: 3 hours**

1 or 2 grouse or pheasants, cut into serving pieces

1 bottle decent red wine (something you would drink)

⅓ pound diced bacon

1 pound mushrooms

1 large sweet onion, sliced thick

1 head garlic, cloves peeled but whole

2 tablespoons flour

Salt

Pepper

1 tablespoon dried thyme

2 bay leaves

2 tablespoons fresh parsley, minced fine

½ cup brandy

Pheasant or chicken broth

Marinate the grouse in wine, bay leaves, and thyme for a day or two in the refrigerator.

When you're ready to cook, cook the bacon over low heat in a heavy, oven-proof pot, ideally a brazier or a Dutch oven. When it's crispy, remove the bacon with a slotted spoon. Turn the heat up to medium.

Pat the grouse pieces dry and brown them in the bacon fat. Take your time, and do this slowly but surely. It could take 15 minutes. Remove grouse pieces to a bowl as they brown.

Brown the onion and mushrooms. Once they're just turning color, add the garlic. Cook another 2 minutes.

Sprinkle the flour over everything and stir to combine. Cook this, stirring often, about 10 minutes.

Pour in the brandy, and stir it in to incorporate. The stew will become very thick. Add the wine from the marinade, and stir that in, too. Return the grouse to the pot, along with any juices that accumulated. If you need it, add enough broth to cover everything by an inch or so. Stir in the herbs and add salt to taste.

Bring to a boil over high heat, then reduce heat to a gentle simmer. Cook for at least 90 minutes, then start checking to see if the leg/thighs are tender. You want them almost to the point of falling off the bone.

When the meat is tender, remove it, along with the mushrooms and onions, and put them in a bowl. Put foil over them to keep them warm.

Turn heat up to high in the pot. Boil down the liquid by half or until it thickens to the point of being a sauce or loose gravy. I like to put everything through a food mill's medium plate for a smooth and silky sauce, but it's not necessary. You could strain it to get the loose bits out if you wanted.

Return the vegetables and meat to the sauce and serve at once.

TORTELLINI EN BRODO

This is the great Tuscan classic, tortellini en brodo, little filled dumplings floating in broth. A perfect example of why simple is not necessarily easy. At first glance, there's not that much going on in this pretty bowl of soup, just a clear broth and a bunch of little dumplings, maybe a parsley leaf or two. But look closer.

First, you need to make the broth. Yes, you can use store-bought broth, but why would you? If you're going to the trouble to make tortellini, you might as well make the broth while you're at it; you can make them both at the same time, and they take more or less the same amount of time. I use leftover pheasant or grouse carcasses, along with the wings for some added meat.

With the broth simmering away, you make the pasta dough, which of course has lots of egg yolks in it—golden yellow is the color you're looking for in this whole dish. Then the filling, which is from some leftover breast or thigh meat, Parmesan cheese, and a touch of nutmeg.

Making tortellini is a labor of love. Tortellini can be fiddly, but you get used to it, and, after the first few dozen or so, you start banging them out quickly. That's the way it is with pasta.

Making this dish is a thing to do on a rainy (or snowy) weekend, a chance to be quiet, to occupy your mind not with the troubles of the work week, but with the creation of one of the great gifts anyone can give to another: A bowl of homemade soup. A bowl of love.

Traditionally, you'd use a leftover roast chicken carcass and leftover meat to make this recipe. But any white-meat bird (or rabbit, for that matter) will be just as good. Note that you can do something like this with red-meat animals like hares and pigeons, but that's a different dish (Dove or Pigeon Tortelli, page 273).

Serves 4 to 6 | **Prep Time: 2 hours** | **Cook Time: 4 hours, for the broth**

BROTH

Carcass and wings of a pheasant, or 2 ruffed grouse

1 chopped onion

1 chopped celery stalk

1 chopped carrot

Chopped stems from a bunch of parsley

2 bay leaves

Salt

A pinch of saffron (optional)

Parsley leaves, for garnish

PASTA

2 cups all-purpose flour

2 whole eggs

4 egg yolks

If not already done, roast the pheasant carcasses at 400°F until nicely browned, which will take 45 minutes to an hour.

Start by making the broth. Hack or chop the roasted carcasses into pieces with a cleaver or poultry shears and put them in a pot. Cover with water by about 1 inch and bring to a gentle simmer. Don't let this boil. Partially cover the pot so some steam can escape but without allowing the broth to reduce too much.

Let the carcasses simmer very gently for at least 2 hours, and up to 4 hours. When you think you are about 90 minutes away from being done, add all the remaining broth ingredients except the salt. Simmer for 90 minutes, then strain the broth. To get maximum clarity, a) don't let the broth boil at all during the whole process, and b) strain it through a paper towel set into a strainer by ladling the broth through, not dumping the contents of the pot into the strainer. This is how I got my broth so clear without going through the rigamarole of clarifying it with a raft like a French consommé. Clean the pot and pour the strained broth into it and set it under low heat. Watch that pot, and don't let it boil! Add salt to taste.

While the broth is simmering, make the pasta dough. Pour the flour into a large bowl and make a well in the middle of the mound of flour.

FILLING

½ pound cooked, chopped pheasant meat (or cooked meat from another white-meat bird or rabbit)

75 grams finely grated Parmesan cheese, about 2 ½ ounces

Zest of a lemon, finely grated

1 egg

A few gratings of nutmeg, about ¼ teaspoon

Salt and pepper to taste

Put the eggs and yolks into the well and mix to make a dough. Knead for at least 5 minutes and up to 10 minutes. Remove the dough from the bowl and wrap in plastic wrap. Let the dough rest for 1 hour. Or, if you have a vacuum sealer, seal the dough in a vacuum bag; it will hydrate instantly, and will not need to rest. I do this because making the tortellini is time consuming.

Make the filling. Mix the chopped pheasant meat, lemon zest, cheese, and nutmeg in a bowl. Taste it. It might not need more salt because the cheese is salty. Add salt if you need to, then put everything in a food processor with the egg. Pulse until you have a paste. Remember: this filling is going into little tortellini, so it needs to be fairly smooth.

Now it's time to make the tortellini. Get a good work surface ready. I use a big maple board, but any large, clean surface will work. Set a little bowl of water near you to paint the edges of the tortellini with your finger. Get something to cut the tortellini—a ruler and a knife work well, since you'll be cutting squares of dough here. I actually use a square cookie cutter, which makes things go much faster. Stuff the tortellini filling into a sturdy plastic bag and squeeze it into a corner. Snip off the corner so you can use the plastic bag like a fancy pastry-piping bag.

Cut your dough into about 8 pieces or so. Keep all the dough you're not using wrapped in plastic. Roll the dough out to position 7 or 8 on your pasta roller; on my Atlas, position 9 is the thinnest setting. Cut out the squares of pasta. How large? Tortellini are supposed to be small, so squares of about 1½ inches are best. If your fingers are too big to manage those little tortellini, make them larger.

Pipe about ½ teaspoon of filling into the center of the square, about the size of a bean. You'll figure out how much is correct as you go. Fold the square over to make a triangle—you'll need to paint the edges with water after the first couple of tortellini, since the dough dries quickly. Make sure there's no air in the triangle. Now fold the triangle around your forefinger and pinch the edges together. Set each tortellino on a baking sheet that you've dusted with either semolina flour or cornmeal. Keep at it until you've used all the filling. This takes me about 2 hours, which is a fair bit of time, but your broth needs to cook anyway, so it's time well spent.

To finish, boil the tortellini in a large pot of salty water—not the broth, as the starch from the pasta will cloud the broth. When the tortellini float to the surface, let them cook another 30 seconds, then drop a bunch in everyone's bowl. Ladle the hot broth over the tortellini and garnish with parsley leaves.

CHAPTER 6

WILD TURKEYS

Turkey hunters will notice this section is slimmer than you might have expected, given the popularity of turkey. That's because virtually every recipe you can make with a pheasant (see the previous chapter) can be made with a turkey. So if you're not finding what you're looking for in this chapter, check back a few pages.

The recipes in this section are *best* with turkey, but again, they can easily be made with other meats, like pheasant or rabbit.

TIPS ON COOKING WILD TURKEY

A wild turkey can be tricky to cook. If you have your heart set on a long-bearded tom, then get ready for some tough meat. But if you're more interested in the eating, aim for the jakes or even the hens in those states that allow you to hunt them. A young jake or hen will be indistinguishable from a heritage turkey that you buy from a farmer's market.

No turkey will be especially gamy—they all taste like the turkey you're familiar with, only more so. Turkeys have a widely varied diet, but they're especially fond of bugs; grasshoppers are a favorite fare. That balance translates into a level of flavor that's hard to replicate with a domestic turkey, although some specialty heritage producers get close.

If you've shot an old tom, here are some tips:

- **Skin it.** I do love crispy turkey skin, but the skin on an old bird will be too thick and leathery to enjoy. Sad, but true. At least it makes it easier to dress the bird, since plucking a turkey can take a while.

- **Break it down.** Cook the legs, thighs, wings, and breasts separately. Don't even try to do that classic roast turkey with an old tom. Braise the drumsticks and wings slowly and pull the meat from the rock-hard sinews. It can sometimes

take more than four hours for the drumsticks to become tender, but be patient: they will submit. Thighs will be more tender.

- **Pound it.** Old turkeys will be so tough that even the breast meat can be chewy. Better to slice it into slabs and pound it into thin cutlets. Breaded and fried as schnitzel (page 74) or piccata (page 78), this is a divine way to cook turkey breast.

If you've shot a young bird, a jake or a hen, try this:

- This is a bird you can cook like a domestic turkey, so use your favorite method to roast the whole bird and enjoy a marvelous Thanksgiving.

- You can also throw the legs and thighs into a pot and braise until tender. The drumsticks should only take a little longer than the thighs.

- Save the skin and either eat it on the meat or remove it and fry it in its own fat, slowly in a frying pan set on medium-low heat. Turkey "bacon" is one of God's great gifts. Of course, the price of turkey bacon is plucking the bird, which happens to be easier with jakes and hens.

In all cases, save the carcass for turkey broth and save the giblets for turkey gravy. You killed this bird, you might as well use as much of it as you can.

ROAST WILD TURKEY

Let me state at the outset that I don't really recommend roasting a whole wild turkey. By the time you get the wings, legs, and thighs tender, the breast meat is hammered. But I recognize that many people want a roast turkey for the holidays, so with all disclaimers aside, here's how it's done.

First rule: don't do this with a big longbeard. It will be very tough all around, and roasting won't solve that. Only hens and younger toms or jakes should be roasted whole. A twenty-four-hour brine is an absolute must here. Brining the turkey is an insurance policy against dryness. How do you brine a bird as large as a turkey? In a cooler. You'll want a cooler that just about fits your bird so you aren't forced to use more brine than needed.

Second rule: roast upside down. Roasting a turkey upside down means the juices will run down to the breast, not away from it. Use a roasting rack and some root vegetables to prop up your bird. One option that also works well is a roasting bag, which helps the turkey retain a bit more moisture. A greased paper grocery bag works for this. Also, do not stuff your bird in the traditional way. You want better airflow working inside the bird, and stuffing will obviously stop that. A few wedges of citrus that have already been juiced, some onion wedges, and some herbs are all good choices to get a bit more flavor going. Just don't pack them in.

Finally, don't truss your turkey. Trussing is great with smaller birds whose legs are reasonably tender because a trussed bird cooks more evenly. You want your legs and thighs to cook faster on a turkey, however, so trussing would be counterproductive. You generally want to cook turkey at about ten minutes per pound. A typical wild bird will serve six hearty eaters, and up to twelve, depending on size.

Serves 6 to 12 | **Prep Time: 45 minutes, not including brine time** | **Cook Time: 100 minutes (see above)**

BRINE

1 gallon water

1 cup kosher salt

½ cup brown sugar or maple syrup

TURKEY

A plucked wild turkey, between
    6 and 12 pounds

5 tablespoons butter

3 to 5 pounds root vegetables
    (like carrots, turnips, or parsnips)
    cut into large chunks

1 cup apple cider

Salt for the vegetables

Black pepper

Pour the water into a very large pot or smallish cooler. Add the salt and sugar or maple syrup into the water and dissolve to make the brine. Submerge the turkey in the brine, and refrigerate overnight. If you're using a cooler, add ice packs to the brine to keep it cold.

Remove the turkey from the brine. If you have the time, set it breast-side up in the fridge for up to another 24 hours; this will dry out the skin a bit (but not the meat) and will give you crispier skin later. You can skip the drying step if you want.

When you're ready to roast, preheat the oven to 325°F. Get a large roasting pan ready with a way to prop up your turkey, breast-side down. A rack or lots of root vegetables will allow you to do this. Pour the cider into the pan and salt well. Set the turkey breast-side down in the pan and dot its back with the butter. Roast for 1 hour.

Raise the temperature to 375°F, and flip the turkey breast-side up. Baste the breast with the juices in the pan, or with some more butter. Roast this way until the thickest part of the thigh reads 150°F, making sure that your thermometer isn't touching bone (or you'll get a false reading). This second roasting step could take as long as another hour or so, but start checking when 90 minutes total have elapsed.

Remove the turkey from the pan and let it rest for 15 minutes on a cutting board. If the temperature is just barely hitting 150°F in the thigh, tent the bird loosely with foil. If it's higher, keep the bird uncovered. Carve and serve.

POACHED TURKEY BREAST WITH GRAVY

Holly and I often have quiet Thanksgivings. Many times, we wake up early, head out to hunt rabbits or ducks for a little while, then kick back with some football and an easy dinner. Roasting a whole turkey, especially a wild one, is not what I call an easy dinner. But you gotta have turkey on Thanksgiving, right? But who says you have to cook the whole turkey?

This is an easy way to have a lovely Thanksgiving for a couple or a small family. For the full-on recipe, you'll need a couple of turkey wings to make some broth (and to help the gravy), but you can use homemade or store-bought broth instead.

You start with the gravy, which hinges on sherry and those roasted turkey wings that are turned into a simple broth. You need enough broth to poach the turkey breast very gently. Poaching keeps the meat super moist and is infinitely better for a piece of skinless breast than roasting or pan-frying. Finish it off with some simple mashed potatoes and a vegetable of your choice, and there you have it: traditional, with a bit of modern technique.

Perfectly poaching a turkey breast is easy, but you do need to know a few tricks before you begin. First, start with meat that is at room temperature. This means taking the breast out of the fridge and letting it sit for forty-five minutes. Second, quick-cure it by salting the breast heavily on both sides when you take it out; this seasons the meat as it comes to temperature. Third, use a good broth. And finally, never ever let the broth even simmer; you want it to just steam at 150°F to 165°F. If you let the broth boil or even simmer strongly, the meat will dry out and get tough.

Incidentally, if you want a stronger gravy than this one, try my Classic Giblet Gravy (page 300).

Serves 4 | **Prep Time: 45 minutes, to let the turkey come to temperature**
Cook Time: 30 minutes, not including time spent making a broth

OPTIONAL WING BROTH

2 to 4 turkey wings

1 tablespoon vegetable oil

Salt

3 quarts water

2 bay leaves

1 tablespoon cracked black peppercorns

1 teaspoon dried thyme

1 teaspoon dried sage, or 1 tablespoon chopped fresh sage

1 cup chopped onion

½ cup chopped carrot

½ cup chopped celery

If you're making the broth, preheat the oven to 400°F.

Coat the turkey wings in the vegetable oil and salt well. Roast in a cast-iron frying pan or other oven-proof pan until nicely browned, from 45 minutes to an hour. Put the roasted wings in a pot with all the other broth ingredients and bring to a simmer. Simmer gently until the meat wants to fall off the bones. This will take about 90 minutes with a domestic turkey, longer for wild. You can pick off the meat and eat it later, or you can chop it up and put some in the gravy, too.

Once the broth is made, take the turkey breast out and salt it well. Let it sit on a cutting board for 45 minutes or so to come to room temperature.

Bring the broth to a simmer and drop the turkey breast in. The turkey should be submerged by the broth. If it is not, add water or chicken stock. Once the turkey is in the broth, move the pot to your weakest burner and turn the heat to its lowest setting. Cover the pot and let it steep in the hot broth for at least 30 minutes and up to 1 hour if you're using a full half breast. Remember to never let the water simmer! You're looking for a target temperature of 155°F to 165°F. So long as you're in that ballpark, you won't overcook the turkey.

(continued)

GRAVY

3 tablespoons butter

3 tablespoons flour

½ cup sherry or Madeira

1 to 1¼ cup turkey-wing broth

1 tablespoon Worcestershire sauce

Salt and black pepper to taste

TURKEY

1½ to 2½ pounds skinless
    turkey breast

Make the gravy while the turkey is poaching. Heat the butter in a small pot over medium-high heat. When the butter is hot, add the flour and mix well. Cook this, stirring often, until it smells nutty and turns milk-chocolate brown, about 10 minutes. Stir in the sherry. The mixture will seize up, so slowly stir in 1 cup of the hot broth until the gravy has the consistency of melted ice cream. Add salt, black pepper, and Worcestershire sauce to taste. Turn the heat to low, and stir from time to time. If it gets too thick, add a little more broth.

To check if the turkey has cooked all the way through, either test it with a meat thermometer—you want it to read 150°F—or slice the thickest part and look: you want a blush of pink in the meat. Slice and serve with mashed potatoes and a vegetable of your choice. Ladle it all with lots of gravy!

"A turkey never voted for
an early Christmas."

—IRISH PROVERB

TURKEY PARMESAN

Turkey Parmesan. It's Italian-American comfort food at its finest. A chicken parm sandwich was in my weekly lunch rotation when I was a kid in New Jersey, and most of my Italian friends' moms had their own version.

"Parm," whether it's chicken or veal or wild turkey or grouse, can be made with jarred sauce, industrial mozzarella, and pre-grated Parmesan in those cheap green cans. I've eaten it this way, and it's still good—although I get the decided aftertaste of shame when I eat such a sterile version of this truly great dish.

Good parm, like all Italian food, is dependent on the quality of each ingredient: fresh sauce, herbs, and mozzarella, and real Parmigiano-Reggiano cheese. And the meat matters. Not only the quality, but the cutlet. Turkey cutlets require a little more work than those of smaller birds. All bird breasts have a thin end and a thick end. Separate them. Pound the the thin end as-is, and slice the thick end crosswise into slabs. Place each slab between pieces of plastic wrap and pound them to ⅛- to ¼-inch thick with a rubber mallet, a meat mallet, or an empty wine bottle. Use about the same amount of force as you would knocking on someone's front door. Work from the center of the meat outward, and constantly lay your palm over the meat to check how evenly flat you're getting the cutlet. The thinner the cutlet, the faster it cooks and the more tender it will be. It takes practice.

Assembling your turkey parm is easy. Dredge your cutlets in flour or breadcrumbs, sauté them until they're golden brown, then bake them briefly in a bath of tomato sauce and cheese. How to serve? Normally either in a sandwich or alongside spaghetti. But it would be good next to polenta, too.

Serves 4 | **Prep Time: 15 minutes** | **Cook Time: 30 minutes**

SAUCE

1 cup minced onion

2 tablespoons olive oil

2 cloves garlic, peeled and minced

1 tablespoon tomato paste

One 28-ounce can crushed tomatoes

½ cup red or white wine

2 tablespoons chopped fresh oregano, basil, parsley

½ teaspoon red pepper flakes

A pinch of sugar

Salt to taste

TURKEY

4 to 8 turkey or pheasant breast cutlets (about 1½ to 2 pounds)

Salt

2 eggs, lightly beaten

1 cup breadcrumbs

½ cup freshly grated Parmigiano-Reggiano cheese

¼ cup olive oil

½ pound mozzarella cheese, sliced

Make the sauce first. Heat the olive oil in a medium-sized pot and sauté the onions, stirring occasionally, until they're soft and translucent, about 6 to 8 minutes. Add the garlic and cook another minute. Add the tomato paste, mix well, and cook for 3 minutes, stirring often. You want the tomato paste to darken to a brick color.

Add the can of crushed tomatoes, the wine, the salt, the red pepper flakes, the sugar, and the herbs. Mix well, and let this simmer gently while you finish the dish.

Mix the Parmesan cheese with the breadcrumbs. Salt the turkey cutlets well, dip them into the beaten eggs, and then dredge them in the breadcrumb-cheese mixture. Heat the ¼ cup of olive oil in a large pan and fry over medium-high heat until golden on both sides, about 6 minutes.

While the turkey is frying, preheat the oven to 375°F. Find a casserole pan (9 by 13-inch is a good size) and spread a layer of sauce. Put the cooked turkey cutlets on the sauce in one layer. Lay down a little more sauce, then cover each cutlet with the mozzarella cheese. Bake in the oven until the mozzarella just starts to brown on the edges, about 12 to 14 minutes. Serve with spaghetti or in a hoagie roll.

TURKEY CUTLETS WITH MORELS

This is an easy recipe for pounded turkey cutlets with a creamy morel sauce. And nothing goes together quite like turkey and morels. It's not at all uncommon to bag a gobbler and find a mess of morels on the same day, sometimes in the same place. So combining them is a natural.

Serves 4 | **Prep Time: 25 minutes** | **Cook Time: 25 minutes**

1½ pounds turkey breast

Salt

Flour

⅓ cup butter

½ to 1½ pounds fresh morel mushrooms, sliced into discs

2 cloves garlic, minced

½ teaspoon dried thyme

½ cup sherry or bourbon

½ cup chives or wild onions, chopped

½ cup heavy cream, at room temperature

Black pepper to taste

Prepare your turkey breast cutlets as you would in the Turkey Parmesan recipe on page 129. Salt the cutlets well.

Preheat your oven to 200°F and set a cookie sheet inside; this is to keep your cutlets hot. I also set a rack in the cookie sheet to keep the cutlets crisp.

Heat the butter in a large frying pan and dredge the cutlets in flour. Fry the turkey cutlets in butter until golden brown over medium heat, about 2 to 3 minutes per side. Move to the rack when done. Don't let the butter get too hot or it will burn; brown is good, black is not.

When all your turkey is ready, add the morels to the pan. Toss to coat in the remaining butter, and add a little more if you want. Salt the morels, and, when they start to give up their water, add the garlic and thyme. Cook over high heat until the water is almost gone.

Add the sherry, and toss to combine. Add the chives and cream, and bring to a bare simmer. Turn off the heat, add freshly ground black pepper to taste, and serve. Give everyone some cutlets and pour the morels over.

TURKEY BUFFALO MAC-N-CHEESE

This isn't the most highfalutin' dish in the book. In fact, along with Saturday Pheasant (page 98), it might be the most low-brow. Who cares? It's awesome.

I got the idea for it from a cookbook called *Melt: The Art of Macaroni and Cheese* that my friends Stephanie Stiavetti and Garrett McCord wrote a few years back. I decided to add meat to my version. Fair warning: this is not low fat, and you'll eat more than you think yourself possible of eating.

If you're wondering about my naming a specific hot sauce, it's because Frank's is the hot sauce used in Buffalo, where Buffalo chicken originated. There is no substitute.

If you happen to have leftovers, they'll keep in the fridge for several days.

Serves 8 to 10 | **Prep Time: 20 minutes, not including buttermilk soak for turkey** | **Cook Time: 50 minutes**

FILLING

1 pound turkey breast, cut into bite-sized pieces

2 cups buttermilk

1 pound pasta, elbows or little shells

6 tablespoons butter (divided—3 tablespoons for the sauté, 3 tablespoons to finish)

1 medium onion, chopped

2 celery stalks, chopped

2 cloves garlic, minced

¾ cup Frank's hot sauce

SAUCE

3 tablespoons flour

2½ cups whole milk, at room temperature

½ cup heavy cream, at room temperature

2 teaspoons dry mustard (optional)

¼ cup Frank's hot sauce

10 ounces shredded cheddar cheese

⅔ cup sour cream

TOPPING

½ to 1 cup crumbled blue cheese

1 cup bread crumbs

2 tablespoons chopped parsley

Marinate the turkey breast in the buttermilk overnight, or at least for a few hours. Rinse off the buttermilk when you're ready to cook.

Bring a large pot of water to a boil, and add enough salt to make the water quite salty. Preheat the oven to 350°F.

Heat 3 tablespoons of butter in a pan over medium-high heat and add the onions and celery. Cook for a minute or two, then add the diced turkey. Cook another 3 to 4 minutes, stirring often, and add the garlic. Cook 1 more minute, then turn off the heat and mix in the Frank's hot sauce.

Boil the pasta until it's softened but still too al dente to eat; it'll cook more in the oven. Drain and set aside.

Make the sauce. In another pan, heat the remaining butter over medium heat and stir in the flour. Cook, stirring almost constantly, until the mixture turns the color of peanut butter, about 8 to 10 minutes. Mix the cream and milk together and pour it, a little at a time, into the pan, stirring constantly.

Stir in the dry mustard, then the shredded cheese, a little at a time, while stirring constantly—add more cheese only when the last bit has incorporated into the sauce. Turn off the heat, and stir in the hot sauce and sour cream.

To assemble, grease a 9 by 13-inch baking dish or something similar. Lay down half the pasta, then the filling, then the rest of the pasta, then the sauce. Sprinkle the blue cheese evenly over everything. Mix the breadcrumbs and parsley and sprinkle that over everything.

Bake for 40 minutes, then remove from the oven and let it sit 10 minutes before serving.

TURKEY GUMBO WITH ANDOUILLE AND SHRIMP

Like Brunswick Stew (page 217), Gumbo is one of the great American "whatchagot" stews, made with whatever happens to be lying around. I included gumbo in the turkey section because making it with wild turkey drumsticks is especially good. It's one of the great uses of a difficult cut of meat.

This gumbo is made with homemade andouille and Gulf shrimp from Alabama, but any good American shrimp and smoked sausage will do; tasso ham is another good option. And feel free to put any and all meats you want in here. This is a great place for that stray groundhog, jackrabbit, or beaver you have lying around in your freezer.

I use filé powder here to thicken my gumbo, but you can skip that and use eight ounces of okra instead. Gumbos are normally thickened with two of three things: always the roux, then either okra or filé.

Serve this with long-grained, steamed rice.

Serves 6 to 10 | Prep Time: 20 minutes | Cook Time: 3 hours

½ cup peanut oil, lard, or butter

1 cup flour

1 quart stock (turkey or other good similar stock)

2 bell peppers, diced

2 celery stalks, diced

1 large yellow onion, diced

6 cloves garlic, minced

1 tablespoon tomato paste

2 to 4 turkey drumsticks

¼ teaspoon celery seed

2 bay leaves

2 tablespoons Cajun or Creole seasoning

¼ to ½ pound smoked sausage or tasso ham, cut into coins or chunks

1 pound peeled, raw shrimp

½ pound sliced okra, or filé powder

Tabasco or other hot sauce to taste

Chopped green onions, for garnish

Pour the stock and 1 quart of water into a pot and bring it to a simmer.

In a large, heavy soup pot, heat the peanut oil over medium-high heat. Stir in the flour to make a roux and cook this, stirring often, until it's the color of milk chocolate. You'll need to stir this more often as it cooks so it doesn't burn. This should take about 15 minutes.

Add the diced vegetables and the garlic, and mix well. Let this cook over medium heat until soft, about 10 minutes. Stir in the tomato paste, celery seed, bay leaves, and Cajun seasoning.

Bring the stock to a full boil and start adding it ladle by ladle into the soup pot. It will sputter and seize up at first, but keep adding the stock until it has all incorporated. Bring this to a full, rolling boil, and let this boil for a couple of minutes.

Turn the heat back down to a simmer and add the turkey drumsticks. Taste for salt and let this simmer until the meat wants to fall off the bone, a couple of hours. Remove the turkey legs and pull the meat from the bone.

Add the sausage, shrimp, and okra or about a tablespoon of filé to thicken, and let this simmer 5 minutes. Add Tabasco to taste and serve garnished with green onions over rice.

WILD TURKEY GRILLADES WITH GRITS

This is a Creole dish that is easy to make and versatile. I am indebted to my friend Sheamus Feeley for this one. He's an Arkansas boy who grew up with this recipe. Grillades are smallish pounded cutlets simmered in a Louisiana-style stew and, typically, served over grits. It's similar to the gumbo (page 135) in some ways, but this dish uses only one meat, and that meat is larger. You eat this with a knife and fork.

Basically, you want pounded-out pieces small enough so that about three or four is a good serving. A pounded quail or partridge breast is a good size to think about. With turkey breast, you'll want to pound out larger cutlets and slice those cutlets into smaller pieces.

Any meat that you can pound into cutlets works, and this is a great dish for dark-meat grouse.

Serves 4 | Prep Time: 30 minutes | Cook Time: 2 hours

ROUX
½ cup flour

¼ cup fresh lard or peanut oil

GRILLADES
1½ pounds turkey breast, sliced and pounded into ⅛-inch thick pieces

Flour for dredging

5 tablespoons fresh lard or peanut oil

2 cups chopped yellow onion

2 celery stalks, chopped

1 red bell pepper, chopped

2 tablespoons tomato paste

1 tablespoon minced garlic

1 to 3 tablespoons Creole or Cajun spice

3 bay leaves

1 quart stock (turkey or other game)

3 to 5 green onions, sliced thin

Tabasco or other hot sauce, to taste

GRITS
1 quart stock (turkey or other game)

1 cup grits, ideally stone-ground white grits

¼ cup heavy cream

2 ounces shredded cheddar cheese

1 teaspoon garlic powder

Salt to taste

In a small pot, heat ¼ cup of the fresh lard or peanut oil over medium-high heat. When it's hot, whisk in the flour until there are no lumps. Cook this, stirring often, until the roux turns the color of peanut butter. Drop the heat to medium-low and keep cooking, stirring often, until the roux turns the color of milk chocolate. Remove the pot from the heat and set aside.

Season the turkey pieces with salt, then dredge in flour.

Heat 3 tablespoons of fresh lard or peanut oil in a heavy, lidded pot over medium-high heat. Brown the turkey pieces in the lard, about 2 to 3 minutes per side. Don't crowd the pot, and do this in batches. Remove the turkey pieces from the pot as they brown, and set aside.

If there's enough oil or lard in the pot, you won't need to add the additional 2 tablespoons; use your judgment. Heat the lard as necessary, add the chopped onion, celery, and red bell pepper, and cook over medium heat; you don't want to brown the vegetables. It should take around 6 minutes for the vegetables to become tender. Add the garlic and cook for 30 seconds, then mix in the tomato paste.

Stir in the roux and cook for about 1 minute. Add the stock a little at a time, stirring constantly. After each addition of stock, make sure the stew comes to a bubble before adding more. Do this until you've used all the stock and the stew is smooth.

Slowly stir in the Creole spice and add the bay leaves, bring the stew to a rolling boil, then drop the heat to a bare simmer. Add the turkey back to the pot, cover the pot, and simmer very gently for 90 minutes.

When you have about 30 minutes to go, make the grits. Bring the stock to a simmer and slowly whisk in grits. Reduce to low heat and stir, adding cream slowly, while grits cook for 20 to 30 minutes, or until they become tender. Once the grits are tender, remove from the heat and add the cheese and garlic powder. Serve the grillades over grits, and garnish with green onion and hot sauce.

POZOLE VERDE

Pozole (puh-ZO-lay) is one of those classic stews every culture seems to hold dear. Pozole is that stew that everyone makes but is slightly different depending on the region and cook, much like chili in Texas, burgoo in Kentucky, Brunswick stew in Virginia (page 217), or chowder in New England.

Most pozole recipes are for pozole rojo, the red stew most of us are familiar with. This is the green version, pozole verde, which is common in Guerrero, a southern Mexican state next to Oaxaca; Acapulco is in Guerrero.

Like chili or Vietnamese pho, pozole is one of those stews where half the fun is adding all sorts of toppings at the table. Many pozole recipes add *chicharróns* (cracklings) and even sardines to their toppings, but I stuck to the more familiar cilantro, avocado, onion, and lime. Chopped green chiles would be another good idea. Just keep it green.

Pozole verde is a cascade of Mexican flavors. The stew hinges on acidic tomatillos, but you get alkaline hominy kernels to balance that out. There's a bit of brightness from the sorrel leaves, lime juice, and chiles. It's not supposed to be über hot, but it does have a nice, gentle heat. The stew broth gets a lot of body from toasted, ground-up pumpkin seeds (pepitas), and little shreds of meat round everything out. It is truly one of the great stews of the world.

You do need access to Mexican ingredients to make this recipe, but fortunately most of these ingredients are in larger supermarkets and in any Latin market.

There are two optional items here that make the dish better, but which you can skip if you must: epazote, a strange-smelling green herb, and sorrel, a lemony green. Epazote is pretty easy to find in Latin markets (it's also a common urban weed), and sorrel can sometimes be found in farmer's markets.

This is a one-pot meal, but you could serve it with rice if you wanted to.

Serves 4 to 6 | **Prep Time: 45 minutes** | **Cook Time: 2 hours**

2 to 4 pounds of turkey or pheasant legs

1 quart of chicken broth

20 tomatillos (not the little ones)

10 large sorrel leaves (optional)

2 to 3 hot green chiles, serrano or jalapeño, chopped

2 or 3 tablespoons lard, corn oil or other cooking oil

½ cup (2 ounces) pepitas, toasted in a frying pan until aromatic and then ground

One 28- to 32-ounce can of white hominy

1 teaspoon dried oregano, Mexican if possible

1 small bunch of epazote (optional)

1 small onion, minced

1 avocado, diced

½ cup chopped cilantro

Lime wedges

Simmer the turkey in the broth, plus enough water to cover, until it's tender enough to shred, about 90 minutes to 2 hours. You can do this up to 5 days in advance if you want, or use leftovers. Basically, you simmer the meat (or meats) until tender, then shred, then set aside. Save the cooking liquid.

Cover the tomatillos with just enough water to cover and boil. Drop the heat to a bare simmer and let this cook for 15 minutes. Move the tomatillos to a blender and add to the blender the sorrel and the chopped chiles. Buzz into a rough purée; you might need to add some of the tomatillo cooking liquid.

Heat the lard in a Dutch oven or other large, heavy pot and add the tomatillo purée. Cook this over medium-high heat for a few minutes. Add the ground pumpkin seeds, the shredded meats, the oregano, hominy, and the epazote if you have some. Add enough of the reserved liquid from cooking the meats to make this a stew. Simmer this gently for 25 minutes. Add salt to taste.

Serve everyone some of the pozole and let everyone top it with the onion, avocado, cilantro, and lime.

TURKEY YUCATÁN

Perhaps nowhere in the world are there more or better recipes for turkey than in Mexico. After all, it was in Central America and the upper part of South America that turkeys were first domesticated. And the best evidence suggests that it was the Maya who first managed this feat. As it happens, the part of Mexico that is most Mayan now is the Yucatán. This recipe may well have its origins before the Spanish arrived there in the 1500s.

I first learned about this dish, called *pavo del monte en k'ool rojo*, in the late David Sterling's excellent book *Yucatán: Recipes from a Culinary Expedition*. This recipe is a slight adaptation from his. The Yucatecan *pavo del monte*, or "mountain turkey," is the famed ocellated turkey—the hardest of the six subspecies to get. It's smaller than the others, and it looks a bit more like a peacock, since its face lacks the droopy snood of the others. It's also psychedelically iridescent. Think Lucy in the Sky, with Turkey.

But, of course, any turkey will do. I used a Rio Grande. You can use whatever's available.

What attracts me to this recipe is not just the exotic and fascinating flavors of the Yucatán, but also the technique. The combination of grilling and then braising an otherwise tough piece of meat to produce something so tender you can easily bite though big pieces in a taco is nothing short of miraculous—especially for an old tom turkey. And I mean that: we slapped the pieces you see in the picture on a small corn tortilla and could easily bite through them. If you've ever bitten a piece of meat in a taco only to have it completely pull out of the tortilla, you know how nice this is.

The other attractive thing about this dish is its flavor. It looks like a standard Mexican mole. But looks are deceiving. There's only a hint of chile in this sauce. It's mostly a mixture of charred, puréed onions, garlic, and tomato, with a hefty dose of ground annatto, or achiote, seeds; that's the red color. It starts out almost tandoori red but mellows with the long braising you need to tenderize the turkey legs.

The result is floral, fairly mild—the chipotle adds a touch of smoky heat—and bright with citrus. Ideally, you would use the bitter juice of the Seville orange, but this hard-to-find citrus can be reasonably replicated with a combination of regular supermarket oranges, limes, and grapefruit.

There are all sorts of substitutions you make do here, but some things are vital. First, it's important to actually char your vegetables for the sauce. If you don't do this, the signature flavors just won't be there. Also, you absolutely do need the achiote rojo. You can't do this recipe without it. Thankfully, achiote rojo is available in most Latin markets. You can also buy it online.

Needless to say, this recipe is more about method than meat choice. The Yucatecos also do this same dish with both chicken and venison, and anything you think might taste good here will work.

Serve your turkey with tortillas or rice, along with a fresh salsa if you want, cilantro and maybe some roasted and sliced poblano peppers. Chopped chives mixed with the cilantro is a good idea, too.

If you happen to have leftovers, they will keep for a week in the fridge.

Serves 6 to 8 | **Prep Time: 45 minutes, to let the turkey marinate and to char the vegetables**
Cook Time: 3 hours, depending on how old the turkey was

TURKEY

Kosher salt (for optional brining of the turkey)

Drumsticks, thighs and wings from a turkey

Gizzard and heart of a turkey, sliced into a few pieces (optional)

Brine the turkey pieces at a ratio of ¼ cup kosher salt to 1 quart of water for a few hours (this step is optional, but if you have an old turkey, it's best not to skip it).

Next mix all the remaining turkey ingredients together to make a mixture that has the consistency of BBQ sauce. Once the turkey pieces have brined, coat them with this and marinate in the fridge at least 30 minutes, and up to a day.

(continued)

½ cup achiote paste

2 teaspoons salt, smoked salt if you have it

2 tablespoons melted lard or vegetable oil

⅓ cup Seville orange juice, or see below

SAUCE

2 heads garlic

1 white or yellow onion, quartered

3 Roma (paste) tomatoes, sliced in half lengthwise

2 tablespoons lard or vegetable oil

1 tablespoon oregano, Mexican if you can get it

1 teaspoon achiote verde (optional)

2 sprigs fresh epazote (optional)

¼ cup achiote paste

1 or 2 chipotles in adobo (optional)

Masa harina

SEVILLE ORANGE JUICE SUBSTITUTE

1 tablespoon lime juice

2 tablespoons regular orange juice

1 tablespoon grapefruit juice

If you want to save time, while the turkey is marinating you can char the 2 heads of garlic, onion, and tomatoes on the grill. Or you can do all your grilling at once. A wood-burning grill is obviously best, but any type will be fine. You want a good char on all the vegetables. Char only the cut side of the tomatoes. Get some good char marks on the turkey, too, but don't worry about cooking the pieces all the way through—that's what the braising is for. Once everything is nicely charred, set it aside.

To make the sauce, coarsely chop the onion and tomato, and peel the cloves of 1 head of garlic, plus at least 4 more cloves from the second head. I like to use all of both heads of garlic. In a large, heavy pot or Dutch oven, cook the vegetables in the lard or vegetable oil over medium heat for about 5 minutes, stirring occasionally. Remove from the heat and move everything into a blender or food processor.

Add to this the oregano, achiote paste, and epazote (if using), chipotles, and a cup or so of water. Purée until more or less smooth.

Put the turkey pieces into the pot and cover with the sauce. Pour some more water into the blender to get every bit of the sauce stuck to the sides and pour that into the pot, too. You want the turkey to just barely be submerged. Bring this to a simmer and add salt to taste. Cover the pot and simmer gently over low heat, stirring once in a while, until the turkey is tender. A jake should take maybe an hour or 90 minutes, and an old tom up to 3 hours.

By now the sauce should be plenty thick. If it's not, whisk in some masa harina until it thickens to the consistency of BBQ sauce.

To serve, you have a few choices. You can lift away large pieces of turkey from the bones (make sure to remove all the drumstick tendons!) and serve in the sauce with rice or tortillas. Or, if you want to go the taco route, shred the meat more completely. Top with any of the accompaniments listed in the headnotes.

TURKEY CARNITAS

Let's face it: wild turkey drumsticks can be unbearably tough, and the tendons are often as tough as bone. The answer? Braise them. For a long time. Eventually, the meat will get tender, and you then pull it off the bone. You can do all sorts of things with that meat, but my go-to is to make wild turkey carnitas.

Carnitas is a Mexican dish made with meat that's first braised in a nice broth until it gets tender and is then browned, on one side only, in some lard or vegetable oil. The result is both tender and crispy, which is genius. If you've had carnitas, I'm guessing it's been made with pork, and I'm guessing you know why it sells out at Chipotle so often.

If I can give you one piece of advice here, it is to take your time. Turkey will get rubbery and nasty before it submits and becomes smooth and luscious. If you need more water, add more water. This recipe will require at least three hours of your time, maybe more if you're cooking an old tom. Be patient. It's worth it.

I prefer carnitas in soft tacos and with the traditional accompaniments: limes, onions, maybe a hot sauce or two, roasted chiles, and cilantro or parsley. A homemade salsa verde is a great sauce here.

Once you make this, the finished carnitas will keep for a week in the fridge. I usually reheat it in a frying pan with a little oil.

Serves 4 | **Prep Time: 10 minutes** | **Cook Time: 3 hours**

---

2 skinless turkey legs plus wings,
    or 2 turkey thighs

Kosher salt

1 tablespoon juniper berries,
    crushed (optional)

1 tablespoon black peppercorns,
    cracked

1 tablespoon coriander seed, cracked

1 tablespoon cumin seed

1 tablespoon oregano,
    Mexican if possible

1 small cinnamon stick

2 cloves

3 dried small chiles,
    such as an árbol or Thai

3 bay leaves

5 tablespoons lard or olive oil

1 tablespoon honey

Juice of ½ an orange

Juice of 1 lime

Salt the turkey well and put it into a Dutch oven or large lidded pot, add all the herbs, spices, and enough water to just barely cover the meat in the pot. Cover and simmer for 3 to 4 hours, or until the meat is falling off the bone. Don't worry, it will. Eventually. A jake or domestic turkey will be tender in about 90 minutes to 2 hours, and old tom might be double that.

When it's tender, remove the turkey from the pot and let it cool. Shred with two forks or your fingers. Discard the bones and any tendons. You can store the meat for up to a week at this point.

To finish, add the lard to a frying pan and brown the meat as much as you like. I like a mix of soft and crispy. At the very end, drizzle in about a tablespoon of honey and the citrus juice. Mix and serve. I serve this as part of a taco plate. But you can eat it any way you like it—sandwiches, ravioli filling, a topping for rice, in a burrito.

TURKEY TAMALES WITH PUMPKIN

Tamales, like all good things stuffed into other good things, are long labors of love.

This is not a quick and easy recipe; it requires some time in the kitchen. I make no apologies for that. But the result of your efforts are packets of autumnal goodness that are a joy to eat and make use of two classic fall ingredients—pumpkins and turkey—both of which, you should know, originated in Mesoamerica. Both the Mayans and Aztecs domesticated the turkey, as well as the various winter squash we all know and love. While not entirely pre-Contact, this recipe for turkey tamales is pretty close—only the lard, the garlic, a few spices were brought to Mexico by the Spaniards.

A tamal, the individual dumpling in a batch of tamales, is a light packet of corn dough—the masa—filled with something good, in this case, shredded turkey meat coated in a red chile sauce. They are then steamed in corn husks or banana leaves or something similar, unwrapped, and eaten, sometimes with a sauce, and sometimes not.

I happen to love pipian sauces, which are made primarily from pepitas, the green centers of pumpkin seeds. You can often find them in the health food section of your supermarket or in any Latin market.

If you can't find them, you can use roasted regular pumpkin seeds, but be sure to grind them well, since they include a thin shell. Sesame seeds are another authentic variation.

And if you don't feel like making the pipian, no biggie. The tamales are fine without them. Or you can use a different sauce.

Since these require a bit of work, you may want to double this recipe. Most Mexican families that make tamales do it in an industrial scale. After all, making seventy-five tamales isn't that much harder than making twenty-five. And tamales freeze really well. Reheated premade tamales (even microwaved!) can then become fast food for busy nights. What's not to love about that?

A few tricks: the filling can be made several days in advance. The pipian sauce can also be made a day or two ahead, but not much more. And, once made, the tamales store in the fridge for a week or so and, as I mentioned, they freeze well.

If you want to reheat refrigerated tamales, bring them out about thirty minutes before you eat them, and heat up a *comal* (the traditional Mexican griddle) or a skillet. Toast the tamales in their husks until the husks get mostly charred, then serve. This is arguably tastier than eating the tamales fresh. For frozen tamales, put them in a steamer while still frozen, and steam for about twenty minutes or so.

You have lots of leeway with ingredients here. No turkey? Use any white meat. Don't have the exact chiles? No biggie—any combination of mild chiles is fine. And needless to say, it doesn't have to be a pumpkin in the masa dough. Any winter squash (except spaghetti squash) works fine.

When looking for lard, get the refrigerated stuff. If you don't see it at a Latin market, ask. They often have fresh lard in the back. Ditto for masa. Many Mexican markets will have freshly made masa in the back, and are happy to sell it to you.

Makes about 25 tamales | **Prep Time: 2 hours** | **Cook Time: 1 hour**

TAMALE DOUGH

1 butternut squash or pumpkin

2½ cups masa harina
(*masa harina para tamales*)

⅓ cup lard

1 teaspoon salt

1 teaspoon baking powder

Corn husks

Cook the pumpkin. Roast the pumpkin or squash at 350°F until it's soft, about 45 minutes to 1 hour. Scoop it out of the shell and purée in a blender. This step can be done a few days in advance.

Soak the corn husks. Submerge the corn husks in hot water and let them soak until you need them, at least an hour or two and up to overnight.

TURKEY

1½ pounds boneless meat

2 bay leaves

2 cloves

8 allspice berries, cracked (optional)

10 to 12 black peppercorns, cracked

1 onion, roughly chopped

TURKEY SAUCE

3 tablespoons lard, duck fat, or
    other cooking oil

½ a white onion, chopped

1 large garlic clove, chopped

6 dried guajillo chiles, seeded
    and torn up

½ teaspoon thyme

½ teaspoon cumin

½ teaspoon allspice

2 plum tomatoes, chopped

2 cups water or broth from the turkey

Salt, smoked if you have it

PIPIAN SAUCE

¼ cup lard, duck fat, or
    other cooking oil

1 cup chopped white onion

2 cloves garlic, chopped

2 plum tomatoes, chopped

1⅓ cup pepitas or 1 cup sesame seeds

2 green onions, chopped

½ cup cilantro, chopped

6 epazote sprigs, chopped (optional)

Salt, smoked if you have it

Prep the turkey. If you are using leftover turkey, shred it up and chop it a bit. Remember it's going into tamales, and you don't want all the meat to come out when you cut off a piece with your fork later. If you are using fresh turkey, simmer it in the rest of the turkey ingredients until it's tender, then shred. Keep the broth.

Make the turkey sauce. While the turkey is simmering, make the sauce for it. Heat the lard in a pan and cook the garlic and onions over medium heat until they are translucent, about 5 minutes. Add the torn up chiles and cook a minute or two, then add the remaining sauce ingredients. Simmer gently for 45 minutes. Let the mixture cool a bit before puréeing in a blender. You want this sauce smooth. Mix with the shredded turkey.

Make the pipian. After you're done blending the turkey sauce, rinse out the blender and pan. Wipe the pan down and add the next batch of lard, onions and garlic, and sauté over medium heat until soft but not browned, about 4 minutes. Add the tomatoes and pepitas and cook, stirring often, another 2 or 3 minutes. Turn off the heat and let this cool. Add the contents of the pan to the blender along with the remaining pipian ingredients. Blend until smooth, adding 2 to 3 cups of broth or water to loosen.

Make the tamale dough. In a large bowl, add the masa and 2½ cups of pumpkin purée, along with the remaining ingredients and mix well. Add just enough hot water to make something between a batter and a dough: You will want to be able to spread it on the corn husks.

Form the tamales. With a corn husk placed in front of you, narrow-side pointing at you, smear some dough over the center of the husk, leaving about ⅛ to ¼ inch free on the edges. Place a heaping tablespoon of turkey filling in the center. Fold over the corn husk to seal the dough, then roll it a little to make a cylinder. Fold up the narrow end of the husk to form a stable bottom to the tamal. You can either stack them in a steamer that way or tie them off with strips of corn husk or twine.

Cook the tamales. Set a steamer insert into a large pot. Add water to the level of the steamer, but not so much the husks get soaked. Line the steamer with spare husks and arrange the tamales open-side up into the steamer. Cover the pot and steam for 1 hour. Check the level of the water in the pot, and make sure it doesn't all boil away.

To serve, heat the pipian gently—don't let it simmer, or it might break. Unwrap some tamales and cover with the sauce. Garnish with cilantro.

BAKED BEANS WITH SMOKED TURKEY WINGS

Baked beans with something smoked is a winning combination, no matter the bean or the smoked meat. In this case, it's a smoked turkey wing (see Smoked Turkey Drumsticks or Wings, page 322) and a host of flavors of the Desert Southwest.

Feel free to substitute almost anything else to make this recipe your own (I'll offer some suggestions below). Keep in mind that baked beans is an all-day thing, so get it together before work or on a weekend. You don't need to dote on it all day, but it does take a while to come together. And remember that the dried beans will have to soak overnight, so a little pre-planning will be called for as well.

If you don't have turkey wings to smoke, smoked wings and legs from pheasants work well, too.

Serves 4 | **Prep Time: 10 minutes, not including overnight bean soak** | **Cook Time: 8 hours**

---

1 to 2 cups tepary, pinto, or other dried bean, soaked overnight

6 cups stock (turkey or chicken)

1 smoked turkey wing

⅓ cup molasses

1 teaspoon crushed chiltepin or other hot, dried chile

½ teaspoon Mexican or regular oregano

1 large sprig epazote (optional)

½ teaspoon ground cumin

1 tablespoon tomato paste

A healthy pinch of salt, smoked if you have it

Lime juice to taste

Simmer the wing in the stock until it's tender, about 90 minutes. Shred the meat and discard the bones and skin.

Mix the broth you just made with the molasses and tomato paste.

Mix all the remaining ingredients together in a lidded pot and set in the oven at 250°F. Let this cook for at least 4 hours, and up to 8 hours.

If you want, cook some white rice in the extra turkey broth and serve that with the beans. Give everyone a few lime wedges so they can add as much as they want at the table.

FRENCH TURKEY WINGS À LA NICE

I first saw a recipe like this one in Calvin Schwabe's *Unmentionable Cuisine*, which has become a cult favorite in adventurous gastronomic circles. His recipe calls for the last digit of the turkey wing, which, to my mind, is hardly worth it. The first two digits, however, are well worth the effort.

Here you'll see echoes of the well-known salade Niçoise: olives, capers, tomato, and tarragon. It's a lovely meal, and a great way to work with an unloved part of the turkey. You could also use pheasant or grouse thighs here, or a rabbit.

Serves 4 | **Prep Time: 20 minutes** | **Cook Time: 2½ hours**

2 tablespoons pheasant fat or turkey fat, or butter

2 tablespoons olive oil

Wings from 2 turkeys, separated (8 pieces)

Salt

¾ pound button mushrooms, sliced

1 large onion, sliced

1 teaspoon dried thyme

1 teaspoon chopped fresh rosemary

I teaspoon chopped fresh sage

2 bay leaves

3 cloves garlic, sliced thin

1 ½ cup diced tomatoes

1 cup white wine

18 to 24 black olives, sliced

2 tablespoons fresh tarragon, chopped

1 tablespoon fresh parsley, chopped

Heat the fat in a large, heavy lidded pot. Brown the turkey wings in this over medium-high heat. Take your time on this, and get some good browning. Salt them as they cook. Set aside pieces as they brown in a bowl.

When the turkey has browned, add the button mushrooms and sliced onion and brown them; add some more fat or oil if you want. Salt them as they cook.

When the onion and mushrooms are nicely browned, return the turkey wings to the pot and add the thyme, rosemary, sage, bay, garlic, tomatoes, and wine. Scrape up any browned bits stuck on the bottom of the pot with wooden spoon. Cover the pot and simmer very gently for 2 hours.

Check the pot after about 1 hour, and add water if needed; you want the wings to braise, not be in a stew.

When the wings are nearly done, add the olives and cook for another 5 minutes. Mix in the tarragon and parsley and serve with crusty bread, rice, or potatoes.

MAPLE-GLAZED MEATBALLS

If you've read any of my cookbooks, you'll know that I'm more than a little fond of meatballs. Meatballs in all their forms, from all ethnicities, made from any kind of meat. Here's a great American appetizer that marries two ingredients made for each other: turkey and maple. The sweet-tart-hot glaze boosts the flavor of the meatballs themselves and makes for one helluva good appetizer. Make this one for parties, Sunday football, whenever.

If you have ground turkey or any ground meat, great. If not, grind about one pound of meat to a quarter pound of pork fat or bacon. If you use bacon, you won't need to salt the meatballs.

Serves 6 as an appetizer | **Prep Time: 15 minutes, if you've already ground your meat** | **Cook Time: 25 minutes**

MEATBALLS

1 ¼ pounds ground turkey (see above)

1 egg, lightly beaten

1 cup breadcrumbs

½ teaspoon ground ginger

½ teaspoon black pepper

½ teaspoon onion powder (optional)

¼ teaspoon Bell's poultry seasoning (optional)

1 teaspoon salt, smoked salt if you have it

¼ cup milk

Oil for frying

GLAZE

½ cup maple syrup

⅓ cup Worcestershire sauce

2 teaspoons tomato paste

Tabasco or other hot sauce to taste

Make the meatballs by combining all the meatball ingredients except the oil. Mix well, but don't overwork the meat, or you'll have tough meatballs. Scoop out about 1 tablespoon at a time, and roll them into balls. Set aside on a baking sheet. You can set these in the fridge for a few hours if you need to.

Pour enough oil into a pan to come about halfway up the side of the meatballs. Heat the oil to somewhere between 325°F and 350°F. Brown the meatballs well. You'll probably need to do this in two batches.

When the meatballs are all nicely browned, drain the oil; you can reuse it later. Leave about 1 tablespoon in the pan. Mix all the glaze ingredients in a bowl to combine, then put the mixture into the pan and turn the heat to high. When it boils, add back all the meatballs. Roll the meatballs around to coat, and cook, shaking the pan constantly, until the sauce cooks down into a glaze. Remove from the heat and serve.

TURKEY KEBABS

While turkey kebabs aren't overly unusual, this recipe comes from a long way away from the turkey's native home of North America. It's from Azerbaijan, as in the former Soviet Republic. I read about this in Naomi Duguid's cookbook *Taste of Persia: A Cook's Travel through Armenia, Azerbaijan, Georgia, Iran, and Kurdistan*, and it's a winner. Boneless turkey—breast or thigh meat—marinated in a mix of onion, something acidic, and sumac, and then grilled.

Sumac is a tart addition common in Persia and its environs. And yes, it is, more or less, the same red sumac you see on roadsides here in the United States. You can buy it online or in Middle Eastern markets, or you can just skip it and maybe add some paprika for color.

The *ajika* sauce is great with this, as it adds a ton of flavor. It's like a red pepper pesto. You can make it a few days ahead of time, and it will keep in the fridge for a month or more. Use it as a side sauce for any meat, fish, or eggs, or thin it out a little with oil and water and use it as a salad dressing.

Serve these kebabs with rice and a cucumber salad.

Serves 4 | **Prep Time: 8 hours, marinating time** | **Cook Time: 20 minutes**

1 to 2 pounds boneless turkey

1 onion, grated

¼ cup verjus or cider vinegar

1 tablespoon sumac (optional)

¼ cup sunflower or olive oil

Salt and black pepper

AJIKA SAUCE

1 head garlic, peeled and chopped

¼ pound walnuts, chopped

4 red bell peppers, seeded and chopped

4 to 10 hot red chiles, such as jalapeño or serrano, chopped

1 tablespoon fenugreek

2 tablespoons fenugreek leaves (optional)

1 tablespoon ground coriander

1 tablespoon salt

Cut the turkey into pieces about 1½ inches across. Salt them well. Mix the meat with the grated onion, the verjus or vinegar, and half the sumac. Let this sit in the fridge for at least 2 hours, and up to overnight.

While the turkey is marinating, make the *ajika* sauce. Put all the sauce ingredients into a food processor and buzz into a paste. It should be rich, spicy, and a little salty. Set it aside at room temperature until you cook the turkey; yes, it can sit out all day.

When you're ready to cook, fire up the grill. Thread the turkey onto skewers, leaving a little space between each piece of meat. Paint with the oil and grill over a hot fire with the grill cover open until you get nice grill marks and the meat is done, anywhere from 5 to 15 minutes, depending on how hot your grill is; don't overcook the meat if you can help it. As you cook the kebabs, sprinkle the turkey with a little more sumac if you're using it.

When they are done, serve with the *ajika* sauce on the side.

POLISH BIGOS WITH TURKEY

Bigos, pronounced something like BEG-oh-ss, is one of the national dishes of Poland. It's a hearty stew often studded with lots of wild game, served in blankets of sauerkraut, cabbage, shredded apple, and onions. Usually it will have some sausage tossed in, too.

Let me state that there are as many recipes for bigos as there are cooks. It's one of those dishes. Sorry in advance if my bigos is not like yours. It's still damned good.

Needless to say this stew can be made with anything, and it will be better the second and third day after you make it.

Serves 8 to 10 | Prep Time: 20 minutes | Cook Time: 3 hours

Wings, drumsticks, and thighs from a turkey, about 5 pounds total

¼ cup duck fat, lard, or butter

Salt

2 or 3 large onions, sliced

1 ounce dried mushrooms, rehydrated in 2 cups water

A smoked turkey wing or two

2 cloves garlic, chopped

1 tablespoon chopped lovage (optional)

1 teaspoon dried marjoram

1 or 2 bay leaves

1 or 2 tablespoons tomato paste

4 cups shredded cabbage

2 cups sauerkraut

1 apple, peeled and coarsely grated

A dozen prunes, chopped in half (optional)

1 pound smoked kielbasa, sliced into discs

Lots of freshly ground black pepper

Brown the turkey in the duck fat or lard over medium-high heat. Do this in batches and take your time. Salt them as they cook. Set the turkey aside in a bowl when each piece has been browned.

When all the turkey has been browned, add the onions and toss to coat in the fat. Add more if need be. Cook the onions over medium-high heat for 6 minutes. Salt them as they cook.

Chop the rehydrated mushrooms and reserve the soaking water. Add the mushrooms to the pot and cook for a minute or two. Add the garlic and cook another minute.

Add the smoked turkey wings, lovage (if using), marjoram, and bay leaves. Mix the tomato paste with the mushroom soaking water and add it to the pot. Add about 2 more quarts of water and bring to a simmer. Simmer, covered, for 90 minutes.

Add the cabbage, sauerkraut, and grated apple, and keep cooking the stew until the turkey is tender, about another hour or so. Remove the meat and separate it from the bones, then return the meat to the pot.

Add the prunes, kielbasa, and black pepper, then cook another 10 minutes. Serve with bread.

CHAPTER 7

QUAIL, PARTRIDGES, AND CHUKARS

These are all small, mild-tasting game birds usually cooked whole, whether with their skin or skinless. Their flavor plays well with any of the pheasant or grouse recipes in the first chapter, but since they are significantly smaller, I decided that they needed a chapter of their own.

I have yet to meet a strong-tasting quail or partridge, although I have met many with subtly fascinating flavors. Key word: subtle. Sure, you can use strong flavors with these birds, but if you cook a quail or chukar correctly, it needs nothing more than salt and maybe a little pepper.

CHAOS THEORY AND ROAST PARTRIDGE

We can all envision the Platonic Ideal of a roasted game bird: crispy skin, juicy, gently cooked breast meat, and fully cooked, tender legs and wings. The bird will be a little salty and bathed in butter or olive oil or whatever oil or fat makes you swoon. Most of all, it will taste of itself. On this I think most of us can agree.

Cooking any game bird is really an exercise in taming chaos. In mathematics, chaos theory states that "small differences in initial conditions yield widely diverging outcomes ... rendering long-term prediction impossible." This is true of cooking in general, but especially so with finicky birds like partridges, grouse, quail, woodcock, and pheasant.

Consider these questions and think about that quote above. How large is your bird? What temperature is it when you start cooking? How hot is your oven or pan? Is there air circulation? Is the bird trussed or not? How old is your bird? Is crispy skin more important to you than perfectly cooked breast meat? How many birds are you cooking? All are small differences in initial conditions that can yield widely diverging outcomes.

That said, game birds are all alike in several important ways. First, the breast meat must be cooked more gently than the meat on the legs and wings. You generally want your quail or partridges slightly less done than your chicken—a solid medium toward medium-well, fully cooked but with a blush of pink (but not rare or even medium rare). That generally means a breast temperature around 148°F and no warmer than 160°F. Second, know that a bird's physical architecture makes this difficult to achieve and still have fully cooked legs. Third, if crispy skin is what we all want, how do we get there without annihilating the breast meat?

In an oven, the answer is high heat. And the smaller the bird, the hotter the oven. Roasting a snipe should be hotter and faster than roasting a wild turkey. It has to do with the surface-to-mass ratio of the bird—small birds heat up faster. But even a roaring, 500°F oven won't really cut it for dainty upland birds like partridges, grouse, woodcock, or quail. And snipe? Unless you have a wood-fired oven that can hit 600°F or 700°F, you won't get close to realizing that Platonic Ideal of a perfectly roasted snipe.

Yes, I have oven-based recipes for all these birds. And I do support them because they work pretty well and are not at all labor intensive. But even with these recipes, which will get you close to the Ideal, there's one major problem: crisping the breast skin at the end. For me, juicy breast meat trumps crisp skin.

One techno hack way to get both is to use a device called a Searzall. It fits on a torch that you hook up to a small propane tank. The device heats a metal grate to glowing, and this heat sears things without the stink of propane on your food. It's a great tool, one I use all the time.

But there's another way, one that requires nothing more than a sauté pan and a spoon.

My initial steps toward this perfection came in the form of a recipe for partridge with cranberries, which uses a technique I read about in the great cookbook *Fäviken* by Magnus Nilsson. It entails moving the birds around constantly and then letting them rest a bit in between. It works. Really well, in fact. But it requires some two-handed action with tongs and some delicate balancing of the birds. It's tough to cook more than two at a time this way.

Then came a trip up north to Alberta to hunt grouse with my friend (and Canadian doppelgänger) Kevin Kossowan. We were camping in the boreal forest, so I cooked our grouse on a flat rock in front of a roaring alder fire. I'd never done this before.

It was a revelation. I had to move the birds here and there on the rock to cook them just right. We'd brought some homemade butter, so I basted the grouse often with this. Soon, the grouse were sizzling in browned butter. Being able to move the birds to hotter or cooler places was a game changer. Primitive precision. And let me tell you, those grouse were some of the best I've ever cooked or eaten.

I lack a flat rock and an open fire in my kitchen. But I do have a sauté pan. By combining the *Fäviken* and open-fire techniques, I've found the best way to cook game birds. I'm certain this method is not unique to me, but I came by it honestly. And I present it to you on the following page as Pan-Roasted Quail or Partridge. For those who don't want to use the pan-roasting technique, Oven-Roasted Quail and Partridge (page 159) is almost as good.

Chukar feathers

PAN-ROASTED QUAIL OR PARTRIDGE

Serves 2, and can be scaled up | **Prep Time: 45 minutes, to let the birds come to room temperature**
Cook Time: 15 minutes

4 whole, plucked quail or partridge

Lard, butter, or olive oil

Salt (fine, not coarse)

Even before you cook your birds, it's best to set them, uncovered, in the fridge for up to 24 hours. The arid, cold environment of the refrigerator dries out the skin of the birds a bit, which will help it become crisp later. The skin may start to look splotchy, but that's normal.

When you're ready to cook your birds, set them out on a paper towel on a plate for a solid 45 minutes. Salt them inside and out using fine salt, not coarse; coarse salt will create odd-looking spots on the skin. It's very important that your birds start the cooking process at room temperature.

Get a sauté pan large enough to hold your birds (four are as many as I've been able to handle at one time). Add a fair amount of fat or oil to the pan, and include some butter in the mix; I like about 3 tablespoons of vegetable or olive oil along with 3 tablespoons of butter. Clarified butter is a good choice, but I like the browning of the solids in the butter, which adds something to the birds. Turn the heat to medium-high.

When the butter melts, set the birds breast-side up in the pan. It'll be a minute or so before they sizzle. Drop the heat to medium-low. You want a gentle sizzle here, lower than that of bacon sizzling. This helps prevent the butter from blackening and gives you the time you need to get to that perfect bird.

Once you're at a nice sizzle, use a soup spoon to ladle the hot fat over the bird. Tilt the pan with one hand and spoon with the other. Do this continuously.

When the breast meat and legs have contracted a little and have turned opaque, tilt the birds on their sides. You want the legs to be in full contact with the pan. Ladle hot fat on the inside of the leg touching the pan, and then on the gap between the leg and wing on the side facing you. Ladle a little in the cavity, too. When the legs and wing on the bottom are golden brown, flip the birds and repeat on the other side.

Once both sides are browned, set the birds breast-side up again. This is a good time to take a break, as you will leave them there, sizzling happily, for 3 to 5 minutes.

To finish, turn the heat up to medium-high again and ladle fat over the breast until the skin browns; this is where the butter comes into its own—butter browns things faster than most other fats. Remove the birds from the heat and let them rest, uncovered, on a cutting board for a few minutes before serving.

The result is nothing short of amazing. It's as close to that Platonic Ideal as I've ever been, and it takes no longer than roasting in an oven. If you can spoon hot butter on a little bird, you can do this. It's that easy.

OVEN-ROASTED QUAIL OR PARTRIDGE

Regardless of species, all quail roast the same, as do all species of partridge. The basic rule is hot and fast. In the case of quail, really hot and really fast. I like about 500°F for about fifteen minutes or so. Partridges need about twenty minutes. This will cook your little birds nicely, although they will be a little pale—a price to pay for juicy and tender meat.

If you really want that pretty brown look, there are two ways to get it. The traditional way is to brown the bird in lots of butter; butter will brown birds faster than oil and, well, it tastes good. Another way is to blowtorch the bird after it comes out of the oven, which is what I do because I went and bought myself a Searzall, which is a device that allows you to brown foods very fast without getting that weird butane smell on it. Either way works, but if you do it, roast the quail a bit less, closer to twelve minutes.

Finally, if you have access to a pizza oven or something else that gets to 600°F or even hotter, you can just blast your quail for about five minutes. This would be ideal, although few of us have a pizza oven.

Whatever you do, keep things simple. The flavor of quail and partridge is chicken-like, but subtly different. You want to enjoy it, especially if you've worked so hard to bring a few birds home with you.

I include a brining step here if you like brining. If you do brine your quail, they will be more tender and you can cook them a few minutes longer—but you run the risk of their becoming too salty. Don't brine too long! If you don't brine, the meat will have a nicer texture, but you have less room for error when you roast them.

Figure on two quail per person as a main course and one per person as an appetizer. One partridge per person is a nice serving. Oh, and put a bowl out for bones. Quail are best eaten with your fingers, and you'll find yourself picking up the legs of your partridges.

Serves 2, and can be scaled up | **Prep Time: 30 minutes, to let the birds come to room temperature**
Cook Time: 15 minutes

OPTIONAL BRINE

¼ cup kosher salt

1 quart water, or white wine

2 bay leaves

QUAIL OR PARTRIDGE

4 whole, plucked quail or partridge

Lard, butter, or olive oil

Salt

2 celery sticks (optional)

Black pepper

Lemon wedges (optional)

If you choose to brine your quail or partridge, boil the water or wine with the kosher salt and bay leaves, then turn off the heat and let cool. Submerge the bird in this brine for 2 to 6 hours.

Preheat your oven to 500°F, or if it doesn't get that hot, as hot as your oven will go. This will take a little while for most ovens, up to 30 minutes. While the oven is preheating, take the birds out of the fridge and pat them dry. Coat with lard, olive oil, or butter (melted butter will brown them better) and salt generously. Set aside at room temperature while the oven heats.

When the oven is hot, get a small roasting pan or cast-iron frying pan and set the birds in it. They will want to tip over, so steady them with cut pieces of the celery stick. To speed the cooking process, try to prevent the birds from touching one another.

Roast quail for 12 to 18 minutes, partridges for 15 to 23 minutes. The lower end of the spectrum will give you birds that are juicy, succulent, and a little pink on the inside—but pale. The higher end of the spectrum will give you a fully cooked, browner bird, but one that is at the edge of being dry. When you take the birds out of the oven, place them on a cutting board to rest for 5 to 10 minutes.

Use this resting time to make the wild-game sauce of your choice, or just squirt lemon juice on the birds before serving.

PARTRIDGES BAKED IN SALT

I'd always been leery about baking things in salt. It seems like such an extravagant waste of salt, and the few times I tried it, the meat or fish I baked tasted ridiculously salty. Then I read Mark Bitterman's book *Salted: A Manifesto on the World's Most Essential Mineral*, in which Bitterman explains why salt crusts, typically kosher salt or, God forbid, regular table, are usually terrible: because these salts are absolutely dry, when they touch moist meat, they suck the moisture right out and destroy its texture. The answer, he says, is *sel gris*, a French sea salt that contains a fair amount of moisture. Is it expensive? Relatively, yes. The several pounds of sel gris you need for this recipe will cost you about $10; kosher salt will cost you about $4.

I've tried this recipe with both kinds of salt, and I have to say it was worth the money. The sel gris really does keep the partridges moister, and the residual salt just tastes better on the bird; sel gris is not pure sodium chloride, so it does have a taste that's different from regular salt. Could you do this with kosher salt? Of course, but it won't be sublime.

Serves 2 | Prep Time: 30 minutes | Cook Time: 45 minutes

---

3 tablespoons olive oil

2 partridges or 4 quail

2 sprigs fresh rosemary or sage

1 teaspoon dried thyme

1 teaspoon black pepper

2 teaspoons sweet paprika

2 pounds sel gris or kosher salt

Take the birds out of the fridge and let them sit at room temperature for 30 minutes.

Heat the olive oil in a large pan over medium-high heat. Pat the partridges dry and brown them on all sides. When they're good and browned, take the birds off the heat and let them cool for 10 minutes or so.

Stuff the rosemary inside the birds' cavities, and dust them with the thyme, paprika, and pepper.

Preheat the oven to 400°F.

Find a baking container just about large enough to hold both birds; I use a large saucier. Spread a layer of salt on the bottom, put the birds on the salt, then add more salt to bury them, patting down the top-most layer of salt after they're completely covered. They should be covered by at least ¼ inch of salt.

Bake the birds—20 minutes for quail or woodcock, 30 minutes for partridge, a full 45 minutes for pheasant. Take the birds out of the oven and let them cool for 5 minutes. Remove all the salt, brushing excess off with a basting brush or your fingers. Serve at once with a bold white wine or a hoppy beer.

VIETNAMESE CRISPY QUAIL

The South isn't the only place that likes crispy fried quail. The Vietnamese also fry their quail, but theirs are laced with spices and are marinated in honey, ginger, and soy.

This recipe is adapted from my friend Andrea Nguyen's fantastic book *Into the Vietnamese Kitchen: Treasured Foodways, Modern Flavors*. It takes a bit of prep time, but it's so worth it. In fact, since these quail are so great as leftovers, you might want to double the recipe.

Other small birds, like doves, snipe, rails, woodcock, and ptarmigan would work well here, too.

Serves 6 to 10 as an appetizer | Prep Time: 3 hours, mostly marinating time | Cook Time: 10 minutes

12 whole quail

2 teaspoons salt

2 tablespoons ground ginger

½ cup Shaoxing wine or dry sherry

4 tablespoons honey

¼ cup soy sauce

1½ cups potato starch, cornstarch, or tapioca starch

Oil for deep-frying

Mix together the salt, ginger, and wine. Coat the quail with this marinade, and do your best to get it into every cavity. Let the birds marinate in the fridge for at least 30 minutes, and up to a day.

When you're ready to cook them, rig up a steamer. I use those expandable vegetable steamer inserts you can put in a regular pot, but Nguyen uses a bamboo steamer in a wok. Put enough water into the pot to come up to the level of the steamer. If you have access to banana leaves, line the steamer with them before adding the quail; otherwise, set the quail in a bowl. Arrange the quail so they aren't touching one another or so they're barely touching, and set this on the steamer. It's likely you'll need to do this in two batches.

Steam the quail vigorously for 8 minutes, then set them, cavity-side down, in a bowl or plate; this makes sure they drain.

When all the quail are steamed, pat them dry with paper towels.

Whisk together the soy and honey, then coat the quail with the mixture. Put the cornstarch into a Ziploc bag and add one quail at a time, shaking to coat. Set each dusted quail on a clean plate so they don't touch. When they're all dusted, put them in the fridge for 2 to 3 hours. They're ready when the starch has turned brown.

Get a deep-fryer ready with enough oil to fry the quail. When you turn on the deep-fryer, take the quail out of the fridge. This will allow the quail to come toward room temperature while the oil heats to 350°F.

Frying doesn't take long, which is why you pre-steamed the birds almost through. Fry one quail at a time, using a slotted spoon and a regular spoon to turn the bird so it browns evenly. If you do this right, it only takes about 45 seconds per bird, but definitely no more than 1 minute.

Set the finished quail on a platter and have at it!

GRILLED QUAIL

Grilled quail is classic outdoor party food—a pile of grilled quail, slathered in sauce, people gnawing away at them all over the yard, drinking beer, laughing. What's not to love?

Start by spatchcocking your quail. I know, that sounds dirty. But it's just a cooking term for flattening the birds. You use kitchen shears to cut out the backbones of the quail, then you flatten them with your hands so they cook evenly. I take the extra step of removing the ribs with a sharp knife and shears. The fewer bones the better. If you're buying your quail, you can often buy them "tunnel boned," which means the only bones left in the birds are those in the legs and the wings.

Grilling them this way is easy. Coat with oil, salt well, and slap them on a hot grill. Start with the breast-side up so you can cook the whole bird well without incinerating the delicate breast meat. Flip them only when one side is well browned—a little char is a good thing here. Paint with the sauce of your choice and you're good to go.

Sauce is your big choice here. You could go European and just use olive oil, lemon, some herbs, and salt and pepper. I do this a lot. Or you could go American BBQ and use your favorite sauce. I'm partial to the mustard-based, South Carolina Barbecue Sauce on page 73. It's the perfect match for the quail.

Break out more quail than you think you need when you make this. Normally, two quail per person is a good portion, but I've eaten six at a sitting and have seen otherwise demure young women gobble down four. And if they don't all get eaten? Don't worry—they're spectacular the next day as a cold lunch.

Serves 4 | **Prep Time: 30 minutes** | **Cook Time: 15 minutes**

8 to 16 quail, backbones removed and flattened

3 to 4 tablespoons vegetable oil

Salt to taste

To flatten the quail, use kitchen shears to remove the backbones of the birds by cutting along either side. Put the quail breast-side up on a cutting board and press to flatten. If you want to be fancy, carefully snip out the ribs and the curved saber bones near the wishbone. Salt the quail and toss them in the vegetable oil.

Heat your grill, and lay your quail on it breast-side up. Grill over high heat with the grill lid down for 5 minutes. If you're using a sauce, paint it on about 5 minutes in.

Turn the quail over and paint the cooked side with sauce. Grill the breast side with the grill cover up for 2 minutes, then turn over again and paint with the sauce one more time. Cover the grill and cook another 2 to 4 minutes.

Take the birds off the grill, paint with sauce one more time, and serve.

BARBECUED QUAIL SOUTHWESTERN STYLE

What's the difference between this recipe and the one preceding it? Grilling is hot and fast; barbecue is slow and low. You set up your grill with a hot side and a cool side and cook your quail on the cool side. It takes longer than grilling, but it's easier—I've seen a lot of grilled quail charred on the outside and raw in the center.

And although you can certainly use any BBQ sauce you like, I love this ode to the Desert Southwest. It's a barbecue sauce, but it hinges on wild foods from the Sonoran Desert: wild chiltepin chiles, wild sage, and either prickly pear syrup or mesquite bean syrup. Oh, and there's a little tequila in there for good measure.

It's everything you want in barbecue: sticky, sweet-and-sour, spicy, savory. It's eat-with-your-hands food, and you'll want to make lots and lots of quail for this recipe because people will fight over the last one. And if by some freak of chance you do have leftovers, they're great cold, too. Now that's a breakfast I can get behind.

Don't despair if you don't happen to be in the Desert Southwest. Many of the esoteric ingredients, such as the chiltepin chiles and the prickly pear syrup, are available online. And if you don't want to go that far, use a habanero or other really hot chile and some good honey. It'll be a little different, but it'll still be good.

Serves 4 | **Prep Time: 30 minutes** | **Cook Time: 45 minutes**

QUAIL

8 to 16 quail, backbones removed and flattened

3 tablespoons vegetable oil

Salt

ARIZONA SAUCE

4 tablespoons unsalted butter or lard

½ onion, coarsely grated

2 shots of tequila (and a third for the cook)

½ cup mesquite bean syrup, prickly pear syrup, or honey

¼ cup cider vinegar

½ cup chicken stock

1 tablespoon chopped sage

1 to 2 teaspoons ground chiltepin or piquin chiles, or hot sauce to taste

Salt to taste

Make the sauce first. Heat the butter or lard over medium heat, add the grated onion, and sauté until the onion turns translucent, about 3 to 4 minutes. Add the remaining sauce ingredients, stir well, and simmer slowly for 30 minutes or more. I always pour the sauce into a blender and purée it, but you can serve it chunky if you prefer.

To flatten the quail, remove the backbones with kitchen shears by cutting along either side of the spine. Put the quail breast-side up on a cutting board and press to flatten. If you want to be fancy, carefully snip out the ribs and the curved saber bones near the wishbone. Salt the quail and toss them in the vegetable oil.

Get your grill hot, but leave an open space with no coals, or with one gas burner left off. Lay your quail breast-side up on the cool part of the grill and barbecue for 10 minutes with the grill lid down. Paint the breast side with the sauce, and repeat this twice until you've cooked the quail for 30 minutes.

Check the doneness, either by inserting a thermometer into the thickest part of the breast (it should read between 150°F and 155°F), or by testing where the legs meet the thighs; they should want to come apart when wiggled but not fall apart. You might need another 10 or even 20 minutes to get to this point, depending on how hot your barbecue is.

Turn the quail over and paint the cooked side with sauce. Grill the breast side for 2 minutes with the lid up, then turn over again and paint with the sauce one more time. Cover the grill and cook for a final 2 minutes. Take off the grill and paint with sauce one more time.

GRILLED PARTRIDGES WITH TOMATO SALAD

This is a recipe I designed for those final warm days of Indian summer, when tomato patches are waning, basil is going to seed, and cucumbers are finally petering out—and, as it happens, partridge season has opened. In the country's northern tier, Hungarian partridge season opens in early September. This is the perfect recipe to mark the event.

All small birds are great on the grill. Doves are great simply plucked and set right on the hot grates. Slightly larger birds cook better when spatchcocked, which is a fancy way to say split down the back. Drop a brick on the birds to flatten them even more, and you can get a perfectly cooked partridge, chukar, grouse, or quail in less than twenty minutes.

A few keys to this technique: make sure the birds are at room temperature when you grill them, otherwise there's a good chance that the center of the breast and the thighs won't be cooked through before the rest chars. Do most of your cooking breast-side up. This prevents the breast from getting too dry.

And you need a hot fire. A screaming hot charcoal or wood fire. Gas will work, but the beauty of this technique is that smoky aroma. Serve your partridges with the remains of your garden, tossed into a salad. Use my recipe only as a guide. Enjoy your last warm days in style!

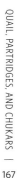

Serves 4 | **Prep Time: 35 minutes, mostly for spatchcocking the birds** | **Cook Time: 20 minutes**

TOMATO SALAD
2 pounds fresh tomatoes, seeded and roughly chopped

1 cucumber, seeded and chopped slightly smaller than the tomatoes (peel if the skin is bitter)

1 shallot, minced

1 large garlic clove, thinly sliced

About ⅓ cup basil leaves, torn into pieces

High-quality olive oil, about 3 tablespoons

Freshly squeezed lemon juice

Salt and black pepper

PARTRIDGES
4 to 8 small birds

Olive oil to coat

Salt and black pepper

Freshly squeezed lemon juice

Start by taking the partridges out of the fridge and setting them on a cutting board to come to room temperature.

While the birds are coming to room temperature, make the tomato salad. Add all the tomato salad ingredients except the basil to a large bowl (since the basil will discolor if left too long, you'll add it later, right before you serve). Toss to combine, and let it sit to marinate.

Spatchcock the birds while the tomato salad marinates. Spatchcocking involves cutting out the backbones of the birds and flattening them so you can grill them faster. Once your birds are flattened and partially deboned, coat them with oil and salt them well.

Get your grill hot and make sure the grates are clean. Right before you start cooking the birds, soak a paper towel in some vegetable oil, grab the oiled paper towel with tongs, and wipe down the grill grates.

Lay the partridges on the grill breast-side up. If you have one, grab a brick, wrap it in foil, and weigh down the partridges with it; this will put the birds in better contact with the grill. Let the birds cook for 8 to 10 minutes. You want to do most of the cooking on this side; it helps keep the breast meat moister. You can also flatten the birds by setting a heavy cast-iron frying pan on them.

Turn the partridges and grill them breast-side down only until they get nice char marks, which typically takes about 2 to 3 minutes. If the birds aren't cooked through—some will be, most won't be—put them back on the grill, breast-side, up for a few more minutes. If they arc upward, put the brick on them.

When they're done, remove the birds from the grill and let them rest on a cutting board for 5 minutes before serving them with the tomato salad.

PARTRIDGES WITH ORANGE-SAFFRON SAUCE

If you've ever seen the movie *Ratatouille*, you may recall that Remy the Rat could see flavors in color. I do this with seasons. Winter is burnt umber and ivory, the colors of deep sauces and stored roots. Summer, on the other hand, is a carnival riot: reds and oranges and purples, and vibrance all around.

Spring is easier. Spring is all about spring green—that vivid, bright emerald that always has a yellow cast to it. This is the green of new growth. Yellow—the canary of mustard flowers or the school-bus yellow of dandelions—compliments that green. So each year, I try to design a dish that celebrates those colors. Some are baroque, others loaded with esoteric ingredients. This recipe is neither. It's a partridge, with simply cooked greens, served with a sauce so easy to make you'll wonder that you haven't made it before. Why orange and saffron? It's a combination that works.

Serves 2, and can be scaled up | Prep Time: 30 minutes | Cook Time: 40 minutes

ORANGE-SAFFRON SAUCE

½ cup white wine

½ cup orange juice

A healthy pinch of saffron, crumbled

A healthy pinch of sugar

1 shallot, minced

Salt

2 tablespoons unsalted butter

GREENS AND PARTRIDGE

1½ pounds tender greens, such as spinach, amaranth, or lamb's quarters

5 tablespoons unsalted butter or vegetable oil (divided— 2 tablespoons to sauté the greens, 3 tablespoons to pan-roast the partridge)

A splash of water, maybe 3 tablespoons

Grated zest of an orange

Salt to taste

2 whole partridges

Sprigs of pea or vetch flowers, for garnish (optional)

Set the partridges on a cutting board and salt them well. Let them come to room temperature.

Make the sauce by bringing the white wine, orange juice, saffron, sugar, and shallot to a boil in a small pot. Simmer strongly for 5 minutes, then turn off the heat and purée the sauce in a blender. Return the sauce to the pot and turn the heat to low. Add salt to taste and keep warm, but don't boil it.

Add 2 tablespoons of butter or oil to a large sauté pan, and cook the greens over high heat, stirring constantly until they wilt. Add the splash of water, the orange zest, and some salt, and cover the pot. Lower the heat to medium-low and steam the greens for 2 minutes. Turn off the heat.

Pan-roast the partridges using the method for Pan-Roasted Quail or Partridge (page 156). Let them rest 5 minutes, then separate them into breast crowns and legs.

To serve, swirl the remaining 2 tablespoons of butter into the sauce, one tablespoon at a time. Pour some sauce on everyone's plate. Top with the greens and then with a partridge.

PARTRIDGES WITH CRANBERRIES AND ROSEMARY

This recipe was my first foray into the pan-roasting technique that I describe at the beginning of this chapter. It results in a perfect bird that needs only a few friends to make a party.

In this case, its primary backup is an oddly fermented cranberry called *vattlingon*, a Swedish preservation technique that translates as "water lingonberries." They fill a jar with lingonberries or cranberries, top it off with water, and put it in a cool place for months. Yes, only water. The reason is because cranberries and lingonberries contain benzoic acid. Sound familiar? It's a naturally occurring form of the preservative sodium benzoate that you can find in most of our processed foods. The net effect is to mellow out the cranberries so they need little or no extra sugar. It also softens them a little, too.

You could use any small bird here: partridges, quail, ptarmigans, or even teal, pigeons, doves, or woodcock if you want to go with a red-meat bird.

Admittedly, the fermented cranberries may be a touch on the exotic side, and you can use thawed, pre-frozen cranberries just as well. Barring that, something like tart grapes or currants would also work. You want tart but not overly sweet. Even a splash of good vinegar would do the trick. Citrusy new spruce or fir tips are best with this recipe, but as you can see it's perfectly good with fresh rosemary as well. You are looking for a piney, resiny element. I also added some pickled mustard seeds, but you can skip that if you'd like.

Serves 2, and can be doubled | **Prep Time: 1 hour, for the birds to come to room temperature**
Cook Time: 25 minutes for partridges, a little less for quail

---

2 whole, skin-on chukars or 4 quail

Salt

⅓ cup high-quality unsalted butter

1 heaping cup cranberries

1 cup (loosely packed) fresh rosemary, kept as little bunches on the stem

1 tablespoon maple sugar or brown sugar

Black pepper and pickled mustard seeds for garnish

Start with birds that are at room temperature. Pat them dry inside and out with paper towels. Heat the butter in a large sauté pan over medium heat. When the butter is hot, lay the partridges on their sides to start cooking the legs. Let them cook undisturbed for 2 to 3 minutes—you want to hear sizzling like you're cooking bacon, not a raging inferno. Flip the birds to the other side and repeat.

Now stand the partridges on their "heads," that is, where the neck was and the wishbone is. You will need to either hold them in this position with your tongs or lean them up against the side of the pan. If you lean them on the pan, move the pan so that only the area that's cooking the birds is over the flame; this prevents the butter in the rest of the pan from burning. Let the partridges cook for 2 to 3 minutes in this position.

Now set the birds on their backs, breast-side up. Baste the breasts with the hot butter, and let the partridges cook on their backs for 3 minutes. Salt the partridges now.

Stand the birds on their legs, leaning forward so the tail end of the breast touches the heat. Again, you might need to hold them there with your tongs or rest them against the sides of the pan; remember that if you do this, slide the pan again so only the part cooking the birds is over the heat. Let the partridges cook this way for 2 minutes.

(continued)

Return the partridges to their sides, as in the first step, only this time use your tongs to gently press the birds into the hot butter; this will help crisp the flanks of the bird and will give you an intense crisp on the legs and wings. Cook them on each side for another minute or two, pressing the whole time.

Now, finally, it's time to cook the breasts. Turn the partridges breast-side down in the pan and hold them with tongs. As you know, breasts have sides—the top of the bird isn't flat. So hold the birds at an angle to hit one side of the breast. You'll need both hands and two sets of tongs to do this. Hold them there for 1 minute. Now switch angles to hit the other side of the breast and repeat. Finally, let them rest however they want on their breasts and cook one more minute.

Finish cooking the partridges for another 2 minutes on their backs. Baste the breasts with the hot butter again. Move them to a cutting board—be sure it's one with gutters, so you can collect the juices—while you make the sauce.

To make the sauce, add the cranberries and rosemary to the butter in the pan and sauté 1 minute. Sprinkle the maple sugar over everything and grind some black pepper into the sauce. Add salt to taste and turn off the heat. Carve the birds, setting each piece skin-side up as you cut them free from the carcass. Pour any accumulated juices into the sauce and pour it over the partridges. Garnish with the pickled mustard seeds and serve immediately.

"Life is just too short to go quail hunting with the wrong people."

—PRESIDENT JIMMY CARTER

SOUTHERN-STYLE QUAIL WITH GRITS AND GREENS

If there's a more Southern way to eat quail than on a bed of stone-ground white grits surrounded by a pool of gravy and eaten with a side of stewed collard greens and ham hocks, I'd like to hear it. OK, maybe fried, but the decision would be a close one.

Quail and grits is a traditional meal in many parts of the South, and I've seen it served both for supper and for breakfast. Everyone has a different mixture of spices for the quail, and everyone's collard greens are a little different, so I make no pretense of having the One True Recipe here. But this is certainly a dish you can see all over the South, especially in Georgia, Alabama, and Mississippi.

Making this the Southern way requires a little attention to detail. First is the grits. If you can possibly find stone-ground white corn grits, use them. To me, there's nothing better than grits made with this process. Barring that, use some other form of grits or polenta. Don't use "quick grits" or somewhere in the South someone's grandmother will cry.

As for the quail, I used plucked birds with the backbones trimmed so I can flatten them; this makes them cook more evenly. If you have skinned birds, it will work almost as well; quail breasts will do in a pinch.

Collard greens are thick, burly cabbage relatives. They need long cooking and should be Army green when done. If you can't get collards, use kale, chard, or turnip or mustard greens instead; just note that they won't need as long to cook, maybe thirty minutes instead of an hour.

Serves 4　|　**Prep Time: 20 minutes**　|　**Cook Time: 2 hours**

**STEWED COLLARD GREENS
WITH A HAM HOCK**

2 pounds collard greens, chard or kale

1 quart stock (quail, pheasant, or chicken)

2 cloves garlic, peeled and smashed

1 ham hock or shank

Red wine vinegar and hot sauce to taste

QUAIL

8 quail

1 tablespoon paprika

2 teaspoons garlic powder

1 teaspoon salt

1 teaspoon black pepper

¼ teaspoon celery seed (optional)

½ cup flour, for dredging

½ cup lard or vegetable oil, preferably peanut oil

Start with the collard greens, since they take the longest time to cook. Bring the stock and an additional 4 cups of water to a boil. Add the garlic and ham hocks and simmer for 1 hour.

While the ham hock is simmering, cut out the stalks of the collards and discard. Roll the leaves into a cigar shape, and slice into ribbons.

After an hour has elapsed, add the collard greens, cover, and simmer for another 45 minutes to an hour. When the collards are tender, fish out the ham hock, pull off the meat and chop roughly. Return to the pot.

While the collards are cooking, start the grits. Bring the water to a boil and add a healthy dose of salt, about 2 teaspoons. Use a wooden spoon to stir the water. Gradually pour in the grits while you're stirring the water. Continue stirring without pausing until all the grits are in. Turn the heat down to medium-low, and gently cook the grits for at least 30 minutes, stirring frequently to keep the grits from scorching on the bottom of the pot. You can add a little more water if they get too thick. You want the finished grits to flow a little.

While the grits are cooking, prep the quail. Use kitchen shears to cut out the backbones of each quail. Flatten the quails against a cutting board so they cook evenly. Mix all the spices together and sprinkle them over the quail.

(continued)

GRITS

1 cup grits

4 cups water

Salt

3 tablespoons unsalted butter

GRAVY

¼ cup minced onion or shallot

2 tablespoons flour

1½ cups stock (quail, pheasant, or chicken)

¼ teaspoon thyme

2 teaspoons Worcestershire sauce

Salt and black pepper

2 tablespoons chopped fresh parsley, for garnish

In a large frying pan, heat the lard over medium-high heat until it's almost smoking. As the fat is heating up, dust as many quail as will fit in your pan in the flour—flour your birds immediately before they can go into the pan; if you flour them too early, they'll become soggy. Lay as many quail as will fit into your pan, breast-side up. Turn the heat down until you hear the quail sizzle like bacon; you don't want a raging sizzle. Cook this way for 7 minutes.

Turn the oven to 200°F and set a cookie sheet or plate inside. While the quail are cooking, spoon hot fat over the breast side of the quail. This sets the flour crust and will help the birds cook better. Do this several times as the quail fry.

After 7 minutes, flip the quail and cook another 3 to 5 minutes. When done, move them to the cookie sheet in the oven and fry the remaining quail.

When all the quail are cooked and out of the pan, make the sauce. Pour off all but about ¼ cup of fat from the pan. Turn the heat to medium-high, and add the minced onion. Cook for 1 minute, then mix in the 2 tablespoons of flour. Let this cook for 3 to 5 minutes, until it gets a nice tan-brown. Start stirring the mixture with one hand, and with the other, slowly pour in the stock. Keep stirring until all the stock is incorporated into the gravy, which should be a little thin. Bring it to a simmer, and add the thyme, the Worcestershire sauce, and the salt and freshly ground black pepper to taste. Let this simmer for 5 minutes.

While the gravy simmers, stir the butter into the grits.

To serve, pour a little gravy into shallow bowls. Top with a big helping of grits. Put the quail on top of the grits. Garnish with the parsley and serve. Serve the collard greens in bowls with vinegar and hot sauce at the table.

QUAIL WITH GRAPES AND PEARL ONIONS

Quail with grapes is a dish seen all over the Mediterranean, most often in North Africa, where it is called *saman bi einab*. It's elegant without being fussy, and it comes together in less than an hour. And while quail is the most traditional, there's no reason you couldn't do this with partridges, cottontails, or pheasant breasts—or switch it up and use dove, pigeons, woodcock, snipe, or ptarmigan and red grapes.

I love making this dish with clarified butter, and for an exotic spin, use my Ethiopian Spiced Butter on page 110.

Serves 4 | **Prep Time: 30 minutes** | **Cook Time: 15 minutes**

1 pound pearl onions

8 quail, backbones removed and flattened

Salt

½ cup butter or olive oil

1 tablespoon minced fresh ginger

1 head garlic, cloves peeled but whole

10 ounces green seedless grapes

Black pepper

Take the quail out of the fridge and salt them well. Let them come to room temperature.

Meanwhile, peel the pearl onions. You do this by boiling them in salted water for 2 minutes. Drain, let cool enough to handle, then slice off the root end of each onion. The peels will slip off. Set aside.

Heat the butter in a pan large enough to hold all the quail plus the onions and the grapes. Over medium heat, cook the quail, breast-side up. During cooking, spoon the hot butter over the tops of the birds to gently cook the breast meat. You can flip the quail if you want them browner, but this risks overcooking. Cook like this for 5 to 8 minutes.

Add the minced ginger, pearl onions, and garlic, and keep cooking for another 2 to 3 minutes. Don't let the garlic burn.

Add the grapes, shake the pan to coat everything with butter, and sprinkle everything with salt and freshly ground black pepper (optional). Cook like this until the grapes start popping, about 2 minutes, then serve with crusty bread.

QUAIL WITH WILD RICE

This is a great dish to make with the rest of the quail, whether you've skinned or plucked your birds. Basically, you simmer the birds to make a simple broth, then use that broth to cook wild rice, which is added to a sauté made from the tender meat from the legs and wings and stray bits from the carcass. Any white meat works here. Grouse is especially good.

Serves 4 | **Prep Time: 3 hours, mostly for making broth** | **Cook Time: 30 minutes**

QUAIL BROTH

Legs, wings, and carcasses
    (everything but the breast meat)
    from 6 to 10 quail

2 tablespoons vegetable oil

Salt

6 cups water

1 bay leaf

WILD RICE

1 cup wild rice

Salt and black pepper

3 tablespoons unsalted butter
    or vegetable oil

⅔ cup minced onion

2 cloves garlic, minced

1 to 3 small hot chiles, sliced
    (optional)

¼ cup chopped chives

½ cup chopped parsley

Worcestershire sauce to taste

Start by making the quail broth. I roast the quail pieces in a little vegetable oil first to give the stock more flavor (you can skip this step if you want—in fact, if you're pressed for time, just use store-bought chicken broth to simmer the quail in). Preheat the oven to 375°F. Toss the quail in the vegetable oil and salt well. Arrange in a single layer in a roasting pan or casserole dish and roast until browned, about 45 minutes.

Move the quail to a pot and cover with 5 cups of the water. Add the bay leaf and turn the heat to medium. Pour the other cup of water into the pan you roasted the quail in and use the water to scrape up all the browned bits from the pan, using a wooden spoon. Add this to the pot with the quail. Add salt to taste and simmer everything for as little as an hour or as long as 2 hours. Don't go longer than that, or the quail meat will lose all its flavor.

Fish out the quail legs and strip the meat off the bones. Set aside. Strain the stock and pour 4 cups into a pot; use the rest for another recipe. Boil the wild rice in the stock until it's tender; real wild rice takes only about 20 minutes, but farmed "wild" rice can take closer to 45 minutes. Add some salt to the broth while it cooks.

Heat the butter in a small frying pan, and sauté the onions until they turn translucent, about 3 to 5 minutes. Add the garlic, chiles (if using), and the reserved quail meat, and sauté another few minutes. Stir in the chives and parsley and turn off the heat.

When the rice is tender, drain it and add the rice to the pan with the onions and the quail meat. Mix well, and add black pepper and Worcestershire sauce to taste. Serve at once.

QUAIL SALAD WITH ROASTED PEPPERS

Most of the quail we bring home get plucked and served whole. I realize that not everyone wants to do this, and I hear a lot from hunters who simply breast out their birds and eat the meat in skinless halves. If you're one of those people, this recipe is for you.

Quail breasts make such a pretty shape on the plate, and each piece makes a perfect two bites (one bite if you're ravenous). This makes them excellent for a main course salad. A good main course salad hinges on a combination of fresh and preserved ingredients, acid, fat, something savory, a little sweet, and maybe a bit of spicy heat. This salad touches all the bases, plus it's a snap to put together.

Cook the quail using my foolproof poaching method: bring hot stock to a boil, turn off the heat, drop the quail breasts in, and walk away.

Everything else about this salad is just arranging things on the plate. I gotta say, this dish is a triumph. It's easy to eat, colorful, with varied textures and flavors. I can imagine eating this in Spain, on the evening after a hunt, with a glass of Rioja rosé or fino sherry and lots of crusty bread. Classy, full of flavor, and—dare I say it—easy to make.

Serves 4 | Prep Time: 15 minutes | Cook Time: 25 minutes, if you're roasting garlic

3 cups stock (game or chicken)

Breast meat from 6 to 8 quail

¼ cup high-quality olive oil

One 12-ounce jar of preserved roasted red peppers, cut into ¼-inch strips

3 green onions, thinly sliced (white parts only)

⅓ cup pine nuts

1 head garlic

Parsley, salt, and black pepper to taste

Lemon juice (optional)

Preheat the oven to 375°F. Cut the top bit off the head of garlic and drizzle olive oil over it. Wrap the head of garlic in foil, and roast for 45 minutes. Open the packet, let cool a bit, and squeeze the cloves from their paper. Set aside.

Bring the stock or broth to a boil. Turn off the heat, and drop the quail breasts into the broth. Let this sit for 10 minutes. If you like your meat less than well done, start checking them at about 5 minutes. When the quail breasts are cooked to your liking, remove them to a bowl and toss them with some olive oil.

Toast the pine nuts in a dry sauté pan over medium-high heat, tossing them frequently to toast all sides. Pay attention to them as they toast—pine nuts go from nicely toasted to burnt in seconds. When the pine nuts have some pretty, browned spots on them, move them to a bowl to cool.

Mix the roasted garlic with the remaining olive oil until well combined.

To compose the salad, toss all the ingredients together with the garlic-oil mix, then garnish with some parsley and ground black pepper. If the salad needs to be a little more tart, add some lemon juice.

Serve at room temperature with some Spanish sherry, a rosé or white wine, or a crisp lager or pilsner beer.

PARTRIDGE ESCABECHE

Escabeche is a cold, vinegary, slightly pickled dish of meat, in this case *perdiz*, Spanish for partridge, and some vegetables. It makes one of the best hot-weather lunches I know.

The dish is steeped in as much controversy as it is in vinegar. Who invented it? What is a "real" escabeche, and which versions are poseurs? Is it a fish dish or a meat dish? Debate even surrounds the dish's pronunciation: Es-kah-BAY-chay, Es-kah-BEH-chay or Es-kah-BESH? The answer to all of these questions is, "It depends."

Scholars say that Arabs invented the technique of cooking a meat or fish and sousing it with a vinegary sauce, probably sometime in the early medieval period. Then again, the ancient Romans were particularly fond of vinegar sauces, so I personally would put my money on either them, or on the Greeks who preceded them, as the inventors.

In its modern form, escabeche is a Spanish creation, and Spain is the country I turn to for my inspiration. The Spanish dispersed the dish throughout their empire in the 1500s, and what has emerged over the centuries are subspecies of the Spanish escabeche in Mexico, South America, and the Philippines. The Portuguese, too, lay legitimate claim to the dish, although every Portuguese escabeche I've seen has been rather nondescript.

Despite the idiosyncrasies of regional escabeches, there's a small list of ingredient common to nearly every Spanish version: olive oil, vinegar (usually made from sherry), thyme, bay leaves, lots of garlic, onion, and black pepper. Paprika, carrots, celery, parsley, rosemary, cloves, and oregano also appear regularly. And a few include saffron (which I do as well) and olives.

What's the real impetus for a preparation like this? Aside from balancing any gaminess in the meat, meat prepared this way will keep for days, even weeks if the weather is cool. And since escabeche is typically made with game birds or fish—which you can have too much of after an unexpectedly productive day—semi-curing the meats makes a lot of sense.

I always make escabeche a day before I serve it, but you could leave it to marinate for as little as eight hours; in other words, you can make it in the morning and serve it that night. It will keep in the fridge for a week or so if it's well covered.

Serves 4 to 6 | **Prep Time: 15 minutes** | **Cook Time: 3 hours, including steeping time at the end**

4 partridges, 2 pheasants or rabbits, or 8 quail

⅓ cup olive oil

Lemon peel from 1 lemon, white pith removed

1 large onion, sliced into half-moons

2 large carrots, peeled and sliced into discs

5 cloves garlic, chopped

½ cup sherry vinegar or white wine vinegar

3 cups white wine

Cut your birds into serving pieces (leave quail whole), and salt them well. Set aside. In a large Dutch oven or pot with a lid, heat the olive oil over medium heat, add the lemon peel, and cook until the lemon peel browns. Remove lemon peel, and either discard it or eat it (it's tasty!). This adds another layer of flavor to the escabeche.

Cook the birds. You have two choices here: either brown them in the olive oil you just flavored with lemon or paint them with that olive oil and grill them over an open fire. I do the former in winter, the latter in summer.

Sauté the onion and carrots in the lemon-flavored olive oil until just beginning to brown. Add the garlic, and sauté for a another minute, stirring often.

(continued)

4 bay leaves

1 teaspoon dried thyme

1 teaspoon black pepper

1 sprig rosemary

2 whole cloves

½ teaspoon saffron

Salt

Add the vinegar, white wine, all the herbs, and the spices, and bring to a simmer. Return the birds to the pot, and add a little water if you need more liquid; you want the birds to be almost submerged, but not completely so. Cover and simmer slowly for 90 minutes. Let the birds cool in the sauce for an hour or so.

Serve cold, warmed, or at room temperature with either boiled potatoes or lots of crusty bread and a white wine or beer.

The grassy desert of southern Arizona. Mearns' quail country.

CHAPTER 8

RABBITS

It may surprise you, but rabbit—not chicken—was once America's most common white meat. Until fairly recently, chicken was only for special occasions—the "chicken in every pot" line that the GOP used in an ad for Herbert Hoover's 1928 presidential campaign suggested as much. Rabbit was more common. That changed after World War II, once breeders developed the "double breasted" chicken we all eat today, after which it was chicken, not rabbit, that had the largest piece of boneless white meat. Also, rabbits are a bit trickier to break down (see page 36) and they are, well, adorable in a way that chickens simply are not. Bunnies slipped into stuffed animal status, and chicken ruled the pot.

That's starting to change, as a new wave of small-scale livestock farmers are learning that raising meat rabbits is uncomplicated and can even be done in cities. It's becoming increasingly common to see rabbit in supermarkets and farmer's markets, and these rabbits are of good quality.

Out in the wild, there are roughly 1.5 million rabbit hunters in the United States, making them among the most numerous hunters in the country. Cottontails and snowshoe hares are the top quarry no matter where you live. They're plentiful, and because they're short-lived, they're tender for a wild animal. Cottontails are one of the few game animals you can fry like a chicken (quail is another).

Most of the meat in a rabbit is in its hind legs, but don't forget the forelegs, which for some reason are often tossed. There's plenty of meat on them to toss into the pot, and they're no more fiddly than a chicken wing—in fact, they make a great "wing" (Honey-Mustard Pheasant Wings, page 105).

Cooking-wise, other than chicken-frying them, rabbits are best braised or stewed. They can be used in most pheasant, quail, and partridge recipes, and they grill or barbecue quite well. If you take the time to debone a bunny, it makes a good Chinese stir-fry, too.

In general, one rabbit will feed two people, a snowshoe hare up to four. Tiny desert cottontails can be single-serving critters, though.

BUTTERMILK FRIED RABBIT

If you like fried chicken—and who doesn't—you'll like fried rabbit, which looks a lot like chicken but definitely tastes like rabbit. You'll likely make this recipe with store-bought rabbits or cottontails, but if you happen to be blessed with a young snowshoe hare or squirrel, use them.

You need a lot of oil for this, but you can reuse it. When you're done, let the oil cool and then pour it through a fine-mesh strainer with a piece of paper towel inside set over a bowl. The paper towel will filter the brown bits, and you can just pour the strained oil back into the container. I generally get three uses from my oil by straining it like this.

Serve your fried rabbit with grits or by themselves with some coleslaw and potato salad on the side. This is picnic food or food to munch on while watching the game. Like I said: comforting, not challenging.

If you're using cottontails, I highly recommend that you brine your rabbits before frying (domestic rabbits don't need to be brined). A simple brine of ¼ cup kosher salt to one quart of water will do—the rabbit will get plenty of seasoning later. Submerge your bunny in this brine for up to twelve hours. This process keeps it moist.

Oh, and should you have leftovers, they're fantastic cold for lunch the next day

Serves 4 | Prep Time: 4 hours, not including brining time | Cook Time: 25 minutes

2 to 4 cottontails, cut into serving pieces

2 cups buttermilk

2 tablespoons Italian seasoning, or mix together 1½ teaspoons oregano, 1½ teaspoons thyme and 1 tablespoon dried parsley

1 tablespoon paprika

1 tablespoon garlic powder

2 teaspoons cayenne, or to taste

1½ cups flour

1 heaping teaspoon salt

About 2 cups vegetable oil

Mix the buttermilk with all the spices except the teaspoon of salt. Coat the rabbit with the mixture and set in a covered container overnight, or at least 8 hours.

When you're ready to fry, pour the oil into a large pan—a big cast iron frying pan is ideal—to a depth of about an inch. The general idea is for the oil to come halfway up the side of the rabbit. Set the heat to medium-high.

While the oil comes to temperature, remove the rabbit from the buttermilk, and place it in a colander to drain. Don't shake off the buttermilk, just leave it there.

Let the oil heat until to about 325°F; this is the point where a sprinkle of flour will immediately sizzle. When the oil is hot, pour the flour and salt into a plastic bag and shake to combine. Put a few pieces of rabbit into the bag and shake to coat it in flour.

Set the coated rabbit pieces in one layer in the hot oil so they don't touch. Fry for about 8 to 12 minutes. Fry gently—you want a steady sizzle, not a raging fry, and you definitely don't want the rabbit to just sit in oil. You might need to adjust the heat. Turn the rabbit pieces, and fry for another 10 minutes or so, until they're golden brown. The forelegs will come out first, followed by the loin, and the hind legs will come out last. You'll probably need to fry in batches, so just leave the uncooked rabbit pieces in the colander until you're ready to flour them up and fry them. Don't let the floured pieces sit.

When the rabbit is good and fried, let them rest on a rack set over a paper towel to drain any excess oil. If you're cooking in batches, set this in a warm oven.

RABBIT WITH MUSTARD

Lapin à la moutarde is a French country dish that can probably be traced back two thousand years or more. There's no reason not to think that the Gauls were making this while Julius Caesar had his eye on the country in 58 BC. Rabbit, mustard, a little cream, an herb or two. Simple.

Serve this dish with crusty bread and a big white wine, such as a white Bordeaux, a white Côtes du Rhône blend, or a buttery California Chardonnay. If you prefer beer, try pairing this with an unfiltered wheat beer or a French *bière de garde*.

Serves 2 to 4 | **Prep Time: 15 minutes** | **Cook Time: 90 minutes**

1 domestic rabbit or 2 cottontails, cut into serving pieces

Salt

¼ cup butter

2 large shallots, chopped

½ cup white wine

½ cup water or stock

½ cup grainy country mustard, like Dijon

1½ teaspoons dried thyme

½ cup heavy cream

4 tablespoons finely chopped parsley

Salt the rabbit well and set aside at room temperature while you chop the shallot and parsley.

Heat the butter over medium heat in a large sauté pan with a lid. Pat the rabbit pieces dry, and brown them in the butter at a moderate pace—you don't want the butter to scorch. Don't let the rabbit pieces touch each other while they brown. Do it in batches if you need to. Once the rabbit is browned, remove it to a bowl.

Add the shallot, and brown it well.

Add the white wine, and turn the heat to high. Scrape off any browned bits on the bottom of the pan with a wooden spoon. Add the mustard, thyme, and water, and bring to a rolling boil. Taste the sauce for salt and add some if needed.

Add the rabbit pieces, coat them with the sauce, then drop the heat to low. Cover and simmer gently for an hour or so. You want the meat to be nearly falling off the bone. It might need more time, but should not need more than 2 hours total.

When the meat is ready, gently move it to a platter. Turn the heat to high and boil the sauce down by half. Turn off the heat and add the cream and parsley. Stir to combine and return the rabbit to the pan. Coat with the sauce and serve.

GERMAN RABBIT STEW

This is an unusual German rabbit stew called *eingemachtes kaninchen*, according to Mimi Sheraton in her excellent book *The German Cookbook: A Complete Guide to Mastering Authentic German Cooking*. It's a Swabian recipe from Southern Germany that doesn't immediately make you think of Germany: lemon, capers, and bay leaves play a prominent role in this stew. It's brothy, meaty, and tart, with just a hint of creaminess. Think *avgolemono* but with more fiscal discipline.

This recipe is a perfect stew for cool nights yet still light enough to enjoy with a chilled white wine outside on the porch as you watch the sunset, thinking about the next time you'll get a chance to chase rabbits.

It's a two-step stew, meaning you make the base and "mount" it with sour cream, white wine, and capers right at the end. Once you add those final ingredients, you're committed, so if you want to make this for dinners or lunches for the week, store just the base (up to step 4) and add the remaining ingredients when you're ready to eat.

Serve this with bread or potatoes and a crisp German white wine. A lager beer would be good, too.

Serves 4 to 6 | Prep Time: 10 minutes | Cook Time: 2 hours

2 cottontail rabbits or 1 domestic rabbit, cut into serving pieces

Salt

3 tablespoons unsalted butter

2 tablespoons flour

2 to 3 cups stock (rabbit or chicken)

1 onion, sliced root to tip

Zest of a lemon, cut into wide strips (white pith removed)

2 to 3 bay leaves

¼ cup lemon juice

2 tablespoons capers

½ cup sour cream

White wine to taste, at least 2 tablespoons

Black pepper

Parsley for garnish

Salt the rabbit pieces well and set aside for 10 minutes or so. Heat 2 tablespoons of the butter in a Dutch oven or other heavy, lidded pot over medium-high heat. Pat the rabbit pieces dry, and add as many to the pot as you can without crowding (you may need to do this in batches). Brown well on all sides. Remove the rabbit pieces once they're browned. This may take 15 minutes or so. Take your time, and don't rush things.

Add the remaining tablespoon of butter, then the sliced onion, and cook until the edges of the onion just begin to brown, about 6 minutes. Sprinkle with flour and stir well. Cook, stirring often, until the flour turns golden, about 5 minutes.

Use a wooden spoon to scrape any browned bits off the bottom of the pot. Return the rabbit to the pot and add enough stock to barely cover. Add the lemon zest, bay leaves, and lemon juice, and bring to a simmer. Cover and cook gently until the rabbit wants to fall off the bone, which will take anywhere from 90 minutes to 3 hours, depending on how old your rabbit was.

Since I happen not to like fiddly stews with bones in them, I prefer to remove the meat from the bones and then add it back into the stew. This is optional, and you could certainly leave everything on the bone if you want. For the deboned version, turn off the heat, fish out the rabbit pieces, and let them cool on a baking sheet. Pull all the meat off the bones, and return the meat to the stew.

You can now store the stew for several days. Or you can serve it at once. Turn the heat to low just to make sure the stew is nice and hot. Don't let it simmer. Add the sour cream, capers, and as much white wine as you want—you want the stew to be a bit zingy. Remove the lemon zest strips. Stir in a healthy amount of black pepper and garnish with parsley.

BRAISED RABBIT WITH GARLIC

I am indebted to the late, great Penelope Casas for this recipe. Casas, who died in 2013, was one of the foremost experts on Spanish food, and her cookbook *The Foods and Wines of Spain* remains an invaluable part of my collection. This dish is from that book.

Spain has all kinds of vinegary-meaty wild game dishes, notably their famous escabeche with partridges or pheasants (Partridge Escabeche, page 181). The theory is that vinegar can offset any sort of gaminess while at the same time helping to preserve things for a few days; it's not a bona fide preservation technique, but it will help keep everything nice for a week in the fridge.

It's ridiculously simple—rabbit, browned in olive oil, braised with vinegar and lots of garlic and onion, served with some sweet peas right at the end. Everything is in balance—the zippy sherry vinegar, the warmth of the slow-cooked garlic, the rabbit that turns luscious after simmering for hours, and even the peas, which really come off as sweet when juxtaposed with everything else in the bowl. Add good black pepper and you need nothing else—except maybe a nice white wine.

The quality of the vinegar and garlic matter here. I use sherry vinegar, and I urge you to use it if possible. But a good cider, white wine, or even malt vinegar would be acceptable alternates. Home-grown garlic is best, as it will often be less harsh and have larger cloves than store-bought garlic, but any garlic will work.

Once made, you can keep this in the fridge for a week or so, but it will become more vinegary each day—and the peas will turn army-green.

Serves 4 | **Prep Time: 20 minutes** | **Cook Time: 2 hours**

3 tablespoons olive oil

1 domestic rabbit or snowshoe hare, or 2 cottontails, cut into serving pieces

1 large yellow onion, sliced ¼-inch thick from root to tip

1 head garlic, cloves peeled but left whole

Salt

⅓ cup sherry vinegar

1 bay leaf

Black pepper

1 cup peas

Heat the olive oil in a large, lidded pot such as a Dutch oven or, if you have one, an earthenware pot. Brown the rabbit pieces well, salting them as you do. Remove each piece as it browns, and set aside. When the rabbit is browned, add the onion and cook, stirring occasionally, until it begins to brown, about 8 to 10 minutes. Add the garlic cloves and cook another minute or two.

Nestle the rabbit back into the pot, sprinkle some salt over everything, and add the vinegar and bay leaf. Pour in enough water to get about halfway up the sides of the rabbit. Cover the pot, and cook slowly for about 2 hours.

When the rabbit is tender, add black pepper and mix in the peas. Serve with lots of crusty bread.

RABBIT RAGU

This is a catch-all white-meat pasta sauce that I chose to make with rabbit. Any light meat will do. I have another, heartier ragu that is better suited to dark meats (Tuscan Hare Ragu, page 211).

The only tricky thing to this recipe is grinding the rabbit meat. If you don't have a grinder, either finely chop the meat or chop it coarsely and pulse in a food processor. You'll also notice that I am grinding pure meat with no fat; you can get away with this because there'll be lots of bacon fat in the pot to smooth things out.

I really like this ragu over polenta, but any pasta is great, too.

Serves 6 to 8 | **Prep Time: 35 minutes** | **Cook Time: 2 hours**

Boned out meat from 2 to 3 cottontails or 1 large domestic rabbit

¼ pound bacon

1 cup chopped fennel bulb

1 cup chopped onion

1 celery stalk, chopped

1 teaspoon chopped fresh sage

1 teaspoon chopped fresh rosemary

½ teaspoon dried thyme

1 cup sherry or white wine

3 tablespoons tomato paste

1 quart stock (rabbit, chicken, or other light stock)

2 cups crushed tomatoes

Salt and black pepper to taste

Grind the rabbit meat finely in a meat grinder, or, if you don't have a grinder, chop the meat into small bits with a knife.

In a large, heavy, lidded pot such as a Dutch oven, fry the bacon as you normally would. Eat the bacon or chop it up and put it into the sauce; it's the salty fat you really want.

Brown the ground rabbit in the bacon fat over medium-high heat.

While the rabbit is browning, pulse the fennel, onion, and celery in a food processor until chopped very finely but not puréed. When the rabbit is ready, add the vegetables and mix well. Use a wooden spoon to scrape any browned bits off the bottom of the pot.

Mix the tomato paste with the wine. Add the herbs to the pot and then the wine-tomato paste mixture. Add the stock and tomatoes and bring to a simmer. Add salt to taste.

Simmer this soupy-looking stuff slowly for an hour or three until it cooks down to a nice sauce. Add more salt if you need to, and add freshly ground black pepper. Serve with pasta or over polenta.

SPANISH PEPPERED RABBIT

If you don't like black pepper, don't make this dish. It's all about the black pepper, and while it will seem almost toxic the moment you put it into the pot, the pepper will mellow as the rabbit cooks.

I learned about this recipe in Clifford Wright's *A Mediterranean Feast*, a vast compendium of all things Mediterranean that is unquestionably the best book of its kind. The basic recipe would work with almost any meat, light or dark. So play with it. I can see it being every bit as good with stewed sharp-tailed grouse or hare as it would be with rabbit or partridge.

Serves 4 | **Prep Time: 15 minutes** | **Cook Time: 2 hours**

1 domestic or 2 cottontail rabbits, cut into serving pieces

Salt

¼ cup olive oil

4 cloves garlic, chopped

2 tablespoons chopped parsley

2 tablespoons chopped cilantro

1 to 3 tablespoons freshly cracked black pepper

2 cups hot water

½ teaspoon ground cinnamon

Grated zest and juice of a lemon

Salt the rabbit pieces well and let them sit while you chop the garlic and herbs.

Heat the olive oil in a large, lidded pot over medium-high heat. Pat the rabbit pieces dry, and brown well. Take your time to do this well—the better you brown the rabbit, the better the finished dish will taste.

When the rabbit is ready, add the garlic, and cook another minute, stirring often. Add the herbs, black pepper, hot water, and cinnamon, stir well, cover the pot, turn the heat to low, and simmer gently until the rabbit is tender. This will be about an hour for a store-bought rabbit, longer for wild ones.

When the rabbit is tender, add the lemon zest and juice, and serve with crusty bread or rice.

"Depend on the rabbit's foot if you will,
but remember it didn't work for the rabbit."

—OLD AMERICAN SAYING

MEXICAN GRILLED RABBIT

I fell in love with this method of cooking during duck season, of all things. When driving home after a morning in the marsh, I always want lunch. Passing through the tiny town of Live Oak, California, there's often a huge plume of smoke emanating from somewhere near the road that smells intoxicating. The smoke comes from a rusty old grill tended by an old man. Inside that grill are a great many spatchcocked chickens, marinated in a bright-red, citrusy sauce.

Finally, one day, I stopped and ordered one. For $10, it was one of the best grilled chickens I'd ever eaten. I later learned that the recipe was a pretty typical *asado*, a traditional Mexican barbecue. And I also learned that it works well with rabbits, quail, and pheasants.

Rabbits are my favorite because they're rarely tough—and I mean rabbits, not hares, here. Quail or partridges would be the next best, followed by pheasants. Pheasants have a problem in that their drumsticks are too sinewy for this method, but breast meat would do well here, as would turkey breast meat. Remember with all these alternative meats that the cooking time will be much less than for rabbits. Keep an eye on it.

To make this recipe, you'll need achiote paste, which is easily found in Latin markets or online.

Serves 4 | Prep Time: 20 minutes, not including marinating time | Cook Time: 45 minutes

1 domestic rabbit or 2 cottontails

One 3½-ounce box of achiote paste

1 grapefruit

1 orange

1 lime

2 tablespoons room-temperature lard or vegetable oil

2 teaspoons salt

You'll want to cut your rabbit a bit differently for this recipe. Using kitchen shears, a stout chef's knife, or a cleaver, slice through the rabbit's backbone where it meets the hind legs. Cut through the hips to separate the two hind legs. Now use the shears to cut the backbone right behind the front legs, and then cut the spine down the center to separate the two front legs. That leaves the torso. Cut the flaps off each side, then the loin into two pieces.

Juice all the citrus into a bowl. Mix the achiote paste into the citrus juice. This is best done with your fingers, and it'll be messy. Be near a sink. Mix in the salt and the lard. You want this marinade to be like barbecue sauce.

Mix the rabbit and marinade well. I put them into a heavy freezer bag that I then set in a bowl in case of leaks. Put this in the fridge for at least an hour, and up to a day.

Get your grill nice and hot on one side and cooler on the other. Grill the rabbit on the hot side of the grill until the marinade sets, turning once or twice. Move the rabbit to the cooler side of the grill and close the lid. Roast this way until the meat is cooked through, anywhere from 30 minutes to an hour, depending on the size of the rabbit and how hot your grill is. Paint the rabbit with the extra marinade from time to time.

Serve with a chopped salad or salsa, Mexican rice or tortillas, and a beer.

GREEN CHILE RABBIT

Another Mexican-inspired take on rabbit, this recipe features all the good things in the green part of the color spectrum: green chiles, tomatillos, cilantro and other herbs, and avocados. This is a perfect dish for September, when the tomatillos and green chiles are ready, but you can use frozen or canned versions if you want to make this at other times of the year.

Serve this over rice, or break up the meat and serve it in tortillas as a taco or wrapped up in a burrito. It can also be used as a filling for enchiladas, like the Dove Enchiladas on page 263.

Any white meat works here, as would squirrels or the legs from dark-meat grouse.

Serves 4 | **Prep Time: 45 minutes, if you're roasting chiles and husking tomatillos** | **Cook Time: 2 hours**

---

4 green chiles, such as Hatch, poblano, or Anaheim

1 pound tomatillos, husked

4 cloves garlic

1 white onion

1 bunch cilantro

2 tablespoons chopped epazote (optional)

1 teaspoon dried oregano, Mexican if possible

¼ cup fresh lard or vegetable oil

1 domestic rabbit or 3 cottontails, cut into serving pieces

Sour cream, for garnish

2 avocados, diced, for garnish

This recipe goes much faster if you already have some roasted chiles and prepped tomatillos on hand. But if you don't, start with the chiles. Blacken their skins on a grill or a gas burner, turning often to char the whole chile. Put them in a plastic bag to steam.

While the chiles are steaming, husk the tomatillos. Slice large ones in half. Cut the onion in half, and cut one half in quarters. Coat the quartered onion, garlic, and tomatillos with vegetable oil and salt well. Arrange on a baking sheet in one layer, and broil over high heat until the tomatillos start to blacken. Remove from the broiler and set aside.

By now, the chiles should have cooled enough to handle. Peel off the skins, remove the stem and seeds, and set aside. Cut half the chiles into large chunks.

Put the rest of the chiles, the tomatillos, charred onion, and garlic cloves into a blender along with the stems from the bunch of cilantro, the oregano, and the epazote if you are using it. Add a big pinch of salt, and purée in the blender. It might seize up, and if it does, add water until the blender whirlpools correctly.

Heat the lard in a large, lidded pot over medium-high heat. Brown the rabbit pieces well. You may need to do this in batches, so take your time. Salt the rabbit as it cooks.

When the rabbit is browned, remove it and set aside. Slice the other half of the white onion, root to tip, and add that to the pot to brown. When the onion has browned, return the rabbit to the pot, add the green chile chunks and enough of the blender sauce to come three-quarters of the way up the sides of the rabbit pieces. Stir well, add a little water if you need to, and bring to a gentle simmer. Add salt to taste, cover the pot, and cook gently until tender, about 90 minutes for a domestic rabbit, a little more for cottontails.

You can serve this as is or remove the meat from the bones. Garnish with cilantro, diced avocado, and sour cream.

AFRICAN RABBIT CURRY

Many years ago, my life's goal was to be either a foreign service officer or a journalist serving in Africa. I did go there for a while, but I soon realized that the only way to really make a living as a freelance reporter in Africa was to cover a war zone. Not my thing.

In training for this, I learned Swahili, a trade language common on Africa's east coast from Somalia down to Mozambique. The course was total immersion, and included learning culture and food. This dish was one of my favorites.

Normally done with chicken and called *kuku wa nazi* (koo-koo wah NAH-see) this version uses rabbit, so it would be *sunguru wa nazi*. It's a simple curry you might see all over East Africa, and can be done with any light meat or fish, including the legs off prairie grouse. *Chakula chema!*

For an extra jolt of flavor, use the spiced butter on page 110.

Serves 4 | **Prep Time: 20 minutes** | **Cook Time: 90 minutes**

1 domestic rabbit or 2 cottontails, cut into serving pieces

Salt

¼ cup clarified butter or vegetable oil (see above)

1 large onion, sliced

2 teaspoons ground turmeric

1 tablespoon curry powder, or more to taste

4 cloves garlic, minced

1 tablespoon minced ginger

2 to 6 small, hot chiles, thinly sliced

1 pound potatoes, cut into chunks (optional)

¼ cup lime juice

One 14-ounce can coconut milk

GARNISHES

2 to 4 canned hearts of palm, sliced (optional)

Chopped roasted peanuts or cashews

Chopped cilantro

Salt the rabbit pieces well, and let them rest while you chop the vegetables.

In a large, heavy lidded pot such as a Dutch oven, heat the clarified butter or vegetable oil over medium-high heat. Brown the rabbit pieces well, removing them and setting them aside as they brown.

When all the rabbit has browned and been set aside, add the sliced onion to the pot and salt well. Toss the onions to coat with the butter or oil. When the onion begins to release its water, use a wooden spoon to scrape up any browned bits at the bottom of the pot. Cook the onion until it begins to brown on the edges, about 6 minutes.

Return the rabbit to the pot, add all the remaining ingredients except the garnishes, mix well, and bring to a simmer. Add salt to taste, cover the pot, and simmer gently until the rabbit is tender.

Serve over long-grained rice garnished with the cilantro, hearts of palm, and chopped peanuts.

RABBIT WITH ARTICHOKES

A fantastic recipe from Diane Kochilas's book *The Glorious Foods of Greece*, this is a perfect springtime supper. Everything here is subtle and comforting and delicate.

Artichokes can be persnickety to clean, but don't let that stop you from trying this dish. It isn't too tough, and you can always use canned artichoke hearts if the idea of cleaning fresh artichokes seems a bit too much.

3 cottontails or 2 domestic rabbits, cut into serving pieces

Salt

Flour for dusting

½ cup olive oil

2 large onions, sliced

2 bay leaves

¼ cup lemon juice (for cleaning the artichokes)

6 large or 12 to 20 small artichokes, cleaned, or 20 marinated artichoke hearts

1 bunch dill, chopped

2 teaspoons flour

Zest and juice of 2 lemons

Freshly ground black pepper

Salt the rabbit pieces well and set aside while you chop the onions and clean the artichokes. If you're using marinated artichoke hearts, let the rabbit sit at room temperature for 30 minutes to absorb the salt.

Pour the olive oil into a large, heavy, lidded pot such as a Dutch oven and set it over medium-high heat. Dust the rabbit with flour and brown in the olive oil. Take your time with this, and set aside each piece of rabbit as it browns.

When all the rabbit has been browned, add the sliced onions. Stir them up to catch any browned bits from the bottom of the pot. Salt the onions, and cook them until they begin to brown around the edges, about 8 minutes.

Nestle the rabbit pieces among the onions, add the bay leaves, and add enough water to just barely cover the rabbit. Add salt to taste. Drop the heat to low, cover the pot, and simmer 1 hour.

Large artichoke hearts should be quartered and will need about 20 minutes in the pot. Small ones should be left whole and need only 15 minutes. The rabbit will likely need 90 minutes to 2 hours, so gauge accordingly. If you're using canned artichokes, they need not go into the pot until you're ready to serve.

When the rabbit is tender, put the lemon juice and the 2 teaspoons of flour in a bowl and whisk together. Add a ladle of the broth from the pot and whisk it into the mixture, then add another ladle from the pot and whisk that in as well. Pour the contents of the bowl into the pot and swirl it around to distribute the sauce.

Add the dill, lemon zest, and black pepper, bring to a simmer again, and serve with rice, bread, or potatoes.

HOW TO CLEAN ARTICHOKES

First, get a big bowl of ice water and add ¼ cup of lemon juice to it. Pick leaves off the 'choke until you get to the yellowish leaves near the center. Use a small, sharp knife to trim away the dark green outer part of the bottom of the 'choke, including the skin on the stalk. Trim the bottom of the stalk, too. Rub the artichoke with a halved, squeezed lemon. Finally, slice the leaves about ½ inch above the artichoke heart. Larger 'chokes should be sliced in half (top to bottom). This will reveal fuzzy white-and-purple fibers that must be removed. Scrape it out with the knife. Submerge each cleaned artichoke in the lemon water while you clean the rest.

THE WHITE RABBIT

Eating this dish will make you appreciate rabbit in a whole new way. You'll realize, perhaps for the first time, that rabbit does not, in fact, taste like chicken, although it looks like it. Rabbit tastes like rabbit. And this, you will see, is a good thing.

I draw my inspiration for this recipe Paul Bertolli's *Cooking by Hand*. Chef Bertolli is a master of braised meats, and he argues that rabbit is one of the few foods that doesn't benefit from browning the way, say, duck or lamb does. So this dish skips that step and uses another technique: to prevent your braise from getting a layer of frothy scum on top (caused by coagulating blood and proteins from uncooked meat), you blanch the rabbit for a moment before it goes into the pot.

Serve with mashed potatoes, white polenta, or rice. A green thing alongside is always nice, too.

QUICK RABBIT STOCK

Ribs, neck, and belly flaps from
    the rabbits

2 bay leaves

½ teaspoon fennel seeds

1 teaspoon coriander seeds

10 juniper berries, crushed (optional)

1 teaspoon cracked black peppercorns

Salt

BRAISED RABBIT

2 to 3 cottontails, 2 snowshoe hares,
    or 2 domestic rabbits

Salt

⅓ cup olive oil

1 medium yellow or white onion,
    sliced root to stalk

1 teaspoon dried thyme

½ cup white wine or vermouth

1 cup quick rabbit stock (see above)

5 to 6 cloves roasted or preserved
    garlic

10 to 20 green olives, pitted and
    halved

3 tablespoons chopped fresh parsley

First, you must break down your rabbits (see page 36 for instructions). Save the stray bones in the pelvis, ribs, belly flaps, and neck for the stock.

To make the stock, put all the rabbit pieces—not just the stray ones—into a pot and cover them with cool water by about ½ inch. Bring this to a boil, then turn off the heat. Skim any sludgy stuff that floats to the top. Fish out all the good pieces of rabbit—legs and saddle—and put them in a bowl in the fridge. Add the remaining stock ingredients, return everything to a bare simmer, and cook for 1 hour. Strain and set aside.

Add the olive oil to a heavy, lidded pot such as a Dutch oven, and heat over medium heat. When the oil is hot, add the sliced onions and cook until soft and translucent; do not brown them. Add the white wine, 1 cup of the stock, the rabbit pieces from the fridge, the thyme, and the garlic cloves. Bring to a simmer, and add salt to taste. Turn the heat down to low, cover the pot, and cook until the meat is tender, about 90 minutes to 2 hours.

Finish the dish by adding the green olives and fresh parsley. Cook for 2 to 3 minutes and serve.

RABBIT WITH MORELS AND GNOCCHI

Sometimes you just gotta go for it. Every spring, I am overwhelmed by all the new ingredients that make this such a special season for food: morels, asparagus, fiddleheads, ramps, nettles, green garlic, fava beans—the list goes on. This recipe is concentrated springtime.

Slow-poached rabbit (an almost-confit), shredded off the bone and tossed with a flavorful oil to keep it moist, simply seared morel mushrooms, barely cooked fiddleheads (or asparagus or favas or fresh peas), a little garlic, and some very special gnocchi. Sometimes I add some lemon juice to brighten things up, sometimes I skip it. The flavors shine strongly, and each morsel on the plate tastes somehow clean and fresh.

The gnocchi are made with stinging nettles, but any spring green will work. Spinach is an obvious choice, as is parsley. But you could use miner's lettuce, pea purée, or any other soft, vivid green thing.

It's a deceptively simple plate of food, but you'll need some time to put it all together. I can tell you though, it's worth your time, and what's more, you can do it in stages, even to the point where once you have everything made, you can whip this up in the time it takes to boil water.

There are three distinct parts to this recipe—the rabbit, the gnocchi, and the morels—and each part can be modified without detracting from the whole. For example, I really like the rabbit slow-simmered, but you could cook it another way and it would still be nice. You could also substitute chicken, turkey, pheasant, or quail. And you can certainly use store-bought gnocchi or pasta if you don't want to make it by hand.

Done all at once, the dish as described here is a weekend-type meal. But you can work in stages. You can salt down the rabbit, rinse it, dry it, and keep in the fridge for up to a week ahead of time. Or you can cook the rabbit, pull the meat from the bones, and store *that* in the fridge for up to a week. You can make the gnocchi up to a month or two beforehand and freeze them. And you can blanch the fiddleheads (or other green thing) up to a day or two in advance and they'll still be good. Plan it and pace it according to your schedule and ambition. The dish keeps its springtime charm whether done all at once or piece by piece.

I'd drink a nice, full-bodied white wine here, or maybe a pale ale or hefeweizen beer.

Serves 4 to 6 | **Prep Time: 3 hours, to let rabbit brine** | **Cook Time: 90 minutes**

RABBIT

22 grams kosher salt (about 2 tablespoons) per pound of rabbit

1 rabbit, cut into serving pieces

2 cups broth (chicken, rabbit, or duck)

1 sprig fresh thyme

1 bay leaf

3 tablespoons walnut oil, olive oil, or melted butter

Toss the rabbit with the salt so all the pieces are well coated. Set in the fridge for 3 hours.

While the rabbit chills, prepare the blanched greens. First, set a large pot of salt water on the stove to a boil. While the water heats, fill a big bowl with ice water and set aside. When the salted water is boiling, drop in the nettles, parsley, or spinach. Boil nettles or spinach for 2 minutes, parsley only 1 minute. Remove the greens from the water (keeping the water boiling), plunge them into the bowl of ice water, lift them out, and squeeze to remove excess water (but leaving the greens damp). Add the fiddleheads or whatever spring vegetable you're using to the boiling water: boil fiddleheads 3 minutes, favas, peas or asparagus 2 minutes. When they're done, shock them in the ice water, pat dry, and set aside for now. Turn the heat off the water.

2 ounces blanched nettles, parsley, or spinach

1 egg

1 teaspoon salt

10 ounces ricotta cheese

¼ cup grated Parmesan

A pinch of nutmeg

1 cup flour

MORELS

8 to 12 ounces fresh morels, cut into discs

3 tablespoons oil (the same oil you used with the rabbit)

4 cloves garlic, sliced thin

8 ounces fiddleheads, fava beans, fresh peas, or asparagus

Salt and black pepper to taste

Lemon juice (optional)

Chop the nettles, then put them into a food processor with the salt, the egg, and half the ricotta cheese. Blitz this for about 30 seconds to 1 minute. You want the fibers of the nettles to be well broken down. Put the contents of the food processor into a large bowl, and add the rest of the ricotta, the Parmesan cheese, and the nutmeg. Stir in the flour bit by bit until you have a loose dough that you can just barely roll into a log. You should not need much more than 1 cup of flour. Put a towel over the dough as you make the gnocchi.

Cut off a quarter of the dough. On a work surface that you've dusted with flour, roll the dough into a log about ½ inch thick. Cut the log into little pillows. Carefully pick up each pillow—this is a *gnoccho*—and roll it off the tines of a fork held upside down to give it little ridges; you can skip this step if you're very new at gnocchi. Repeat with the rest of the dough. Set the finished gnocchi in the fridge for now.

When the rabbit has brined for 3 hours, rinse it off and pat it dry. Add the broth to a medium-sized pot that will just barely fit the rabbit, and submerge the rabbit pieces in the broth. If the broth doesn't cover the rabbit, add a little water. Add the sprig of thyme. Cover the pot, and simmer the rabbit until it starts to fall off the bone, about 90 minutes. When the rabbit is ready, pick the meat off the bones and coat in the walnut oil. Set aside.

To finish the dish, get the blanching water hot again and keep it at a simmer. Put the morels in a large sauté pan, and set the heat to high. Soon the morels will steam and sizzle and give up their water. When they do, salt them. When most of the water is gone, add the walnut oil and sauté the morels until they start to brown on the edges, about 3 to 6 minutes. Add the rabbit and the garlic. Now's the time to start boiling your gnocchi. When the gnocchi go into the boiling water, add the fiddleheads to the pan with the morels. Sauté just to get everything hot.

When the gnocchi are ready, add them to the pan with everything else, toss to combine, and add salt and freshly ground black pepper to taste. Add the lemon juice if you want, and serve at once.

PART THREE

DARK MEATS

CHAPTER 9

HARES, SQUIRRELS, AND OTHERS

Hare isn't often eaten in the United States. In fact, with the exception of the snowshoe hare in the north country, we don't even call our native hares by that name. We call them jackrabbits. But make no mistake, a jackrabbit is a hare. How much difference is there between a rabbit and a hare? Quite a bit, actually.

The first thing you notice about a hare are the ears, which are much longer than a rabbit's. Hares also give birth to "precocious" young, meaning they can hop away from danger minutes after birth. Rabbits give birth to helpless little pink things. Hares are larger, smarter, faster—and in the kitchen, tougher—than any species of rabbit. Jacks are to cottontails what pigeons are to doves, geese are to ducks, and elk are to deer.

Oh, and one more thing, especially important to a cook: hare meat is rich and dark, like beef or venison. Rabbit meat is white and subtle, like chicken.

There are many cultural reasons why most Americans don't eat jackrabbits. Suffice it to say that even after all this time, we are still in a Depression hangover, and jackrabbits remain stigmatized as poor-people's food. And there is the issue of parasites, which is a legitimate concern (see page 49).

So what do you do with jackrabbit meat? Braising or stewing are the best methods, but you can debone a hare backstrap—which looks like a little deer backstrap—and use it in stir-fries in place of beef or lamb. You can also chicken-fry leverets (young hares); you'll know you have one because a leveret is half the size of its adult friends, and their ears tend to tear easily.

Squirrels, on the other hand, unlike jacks, are much loved in many parts of this country. Mostly we eat eastern or western gray squirrels, fox squirrels, and in the Southern Rockies, Abert's squirrels. These tree ninjas are generally a single-serving animal, although a big western gray or fox squirrel can feed two in a stew. The meat cooks up dark-ish, like the thigh meat on a good farmer's market chicken. It's dense and nutty.

Like hares, braising or stewing are your best bets, but you can fry the young ones. Or you can simmer older squirrels in broth until they're tender and then fry them using the Buttermilk Fried Rabbit recipe on page 185.

EXOTIC PROTEIN

My friend and squirrel-hunting buddy Joe Keough happens to be a trapper in his spare time. Consequently, every winter he fills up a freezer with the meat of various furbearers that he calls his Box of Exotic Protein. Beavers, muskrats, a woodchuck or two. Maybe a raccoon.

Furbearers are beyond the scope of this book. I just don't get enough muskrat year to year to really develop recipes for them, although they do exist. 'Skrats, as it happens, are something of a local delicacy on the Delmarva Peninsula, where Delaware and the eastern shores of Maryland and Virginia are located. So if you're ever there and see it on the menu, often as "marsh hare," order it.

Broadly speaking, furbearers can be used in recipes for hares or jackrabbits. Anything you can make with a jack will work with a beaver, a woodchuck, or a marmot. And there are some general tips and tricks for dealing with them.

The first tip is about the fat: get rid of it. It's unappetizingly grassy and can be smelly (I've heard "old gym socks" more than once), and generally it should be trimmed. Though I've yet to meet someone who says beaver fat or woodchuck fat is in the same league as, say, duck fat, I've heard tell that raccoon and opossum fat has the consistency of pork fat and that it's good crispy.

Glands. Furbearers seem to be riddled with particularly unpleasant glands—raccoons, beavers, and muskrats above all. When butchering these animals, remove any little grayish packets you find in the undersides of the legs, or in the case of beavers,

the very large castor glands that live between the beaver's hind legs.

Diet. They don't call raccoons "trash pandas" for nothing. And many folks I've talked to who eat opossum will trap them live and give them kitchen scraps and vegetables for several days "to feed out the nasty." I've heard several old timers note that the best time to hunt and eat 'possums is when the persimmons have hit the ground; they love the fruit, apparently. Most other exotics, such as woodchucks, beavers, and muskrats, have pretty mild diets, however.

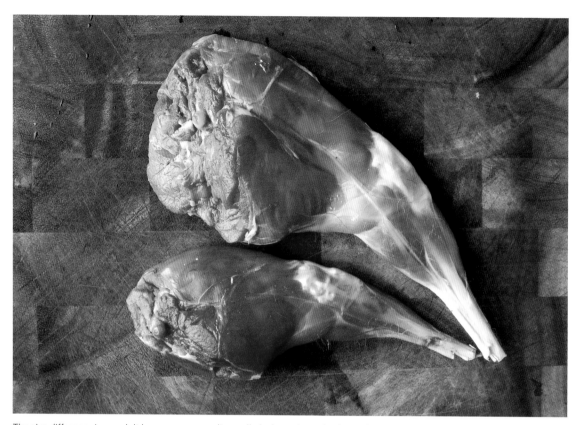

The size difference in an adult hare versus a yearling, called a leveret, can be dramatic.

Texture. Beaver is like beef, and it's widely recognized as the king of furbearer proteins. The texture of a muskrat, on the other hand, is oddly soft, almost mushy. Joe likes to braise it, shred it, and use 'skrat meat in a ravioli filling. You could use it in the filling for the Pigeon or Dove Tortellini on page 273.

As a side note on texture, beaver tail is gnarly—all fat and gristle. You'll read about the mountain men who said they loved it, but that's because they had almost no fat in their diets; their bodies craved fat, and beaver tails are loaded with it. Few modern humans I know can honestly say they like it. Who knows, maybe you're one of them.

A few other animals are worthy of note. My friend Ryan Diener of Missouri says skunk is basically a large squirrel. But be very, very careful around those scent glands! I've heard mixed reviews on porcupine, ranging from superlative to "only if McDonald's isn't open."

As a general rule, these exotic-protein animals are best simmered slow and low in braises or stews—simmered raccoon, with the meat pulled like pork shoulder and mixed with barbecue sauce is a time-honored tradition in the South. Young woodchuck, the only real exception to this rule, can be fried using the Buttermilk Fried Rabbit recipe on page 185.

TUSCAN HARE RAGU WITH PASTA

If there were a classic hare recipe, this one could be a contender: Tuscan hare ragu with fresh pappardelle pasta. It's meaty, rich, and tomatoey without being a true tomato sauce. Hare tastes like well-braised lamb, and a little of the sauce goes a long way. If you've never eaten a jackrabbit before, this would be a good way to start.

Most recipes for hare ragu will have you marinate the meat in wine, vinegar, and herbs for up to two days. I rarely do this, but you can if it makes you happy.

This is a pasta sauce specifically designed for hare or jackrabbit. If you don't have one lying around, don't substitute rabbit—use some other red meat. As for pasta, I make my own pappardelle pasta, which you can certainly do, or you can buy fresh pappardelle. Or just use dried pasta.

This sauce keeps well in the fridge for a week or so, and it freezes well.

Serves 6 to 8 | **Prep Time: 20 minutes** | **Cook Time: 4 hours**

3 tablespoons olive oil

2 pounds hare meat

Salt

2 cups chopped onion

2 carrots, roughly chopped

2 celery stalks, roughly chopped

2 tablespoons chopped fresh sage

2 tablespoons chopped fresh
rosemary

2 bay leaves

1 handful dried porcini mushrooms,
chopped (about 1 ounce)

2 tablespoons tomato paste

1 tablespoon red wine vinegar

One 28-ounce can crushed tomatoes

1 cup red wine

Parsley and grated cheese to garnish

Cut the hare into large pieces with a cleaver or kitchen shears. This will make it cook faster and fall off the bone easier (watch for bone shards—rabbit and hare bones are brittle.) Rinse the hare under cold water, and pat dry with paper towels.

Heat the olive oil in a large Dutch oven or other heavy, lidded pot over medium-high heat. Brown the hare pieces well. Take your time and do this in batches. Salt them as they cook. When browned, set aside.

While the meat is cooking, pulse the onion, carrot, and celery in a food processor until finely chopped but not a purée.

When the meat has been browned, add the onion, carrot, and celery, and cook, stirring occasionally, until the veggies begin to brown. Add the meat back to the pot, then add the sage, rosemary, bay leaves, and dried mushrooms. Mix well and allow to cook for a minute.

Add the vinegar, tomato paste, and wine to the pot. Turn the heat to high to bring everything to a boil, then add the can of crushed tomatoes. Mix well, drop the heat to a bare simmer—only a few bubbles coming up to the surface—cover, and let this cook until the hare meat wants to fall off the bone, up to 3½ hours.

When the meat is tender, fish out the bay leaves and discard. Remove the hare pieces, and pull the meat from the bones. Chop it into small pieces if you want. Return the meat to the pot.

If you want a smoother sauce, ladle out about a third to a half of the sauce and put it into a food mill with a medium grate attached. Alternately, put it into a food processor or blender. Purée, meat and all. If you use a food mill, you'll have some dry, stringy hare meat left in the mill; discard this or feed it to your pets. Return the purée to the pot.

Serve with the pasta of your choice along with some parsley and grated cheese.

SOUTHERN SQUIRREL FRICASSEE

When I was growing up, my mom had a fascinating set of cookbooks. They were well loved, tattered, and dog-eared. They were written by the memorably named Meta Givens, and they were called *The Modern Encyclopedia of Cooking*. I used to read them for hours, marveling at the wonders within.

Sure, there were lots of recipes for old-school foods I couldn't care less about, but the section on game was riveting—and this was decades before I'd even thought about hunting. All of the practical advice about skinning bears and barbecuing raccoons was a window on an unknown world. Among those recipes was one for squirrel fricassee.

A fricassee is really more a method than a dish. You flour something, fry it, then add just enough liquid to keep the thing moist while you simmer it to tenderness. Then you make a gravy from everything and eat it with grits, cornbread, or potatoes. Anything can be fricasseed, but I especially like to do this with squirrels.

A few notes on the recipe are in order. Grate the onion on the coarse side of a box grater; this will help it to disintegrate and become part of the gravy. For the beer, go with a cheap macro-brew beer or at most a light lager or pilsner; don't overthink things. Finally, some people skip the Creole or Cajun seasoning and go instead for lots of dry mustard. That's good, too.

Serves 4 | **Prep Time: 20 minutes** | **Cook Time: 2 hours**

4 squirrels, cut into serving pieces

Salt

¼ cup Creole or Cajun seasoning (optional)

1 ½ cups flour

¼ cup bacon fat, lard, or peanut oil

1 large onion, grated (see above)

2 cloves garlic, minced

Half a can of beer (see above)

2 cups stock (squirrel, pheasant, or chicken)

½ cup heavy cream

Worcestershire sauce to taste

Black pepper and hot sauce to taste

Chopped chives, green onions or parsley, for garnish

Salt the squirrel pieces well and let them sit on the counter while you chop the garlic and grate the onion; if you don't have a grater, mince the onion.

Mix the Creole seasoning with the flour and dust the squirrel pieces in it.

Heat a big frying pan you can put a lid on and add the fat. When it's hot, add the squirrel and brown well over medium-high heat. Remove the pieces as they brown.

When all the squirrel has browned and been removed from the pan, add the grated onion, and cook, stirring often, for 3 minutes. Add the garlic, and cook another minute.

Dust everything in the pan with the flour mixture; you want it to look like a light snowfall. Mix well, then slowly pour in the beer, stirring constantly. You ultimately want a very thin gravy that's the consistency of melted ice cream, so you'll likely need to add the stock as well.

When the gravy reaches the proper consistency, return the squirrel to the pan along with any juices that may have accumulated while they were resting. Cover the pan and simmer very gently until the squirrel is tender, anywhere from an hour to 2 hours.

When the squirrel is tender but not falling off the bone, add the cream, Worcestershire sauce, black pepper, and hot sauce. Let this all cook a bit—5 minutes or so—then serve, garnished with the chives.

SQUIRREL STEW WITH PAPRIKA AND GREENS

It's becoming something of a tradition for me to journey to northeast Ohio in the fall to hunt squirrels with my friend Joe Keough. We'll creep into the sugar bush (maple syrup forest) of one of Joe's friends in search of the wily tree ninja, which is the awesome name given to the various *sciuridae* by another squirrel-hunting friend, Chef Jonathan Wilkins of Arkansas. Almost immediately, I spotted a foolish young Algonquin black squirrel—just a dark color phase of an eastern gray squirrel—and blasted it with the old side-by-side I'd borrowed from Joe. One down. Then things got slow. We wandered for a while, hearing the tree ninjas yell at us (or maybe at each other, or maybe at nothing at all) without seeing them. Ultimately, we ended up with three for the day. Not a ton of meat for the three of us (Joe's wife Dorrie was waiting at home), so I thought I'd make a stew.

This is that stew, made from whatever was at hand at the time. Dorrie had some of the last tomatoes of the season and some beautiful chard. They had good Hungarian paprika kicking around, as well as smoked Spanish paprika. I mixed them in the stew. Finally, we'd just gone to Cleveland's West Side Market, where I'd bought a bunch of smoked sausages. In they went, too.

We sat down to eat our impromptu stew, which seemed somehow Portuguese to us, and very quickly realized that this dish was a keeper. "You better write this one down," Dorrie said. So I did.

There are a lot of ways you can play with this dish. You can use rabbit or pheasant instead of squirrel, red wine instead of white wine, red vinegar instead of cider, kielbasa instead of smoked Portuguese sausages, collards instead of wild greens, and on and on. Have fun with it.

The only trick to this stew, if it can even be called a trick, is to build the flavors bit by bit. Not everything needs as long to cook as squirrel legs do. Follow my instructions on when to add each ingredient, and you'll be fine.

Oh, and as you might guess, this stew reheats well, so you can make it for lunches during the week.

Serves 6 to 8 | **Prep Time: 30 minutes** | **Cook Time: 2 hours, maybe more if they are old squirrels**

---

3 squirrels, cut into serving pieces

Salt

Flour for dusting

⅓ cup olive oil

3 cups sliced onion

3 cloves garlic, minced

1 heaping tablespoon tomato paste

1 cup white wine

¼ cup cider vinegar

1 heaping teaspoon dried savory
or oregano

½ teaspoon red pepper flakes

1 heaping tablespoon paprika

2 to 3 cups whole, peeled
tomatoes, torn into large pieces

Salt the squirrel pieces well, and then dust them in flour. Heat the olive oil in a large Dutch oven or other heavy, lidded pot over medium-high heat. Brown the squirrels in batches, being sure not to overcrowd the pot. Move the browned pieces to a plate or cutting board while you cook the rest.

When the squirrels have been nicely browned, remove them from the pot and add the onion. Sauté the onion until it just begins to brown on the edges, about 6 to 8 minutes. Add the garlic, and cook another minute. Add the tomato paste, mix well, and cook this for 2 to 3 minutes, stirring often.

Pour in the white wine, vinegar, and about 1 quart of water. Add the savory (or oregano), red pepper flakes, and paprika, then the torn-up tomatoes, then the squirrel. Mix well, and bring to a simmer. Add salt to taste, and cook gently until the squirrel wants to fall off the bone, about 90 minutes. Fish out all the squirrel pieces and pull the meat off the bone—this makes the stew a lot easier to eat. Return them to the pot.

(continued)

½ to ¾ pound smoked sausage, such as kielbasa or linguica, cut into bite-sized pieces

1 pound greens (kale, chard, collards, wild greens, etc.), coarsely chopped

Black pepper to taste

Vinegar

Add the smoked sausage and the greens and cook until the greens are done, about 10 minutes (if you're using collards, they need more than 10 minutes to cook, so adjust accordingly). Add salt, black pepper, cayenne, and vinegar to taste, and serve with crusty bread.

The squirrel woods of northeastern Ohio.

BRUNSWICK STEW

If I'd written a small-game cookbook without a recipe for Brunswick Stew, I'm not sure I could live with myself—especially as a former Virginian. Said to originate in Virginia ... or North Carolina ... or maybe Georgia (all stake their claim), this is a rib-sticking, meat-and-vegetable-packed party in a pot.

Pretty much anything goes into this stew, with a few rules. It should have tomatoes in some form, definitely some kind of beans, corn for sure, maybe okra—and squirrel.

Yep, squirrel. Brunswick stew is probably the most famous squirrel dish in the world. "Civilians" can make it with chicken, but we're hunters here. Use boreal rodents.

I like to toss in some other meats, too. Rabbit or pheasant definitely, maybe some wild pork shoulder or venison neck. But if you look at the stew's history, which dates back two hundred years or so, you'll see a lot of 'possums in the mix. I've never cooked an opossum, but I've eaten them, and they're fine in a stew like this. So if you happen to have some 'possum lying around, this is the place to use it.

Serves 8 to 12 | **Prep Time: 45 minutes** | **Cook Time: 3 hours**

Salt

2 to 4 squirrels, cut into serving pieces

1 pheasant or rabbit, cut into serving pieces

1 opossum, cut into serving pieces (optional)

Flour for dusting

¼ cup bacon fat, lard, or butter

2 large onions, chopped

2 celery stalks, chopped

1 head garlic, chopped

2 quarts stock (squirrel, pheasant, or chicken)

One 28-ounce can of crushed tomatoes

3 bay leaves

1 pound potatoes, cut into chunks

2 to 3 cups canned lima beans or butter beans, rinsed

2 cups corn kernels

½ pound okra, sliced (optional)

¼ cup Worcestershire sauce, or to taste

Tabasco or other hot sauce, to taste

Salt the squirrel and other meats well and let them sit out while you chop all the vegetables.

Heat the fat in a large soup pot or Dutch oven over medium-high heat. As the fat is heating, dust all the pieces of squirrel and various other meats with flour.

Brown the meats in the fat. Do this in batches so the meats don't touch each other in the pot. Take your time, removing pieces to a tray as they brown.

When all the meats are browned and have been removed, add the onion and celery, and sprinkle them with a little salt. Move the vegetables around the pot to remove any bits stuck to the bottom. Cook the vegetables until the onion starts to brown.

Add the garlic and the meats back to the pot. Mix well, and cook for a minute or two.

Pour in the stock, tomatoes, and bay leaves. If you need to, add water until the meats are covered by at least 1 inch. Bring this to a simmer and salt to taste. Cook gently for 2 hours.

Fish out all the meats and remove the meat from the bones; this makes the stew a lot easier to eat.

Return the meat to the pot and add the potatoes. Simmer until the potatoes are tender, about 35 minutes. Add the remaining ingredients, mix well, and cook for another 10 to 15 minutes. Serve with corn bread.

HMONG SQUIRREL STEW

Hmong, the Southeast Asian group who fought with us during the Vietnam War, remained in Vietnam after we left—and they faced severe persecution. So the US government let them immigrate here. But the Hmong are different from most immigrant groups: they came here as farmers and hill people. Hunters. And of all the animals the Hmong hunt, they're most famous for chasing squirrels. Squirrels live in the mountains of Laos, so hunting our squirrels was a natural for them. But being unfamiliar with the concept of fish and game laws, when they arrived in the early 1980s, the Hmong decimated California's squirrel population (or so legend has it). By all accounts, things are better now. The Hmong got the message, and the squirrel population has recovered. But the September squirrel opener still draws hundreds, sometimes thousands, of Hmong into the Sierra to chase Mr. Bushytail.

My inspiration for this stew came from the excellent cookbook *Cooking from the Heart: The Hmong Kitchen in America*, whose co-author, Sheng Yang, lives here in Sacramento. Where Vietnamese cooking is refined and occasionally complex, Hmong food is rustic—it's the difference between Paris and Provence. So while this stew looks a little like Vietnamese pho, it's simpler to make. The result is a light, aromatic stew in which the squirrel provides the meaty bass note to an array of high, bright flavors. Each bite will be different, but wonderful.

For a more substantial stew, boil some rice or udon noodles and put them in everyone's bowl before you ladle out the stew.

If you don't have squirrels handy, pheasant, sharp-tailed grouse legs, or rabbit are good substitutes.

Serves 4 to 6 | **Prep Time: 20 minutes** | **Cook Time: 90 minutes to 2½ hours**

2 to 3 squirrels, cut into serving pieces

3 tablespoons vegetable oil

4 cloves garlic, minced

1 stalk lemongrass, minced (white part only)

3 to 5 red chiles, chopped

1 tablespoon minced galangal (optional)

2 tablespoon minced ginger, peeled

1 quart chicken stock

6 lime leaves, or 1 tablespoon lime juice

1 tablespoon fish sauce or soy sauce

1 pound bok choy or chard, chopped

¼ pound snow peas

1 teaspoon ground Sichuan peppercorns (optional)

Salt

Optional garnish: Chopped cilantro, green onion, mint, and a drizzle of sesame oil

Heat the vegetable oil in a large pot such as a Dutch oven. Pat the squirrel pieces dry and brown them over medium-high heat in the oil. Remove them as they brown and set aside.

Add the garlic, lemongrass, galangal, ginger, and chiles, and stir-fry over high heat for 90 seconds.

Return the squirrel to the pot and add the chicken stock, lime leaves, and fish sauce. You want the broth to cover everything by about an inch. If it does not, add some water. Bring to a simmer, and cook until the meat wants to fall off the bone, between 1 hour and 2 hours. Remove the meat and shred it off the bones. Return the shredded meat to the pot.

Add the bok choy and the snow peas, and simmer until tender, about 10 minutes. Add salt to taste and the ground Sichuan pepper.

You can serve it in bowls as-is or over steamed rice. Garnish with the cilantro, green onions, and mint. Drizzle some seasame oil over when you serve.

HARE BILBAO

The Spanish eat hare as much as the Portuguese do, and this recipe is one of the best from the Iberian Peninsula. Also known as Hare with Chocolate, it is an old dish—I'd say about five hundred years. If you look at the ingredients closely, you'll notice something: this is a European interpretation of a typical Aztec or Mayan mole—bitter chocolate and ground nuts, herbs, and onions. All are elements in many moles.

My guess is that this dish originated in the late 1500s, after the Columbian Exchange brought chocolate to the Old World. It's not sweet, but it is exotic.

That said, none of the ingredients are terribly hard to come by. And it reheats well, so you can make it on a weekend and have it for lunches during the week. Serve with smashed potatoes or crusty bread and a salad.

Serves 4 to 6 | **Prep Time: 20 minutes, not including marinating time** | **Cook Time: 2½ hours**

1 whole hare, cut into serving pieces

2 cups Port or red wine

1 pound pearl onions, peeled

1 yellow onion, chopped

2 large cloves garlic, chopped

1 ounce dried mushrooms

⅓ cup olive oil

Salt (smoked if you have it)

2 teaspoons dried thyme

1 tablespoon chopped fresh rosemary

2 tablespoons paprika
   (smoked if you have it)

1 bay leaf

1 cup stock (beef or game)

1 tart apple, peeled and grated
   coarsely

2 tablespoons ground hazelnuts
   or almonds

1½ ounces finely chopped bitter
   chocolate

3 tablespoons chopped fresh parsley

Soak the hare in the Port or red wine overnight, or at least a few hours. Reserve the wine. Rehydrate the dried mushrooms in 2 cups water. Reserve the water.

Pulse the yellow onion, garlic, and rehydrated mushrooms in a food processor until very finely chopped, but not a purée.

Pat the hare pieces dry. Add the olive oil to a heavy, lidded pot, and brown the hare over medium-high heat. Salt the pieces as they cook, and remove to a bowl when browned.

Brown the onion-mushroom mix in the pot. Return the hare pieces to the pot along with any juices that have collected. Mix in the thyme, rosemary, paprika, and bay leaf, then pour in 1 cup of the wine you marinated the hare in, along with 1 cup of game stock and the water you rehydrated the mushrooms in.

Add the grated apple to the pot, bring it to a simmer and add salt to taste. Simmer, covered, until the hare is tender, anywhere from 90 minutes to 3 hours. You can either leave the hare on the bone or debone it. With about 30 minutes to go, add the pearl onions.

When the hare is ready, add the ground hazelnuts and chocolate to the pot and stir to combine. You can purée the sauce if you want; I rarely do. Garnish with parsley and serve.

GREEK HARE WITH TOMATO, LEMON, AND GARLIC

This is a dish from Cephalonia, one of the Ionian Islands of Greece, that I discovered in Diane Kochilas's fantastic book *The Glorious Foods of Greece: Traditional Recipes from the Islands, Cities, and Villages.* Rabbit is what she calls for, while noting that it would most often be done with hare. Well, a jackrabbit is a hare, so there you go.

This is an excellent, easy recipe to introduce someone to jackrabbit cookery.

If you use the other animals that work with this recipe, I'd suggest two cottontails, three to four squirrels, one to two dark-meat grouse or the legs off a turkey.

Serves 4 | **Prep Time: 20 minutes, not including the marinating time** | **Cook Time: 2½ hours**

---

1 hare, cut into serving pieces

2 cups red wine vinegar

2 tablespoons cracked black peppercorns

2 heads garlic (yes, whole heads)

½ cup olive oil

One 6-ounce can tomato paste

½ cup water

Salt and freshly ground black pepper

Grated zest and juice of 2 to 4 lemons

Bring the vinegar and cracked peppercorns to a boil, turn off the heat, and cool. Soak the hare in this overnight in the fridge, or at least for a few hours.

Mix the tomato paste with the ½ cup of water and set aside.

Remove the outside layer of husk from the garlic heads. Set the garlic heads in a small pot and cover with water. Bring to a boil, then drop the heat to a simmer and cook for 15 minutes. Remove the garlic, saving the water. When the garlic is cool enough to handle, squeeze the pulp into a small bowl.

Pat the hare dry. Add the olive oil to a large, heavy pot set over medium-high heat, and brown the hare. Salt the meat as it cooks, and remove to a bowl as it browns. Add the garlic pulp to the pot and cook for a minute or so.

Mix in the diluted tomato paste and the garlic water, then return the hare pieces (and any juices that have accumulated in the bowl) to the pot. If the hare is not covered, add a little water. Bring to a simmer and add salt to taste. Cover the pot.

When the hare is tender, about 2 hours, you can fish it all out and strip the meat from the bones if you'd like; this makes it easier to eat. Add black pepper, lemon zest and as much of the lemon juice as you like. Serve with bread or rice.

CHINESE HARE WITH CUMIN AND LEEKS

There is a Sichuan Chinese dish of lamb with cumin and leeks that I love to order at my local Chinese restaurant, and it occurred to me that it would be just as good with any red meat. I use boneless jackrabbit meat here, primarily from the backstrap and tenderloins, which are very tender.

The great thing about this Chinese dish is that it requires nothing you can't get at a regular grocery store, and it's easy to make. You might be surprised to see cumin in Chinese cooking, but it's a thing, especially in the northwestern, Uyghur-influenced regions like Xinjiang.

Serves 4 | **Prep Time: 25 minutes** | **Cook Time: 15 minutes**

MARINADE
1 tablespoon vegetable oil

2 tablespoons soy sauce

1 tablespoon corn starch, potato starch, or tapioca starch

2 teaspoons sugar

2 teaspoons ground cumin

1 teaspoon ground white pepper

TO FINISH
1 pound boneless hare, or dark-meat grouse breast, sliced into pieces ⅛-inch thick

2 cups canola oil

2 tablespoons minced garlic

6 to 8 very thin slices of ginger

2 to 10 small, hot dried chiles, broken up and seeded

2 medium leeks, white and light-green parts only, thinly sliced

1 teaspoon salt

Cilantro for garnish (optional)

Mix all the ingredients for the marinade in a bowl that will hold all the sliced hare. Using your (very clean!) hands, massage the marinade into the slices, making sure to separate any slices that may have stuck together so marinade gets on every slice. Set the bowl in the fridge for 20 minutes while you chop all the other vegetables.

Bring the 2 cups of canola oil to 375°F to 390°F in a small pot or wok. Set a colander or coarse mesh sieve over a bowl, and have a Chinese spider strainer or slotted spoon, plus a chopstick or butter knife at the ready. Put about a quarter of the meat in the hot oil, and use the chopstick to separate the slices as soon as they hit the oil. Let the meat flash-fry for 10 to 15 seconds, then use the strainer to move the meat to the colander to drain. Repeat with the rest of the meat, a quarter at a time.

When all the meat has been flash-fried, turn off the heat and let the oil cool a bit. You can pour it into a heatproof container, strain the oil, and use it several times before you need to toss it. If you fried in a wok, leave about 2 to 3 tablespoons of the oil in the wok. If not, put 2 to 3 tablespoons of oil into a large frying pan.

Heat the oil over high heat until it's almost smoking. Add the garlic, ginger, and chiles, and stir-fry for 30 seconds. Add the sliced leeks and stir-fry for 1 minute, until they wilt.

Add the hare back to the wok or pan and stir-fry for another minute, sprinkling the salt over everything as you do this. Turn off the heat, and toss in the cilantro, if you're using it, and serve at once with steamed rice.

SARDINIAN HARE STEW

I developed this recipe from a rabbit dish called *coniglio al guazzetto* that I found in Giuliano Bugialli's book *Foods of Sicily & Sardinia and the Smaller Islands*. It's unusual in that it uses capers as a primary flavoring component. The other dominant flavors are saffron, which grows on the island, and red wine vinegar. It's a hearty dish, great for cold weather.

If you can't get hare, substitute lamb first; that just seems more Sardinian to me. You could also go with dark-meat grouse or squirrels, or turkey thighs and legs. Or rabbit.

The dominant flavors here are the gamy hare, vinegar, saffron, and capers. Use the best saffron you can afford; it matters. This dish is a heady mix that needs a powerful red wine. Eat this stew with crusty bread, couscous, or our favorite, a soft polenta with butter and cheese.

Serves 4 to 6 | **Prep Time: 30 minutes** | **Cook Time: 3 hours**

1 hare, 2 dark-meat grouse, the legs and thighs from a turkey, 4 squirrels, or 2 rabbits

4 tablespoons olive oil

¾ cup chopped parsley, separated into ½ cup and ¼ cup amounts

5 chopped garlic cloves

1 chopped onion

8 tablespoons capers

Large pinch saffron

1 cup warm water

¼ cup high-quality red wine vinegar

Salt

Salt the hare well. Heat the olive oil over medium-high heat in a large pot or Dutch oven. Pat the hare pieces dry, and brown them well in the pot. You might need to turn the heat down to medium. Do it in batches and take your time. Transfer each piece to a bowl when it browns, and continue browning the others. This could take 30 minutes.

Meanwhile, chop half the capers. Get your tap water running as hot as it will go, and fill a cup measure. Crush the saffron in your palm and sprinkle it into the hot water. Get every bit, and let this soak as the hare is browning.

Once all the meat is browned and removed from the pot, add the onion to the pot and sauté until browned. Add the garlic and cook for 1 minute.

Add everything into the pot except the extra ¼ cup of parsley, nestling the hare pieces in tight. If the liquid doesn't come up to the level of the hare pieces, add some more water. Do not add wine or stock—the point is to have pure flavors here. Cover tightly and simmer gently over low heat for at least 90 minutes, or until the meat is close to falling off the bone. When it is, pull it out and strip it from the bone.

Return the hare to the pot, add the ¼ cup of parsley and mix well. Turn off the heat and cover for five minutes. Serve over polenta, couscous, Sardinian fregula pasta or with crusty bread. Don't forget the wine: you will want a big, heavy red here.

HASENPFEFFER

Whenever I'm talking to someone about hunting, and the conversation turns to chasing rabbits, I'm invariably asked about hasenpfeffer. It seems to be the only rabbit recipe anyone knows, and I'm pretty sure we can thank Bugs Bunny for that one. There's a 1962 episode of Looney Tunes where the king demands hasenpfeffer from his cook, who is, of course, Yosemite Sam. "Where's my hasenpfeffer?!" Sam grabs a knife and hilarity ensues.

Interestingly, there's a hidden truth in this episode. At the end, Bugs notes that this is the only time a "one-eyed Jack (rabbit) beats a king." Hasenpfeffer, you see, is not a rabbit recipe. It requires a *hase*, the German word for hare. And our most common hare here in North America is the jackrabbit.

Hasenpfeffer is an old dish. Its combination of vinegar, wine, and lots of spices suggests that it's at least as old as the Renaissance, and probably older. One source puts its origins in Westphalia, in the 1300s. The "pfeffer" refers in this case not just to black pepper, which would be the literal translation, but to a general spiciness—not chile spicy, mind you, but highly seasoned with herbs, juniper, and Spice Trade goodies like black pepper, allspice, and cloves.

Like its cousin sauerbraten, hasenpfeffer hinges on a flavorful marinade and a long soak time of up to five days. You then braise it slowly and serve with a vegetable of your choice, plus noodles, potatoes, or dumplings. I love dumplings, and the Germans happen to be masters of the art, second only (in my opinion) to the Chinese.

These are semolina dumplings—balls of semolina dough bound with egg and heavily spiced with nutmeg; it's a perfect accompaniment to the hasenpfeffer. Done right, these dumplings, like all good dumplings, are light and fluffy. Done poorly, they're gut bombs.

While hasenpfeffer should properly be made with hare (snowshoe or jackrabbit in the United States), hares are notoriously hard to find if you're not a hunter. So do what everyone else does: make it with rabbit. Although the actual making of the dish is fairly quick and easy, it'll be far better if you give it the two to five days' worth of marinating time.

Once made, hasenpfeffer lasts a week in the fridge.

Serves 4 to 6 | **Prep Time: 2 to 5 days marinating time** | **Cook Time: 3 hours**

MARINADE

1 cup water

1 cup red wine

1 cup red wine vinegar

1 tablespoon salt

2 tablespoons chopped rosemary

1 tablespoon juniper berries, crushed

1 tablespoon cracked black peppercorns

3 bay leaves

4 cloves

1 teaspoon dried thyme

2 green onions, chopped

FOR THE HASENPFEFFER

Bring all the ingredients for the marinade to a boil, then let cool to room temperature. While the marinade is cooling, cut up a hare into serving pieces. Put the meat into a covered container (plastic, ceramic, or glass) just large enough to hold the cut-up pieces. Cover with the cooled marinade. If you have leftover marinade, put that into a different container. Put everything in the refrigerator, and let it sit at least 8 hours, but 2 days is better.

When you're ready to make the hasenpfeffer, remove the hare from the marinade and pat it dry with paper towels. Save the marinade. Add the butter to a Dutch oven or other large, heavy pot, and heat over medium heat. Dredge the hare in the flour, and brown well on all sides in the butter. Do this over medium to medium-high heat so the butter doesn't burn. Remove the hare pieces as they brown and set aside.

As the hare is browning, preheat the oven to 325°F, and strain the marinade into a bowl. If there was any excess marinade, add that to the bowl now, too.

HARE

1 hare, or domestic rabbit;
    2 cottontails; or 4 squirrels

4 tablespoons unsalted butter

Flour for dredging

2 to 3 cups chopped onion

¼ cup sour cream

SEMOLINA DUMPLINGS

1 cup milk (whole or 2%)

1 teaspoon salt

6 tablespoons semolina flour
    (or use farina or Cream of Wheat)

2 tablespoons unsalted butter

1 egg, lightly beaten

½ to 1 teaspoon ground nutmeg

Once you've browned all the hare and removed the pieces from the pot, add the onion to the pot, and stir to coat with the butter. If there isn't much butter left in the pot, add another tablespoon or two. Cook the onions over medium-high heat until they're soft and a little brown on the edges. Sprinkle salt over them as they cook.

Return the hare to the pot, and add the strained marinade. Bring to a simmer, cover, and put into the oven. Cook at a gentle simmer until the meat wants to fall off the bones; this will take 2 to 4 hours for a wild hare, or between 90 minutes and 2 hours for a domestic rabbit. To finish the hasenpfeffer, remove it from the oven and uncover the pot. Spoon off about a cup of the sauce and put it into a bowl. Add the sour cream to the bowl and mix to combine. Return the mixture to the pot and swirl it around to combine. Serve at once with the dumplings.

FOR THE SEMOLINA DUMPLINGS

When the hasenpfeffer has been cooking for an hour or two, make the dumpling dough. Heat the milk to the steaming point, and add the butter and salt. Start stirring the milk with one hand while you sprinkle in the semolina with the other. Stir well until the semolina absorbs the milk and forms a stiff dough. Take the pot off the heat, and let the dough cool.

Bring a large pot of salted water to a boil on the stove. Once it boils, turn off the heat and cover the pot until the hare is done.

When the hasenpfeffer is ready, turn the heat off the oven but leave everything inside. Now it's time to finish the dumplings. Mix the egg and nutmeg into the semolina dough. Let the dough stand while you bring your pot of salty water back to a boil, which won't take long because you preheated it. Get a bowl of water ready—this is to wet your hands so the dumpling dough doesn't stick to them.

Roll the dough into balls. I like portions that are tablespoon-sized or thereabout, which make dumplings the size of walnuts, but you can make the dumplings any size you like. As you make them, drop each one into the boiling water. Don't crowd the pot. Once the dumplings start bobbing on the surface, let them cook another 2 to 5 minutes, depending on how soft you like them. Remove with a slotted spoon and set aside. Eat the moment the dumplings are all ready.

BARBACOA

Normally a beef dish, this Mexican preparation is fantastic for any red meat (I even included a venison version in my last book, *Buck, Buck, Moose*). I include it here in the hares chapter because it works so well with jackrabbits. Turkey thighs and drumsticks are also good choices.

Basically, you braise the front and hind legs of jackrabbits in a flavorful broth, then shred the meat and mix with a little lard and a simple chili sauce. Serve on tacos or in enchiladas or burritos and you're golden.

It's pretty hard to discern exactly what sort of meat you're eating when you do this, so barbacoa is also an excellent dish for unusual critters like beavers or woodchucks.

Pro tip: save the braising liquid. Strain it through a fine-meshed sieve and freeze it. Then reuse over and over as needed. It just keeps getting better.

Serves 4 to 6 | **Prep Time: 15 minutes** | **Cook Time: 2½ hours**

Legs from 3 to 4 hares or 2 turkeys

2 bay leaves

1 teaspoon smoked paprika (optional)

1 teaspoon ground cumin

1 teaspoon ground cloves

1 teaspoon oregano (Mexican if possible)

1 tablespoon kosher salt

1 sprig epazote (optional)

½ cup lime juice

½ cup cider vinegar

1 quart stock (beef or venison)

¼ cup lard or vegetable oil

Smoked salt (optional)

Cilantro, shredded cheese, sour cream, avocados and hot sauce, for garnish

CHILE SAUCE

4 dried guajillo chiles, de-stemmed, seeded, and torn up

4 dried ancho chiles, de-stemmed, seeded, and torn up

2 dried chipotle or cascabel chiles, de-stemmed, seeded, and torn up

2 tablespoons lard or vegetable oil

1 large onion, chopped

4 cloves garlic, chopped

Salt, black pepper and lime juice to taste

FOR THE MEAT

Put the hare legs into a large, heavy, lidded pot and add the bay leaves, paprika, cumin, cloves, oregano, salt, lime juice, vinegar, and stock. Add the epazote if using. If the hare is not submerged, add enough water to cover. Bring to a simmer, and cook slowly until the meat falls off the bone, about 2½ hours.

Pick all the meat off the bones and mix in the lard or vegetable oil. Sprinkle the meat with the smoked salt. You can serve it as is, or make the following chile sauce to go with it. Serve with one or more of the garnishes.

FOR THE CHILE SAUCE

Heat the lard in a pan and brown the onions in it over medium heat. When the onions are nicely browned, add the garlic and the torn-up chiles and mix well. Cook for 1 minute, then barely cover with water. Add some salt and simmer until the chiles are tender, about 15 minutes.

Put everything into a blender and purée until smooth. You want it to be the consistency of BBQ sauce. Add salt, black pepper, and lime juice to taste.

Once made, this adobo will keep for a week or two in the fridge.

CHAPTER 10

DARK-MEAT GROUSE

SHARPTAILS, SPRUCE GROUSE, SAGE GROUSE, PTARMIGAN, AND PRAIRIE CHICKENS

The birds in this chapter are tricky birds to cook. All have dark breast meat, like a dove or a duck, and a few have white-meat legs and wings, which is unusual in the gamebird world. Like ducks, the ideal temperature for the breast and legs are far apart, making roasting them problematic. Doable, but harder than roasting a pheasant. For the most part, it's best to separate breasts from the rest of the bird. Cook the breasts like a steak, the rest like brisket—slow and low. If the legs are light, as they are with sage grouse, for example, cook them like pheasant legs and thighs. If the legs are dark, as they are in sharp-tailed grouse, cook them like jackrabbits.

The method for cooking skinless pheasant breasts I describe on page 67 (Simple Seared Pheasant or Grouse Breast) is ideal for the breast meat of these birds.

Four species of grouse, plucked and ready to eat. *Clockwise from top left*: ptarmigan, sharp-tailed grouse, blue grouse, sage grouse.

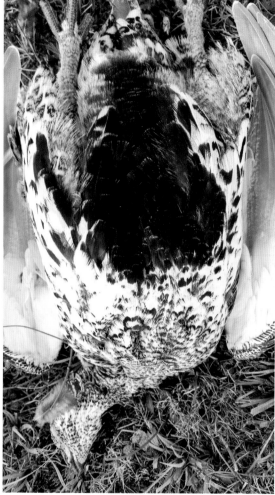

Clockwise from top left: ptarmigan, sage grouse, and prairie chicken.

ROAST SHARP-TAILED GROUSE, SAGE GROUSE, SPRUCE GROUSE, PRAIRIE CHICKEN, OR PTARMIGAN

From a cooking standpoint, dark-meat grouse are essentially giant doves—red meat that needs to be served pink. So don't treat a sharpie like a chicken. The goal here is to get breast meat medium and legs done enough to eat. Note that I do not recommend this recipe for rooster sage grouse; they're just too big and tough to roast whole.

Regarding the serving size for this recipe, one ptarmigan per person is a must. Sharpies and prairie chickens can serve one per person, or two if you have lots of other things going on the plate. A hen sage grouse will serve two hearty eaters or three normal ones.

Serves 2 (see above) | **Prep Time: 30 minutes** | **Cook Time: 20 minutes**

1 or 2 whole dark-meat grouse, plucked

Salt

2 sprigs sage

2 sprigs rosemary

Soft butter, bacon fat, or olive oil to coat the bird

Black pepper to taste

2 to 3 pounds of mixed root vegetables, cut into large chunks

Salt the grouse well and set out at room temperature for 30 minutes or so. Preheat the oven to 325°F.

Put the herbs inside the birds' cavities. Either smear the soft butter over the birds or coat with oil. Sprinkle with salt and grind some pepper over them, too. Put a little butter or oil in the bottom of a cast-iron or other oven-proof frying pan.

Set the grouse in the pan, holding them in place with the chunks of root vegetables. If you want, you can then eat those vegetables with the grouse later. Roast hen sage grouse, prairie chickens or sharp-tailed grouse in the oven for 18 to 20 minutes, ptarmigan for 10 minutes. Remove the birds from the oven.

Set the oven to 500°F, or as hot as it will go. Baste the birds with a little more butter or fat. When the oven hits temperature, return the birds to the oven and roast until the breast meat hits about 140°F at the thickest part, near the wishbone. This should take anywhere from 5 minutes for ptarmigan to 15 minutes for a big prairie chicken or sage hen.

Remove the birds from the oven, set them on a cutting board, and let them rest for 5 to 10 minutes before serving.

ICELANDIC CHRISTMAS PTARMIGAN

This is a popular Christmas dinner option in Iceland and some other parts of Scandinavia. Lots of cooks make it in different ways, some adding blue cheese to the sauce at the end, others adding sweet cream or sour cream. I kept my version more spare.

The dish relies on whole birds served two ways: breast meat seared medium-rare, and leg meat simmered in a grouse broth that is then turned into a sauce; the stock can be made several days ahead of time. The berries are vital to the dish, and they need to be tart. Top choices would be currants, followed by blueberries or huckleberries, then lingonberries or cranberries. This isn't a sweet sauce, but if you want, you can add a bit of sugar.

Serve this with good bread or potatoes, and some braised red cabbage.

Serves 4 | **Prep Time: 20 minutes** | **Cook Time: 2½ hours**

4 whole ptarmigans or pigeons, or
    2 dark-meat grouse

Salt, smoked if you have it

1 carrot, chopped

1 celery stalk, chopped

1 small onion, chopped

1 bay leaf

2 teaspoons dried thyme

10 juniper berries, crushed (optional)

½ ounce dried mushrooms,
    about a handful

3 tablespoons butter

Black pepper

½ cup fresh or frozen tart berries
    (see above)

2 teaspoons potato starch,
    cornstarch, or tapioca starch
    (optional)

Preheat the oven to 400°F. Carve the breasts off the birds and set aside. Salt the rest of the birds well and set them in a pan. Roast them uncovered in the oven until nicely browned, about 45 minutes to 1 hour.

Put the roasted carcasses in a pot with the carrot, celery, onion, bay leaf, thyme, juniper berries, and dried mushrooms. Cover with water by about 1 inch and bring to a simmer. Simmer for 90 minutes. Strain, wipe out the pot, and return the stock to the pot. Boil furiously until reduced by ⅔. If you want, pick off the meat from the carcasses and reserve.

When the broth is almost ready, heat the butter in a pan large enough to fit all the grouse breasts. Salt the breasts well and set them skin-side down in the pan (if there is no skin, place them on the side the skin once was). Sear over medium-high heat, using a spoon to baste the breasts until they turn opaque. Sear this way without flipping until the skin side has a nice crust on it, about 6 to 8 minutes. Remove and let the breasts rest on a cutting board, crust side up.

Finish the sauce by pouring 1 to 2 cups of the reduced broth into the pan. Use a wooden spoon to scrape up any browned bits stuck at the bottom. Add salt and freshly ground black pepper to taste and bring it to a boil. If you want to thicken the sauce, mix a teaspoon of the starch with some of the broth, then pour it into the pan. If you want it even thicker, add the second teaspoon.

Add the berries and reserved grouse meat if using. Swirl together and let this cook a minute or two. To serve, carve the breasts and pour the sauce over them. Serve with good bread or potatoes.

NORDIC GROUSE SOUP

This soup is full of ingredients common to Scandinavian cuisine, so I decided to call it Nordic Grouse Soup; it's not a riff on any particular traditional recipe. Grouse are native to Scandinavia, and if you happen to be there while reading this recipe, use their black grouse or, if you're making a big batch, a capercaillie. But you can use meat from any of the animals covered in this book to make this soup.

I like using rye berries, but they do take a long time to cook, up to two hours. Regular pearled barley would be just as good and just as Nordic. Wheat berries or rice are options, too.

While the ingredients are Scandinavian, the method I use is closer to the way the Japanese make soup: gently cooking the whole grouse in water until each part is perfectly tender and removing them as you go. And you also cook the starch—rye berries, in this case—separately and add them to each bowl as you serve. This keeps the grain from overcooking or clouding your broth.

You can buy smoked salt and dried lovage online, or substitute parsley and regular salt.

The broth can be made several days in advance and stored in the fridge.

BROTH

2 whole grouse, any kind

3 quarts water

Salt

12 to 15 juniper berries, crushed

12 to 15 allspice berries, crushed

A 1-inch piece of ginger, chopped

2 tablespoons dried lovage
    (or parsley)

1 medium yellow onion, chopped

2 carrots, peeled and chopped

½ ounce dried porcini mushrooms

½ ounce other dried mushrooms

SOUP

⅔ cup rye berries or pearled barley

1 medium yellow onion, halved and
    sliced thin

2 tablespoons butter

1 large carrot, peeled and sliced into
    thin discs

1 cup fresh or frozen peas

1 to 2 teaspoons smoked salt

GARNISH

1 to 2 radishes, sliced paper thin

2 to 3 tablespoons chopped parsley

To make the broth, pour the water into a stockpot and add about a tablespoon of salt. Bring to a simmer over medium heat. Once the water simmers, add the grouse and turn the heat down below a simmer, to 170°F if you have a thermometer. You want it steaming, but not bubbling.

Let the grouse cook for 30 minutes, then pull them out. Strip off all the breast meat, and set the meat aside. Return the rest of the grouse to the pot and continue to cook for another 30 to 45 minutes. Pull the birds out again, and strip off all the remaining meat. Put all the grouse meat into a container and set aside. Return the bones to the pot. Simmer for 1 hour.

Add the remaining broth ingredients, and bring everything to a simmer again. Simmer this gently—the water should just barely be bubbling—for 1 more hour.

Turn off the heat. Set up a fine-meshed sieve over another large pot or bowl and put a piece of paper towel into it. Pour the broth through the paper-towel-lined sieve into the other container. You might need to stop and switch paper towels if it gets too gunked up. Add salt to taste to the strained broth. This broth can be stored for up to a week in the fridge.

To make the soup, cover the rye berries with enough water to submerge them by 2 inches. Add a palmful of salt, and boil until tender.

Meanwhile, set a large pot over medium-high heat and add the butter. Once the butter is good and hot, add the sliced onion and sauté until it's translucent but not browned, about 5 minutes.

Pour the broth over the onions and add the sliced carrots. Heat the broth to the steaming point.

By the time the rye or barley is cooked, the carrots in the broth should be, too. Add the peas and the reserved grouse meat to the broth and cook for a few minutes. Add the smoked salt to taste.

To serve the soup, drain the rye berries and divide them among the bowls. Ladle the soup over the grain. Garnish with paper-thin slices of radish and chopped parsley.

SHARP-TAILED GROUSE, PRAIRIE FLAVORS

Whenever I try to figure out what to serve with wild food, I think about something the great British chef Marco Pierre White once said: "Nature is the artist. The chef is just the technician." What goes together in life will go together on the plate. You'll see that I also do this with grouse (Grouse Northwoods, page 77) and doves (Doves with What They Eat, page 270).

Everything on the plate is a flavor of our Great Plains. Sharpies and other prairie grouse love eating rose hips, and it's easy enough to make a sweet and sour sauce with them that the French call a *gastrique*. Grain has to play a role, since the Dakotas, where lots of sharpies and prairie chickens are hunted, are in the group of "amber waves of grain" states we all sang about in grade school. The region also produces a lot of sunflowers, so sunflower seeds and sunflower oil would go in, too.

Wild onions, which grow everywhere, make an appearance as well. Malt vinegar—also from grain—brightens up the flavors. Garnish? Onion flowers and some purple vetch flowers growing in my yard; vetch, a legume, is a relative of the bean or pea, and it grows wild all over the country.

The grouse is meltingly tender, a little smoky and sweet-and-sour from the rose hip glaze, yet still a bit funky (because it's sharp-tailed grouse, after all). The farro is light, and the wheat malt-vinegar sunflower-seed green-onion mixture really works. The magenta vetch flowers add a bit of beauty.

Fear not if you don't have all the ingredients for this dish; there are some perfectly great substitutions. If you don't have dark-meat grouse, you can use breasts of pigeon or dove. If you can't get smoked salt, skip it. You can use red currant jelly in place of rose hip jelly. Use cider vinegar in place of malt vinegar, and wheat berries, rye berries, barley, or brown rice in place of the farro. Skip the flowers if you can't find any, but remember that any pretty, edible flowers are just as good.

Serves 4 | **Prep Time: 10 minutes** | **Cook Time: 45 minutes**

GROUSE
Breasts from 2 sharpies, sage grouse, or prairie chickens

1 tablespoon salt, smoked if possible

2 tablespoons sunflower oil, or other neutral oil

ROSE HIP SAUCE
4 tablespoons rose hip jelly (or substitute red currant jelly)

2 tablespoons cider vinegar

Salt to taste

Sprinkle the smoked salt on the grouse and set aside for 30 minutes.

Make the sauce. Melt the jelly in a small pot over medium heat, then whisk in the vinegar and salt to combine. Turn off the heat and set aside.

Cook the grain. Bring the stock to a boil, add the salt and farro. Simmer gently until the grains are tender, about 30 to 40 minutes. Drain the grain and discard any remaining stock, or use the stock in another recipe.

Make the pilaf. Heat the sunflower oil over medium-high heat in a large sauté pan and sauté the white parts of the green onions for 1 minute, stirring often. Add the cooked farro and the sunflower seeds and toss to combine. Add salt to taste. Turn off the heat.

Cook the grouse. Heat more sunflower oil over high heat. Pat the salted grouse breasts dry with paper towels, then place them skin-side down (or on that side if there is no skin). Sear hard, spooning the hot oil over the breasts until they turn opaque. Do not flip. The grouse are

1½ cups farro, wheat berries, rye berries, or barley

3½ cups stock (grouse or beef)

2 teaspoons salt, smoked if possible

2 tablespoons sunflower oil, or other neutral oil

4 green onions or wild onions, white parts and green parts chopped separately

¾ cup shelled, roasted sunflower seeds

1 tablespoon malt vinegar

Onion or vetch flowers, to garnish (optional)

ready when there's a nice crust on one side and when they lift off the pan easily. This takes about 5 minutes.

To finish, rest the grouse on the cutting board, seared side up. Slice thin. Heat up the grain to warm it through, then mix in the malt vinegar and the chopped green parts from the onions. Bring the rose hip sauce to a boil, then turn off the heat.

Give everyone some farro, and top with the grouse slices. Top with the rose hip sauce, and serve.

"Better one grouse in the bag
than ten on the branch."

—FINNISH PROVERB

PTARMIGAN STROGANOFF

Many think ptarmigan, the smallest and funkiest of the grouse, don't make good table fare. I get it; ptarmigan are strongly flavored, and although I happen to like that, not everyone does. If you're one of those who lean away from strong flavors, worry not. This recipe is for you.

Stroganoff normally relies on thinly sliced beef in a creamy, mushroomy sauce spiked with dill and served over noodles. My version can be done with the breast meat from any dark-meat grouse, pigeon, or dove, or the backstrap off a hare. And I suppose there's no reason you couldn't use pheasant breast here if you wanted to.

Most stroganoff recipes use egg noodles, and that's fine here. But I really like the way homemade spätzle goes with the stroganoff, so I provide a recipe for that below.

This is simple, weeknight food. Enjoy it with a salad and maybe some bread.

SPÄTZLE

2 cups flour

¼ teaspoon nutmeg

¼ teaspoon black pepper

1 to 2 teaspoons salt

1 egg, lightly beaten

½ cup sour cream

Up to ¾ cup heavy cream

STROGANOFF

3 tablespoons butter

Boneless meat from 2 to 3 ptarmigans

2 shallots, minced

2 cloves garlic, minced

6 to 8 ounces shiitake or button mushrooms, sliced

½ cup Madeira or dry sherry

¼ teaspoon nutmeg

A few grinds of black pepper

1 cup sour cream, at room temperature

Heavy cream, optional (to loosen sauce)

2 tablespoons chopped fresh dill

I make the spätzle first. These can be made up to a day ahead and stored in the fridge. Mix all the ingredients except the heavy cream in a bowl. Using the heavy cream as needed, thin the sticky dough into a batter that's a bit like thick pancake batter. I use a spätzle maker to make my spätzle, but you can either use a colander with wide holes or just flick the dough/batter off a cutting board with a knife.

Bring a pot of salty water to a boil over high heat. Keeping the water boiling vigorously, boil the spätzle until they float, then 1 minute more. Skim the boiled spätzle from the water with a slotted spoon or a spider skimmer, and move them to a baking sheet. Toss the cooked spätzle with a little oil so they don't stick together.

To make the stroganoff, salt the ptarmigan well, and let it sit on the cutting board for 20 minutes or so (this is a good time to make the spätzle). Heat 2 tablespoons of butter in a large sauté pan over medium-high heat. Pat the ptarmigan dry and sear until it's just barely rare, about 90 seconds per side. When the meat is ready, move it to a cutting board and let it rest.

Add the shallots and mushrooms to the pan, and turn the heat to high. Soon they will give up their water, and when they do, use a wooden spoon to scrape any browned bits from the bottom of the pan. When most of the water has boiled away, add the rest of the butter to the pan along with the garlic, and sauté everything for 5 minutes, stirring often. Sprinkle some salt over everything.

Add the sherry to the pan, and toss to combine. Let this boil down furiously. While it is doing so, grate some nutmeg over the mixture. When the sherry is mostly gone, turn the heat down to low. Slice the ptarmigan thinly, and return it and any juices that have collected on the cutting board to the pan. Stir to combine and add most of the chopped fresh dill.

Turn off the heat, move the pan away from the hot burner, and stir in the sour cream. Stir to combine, and allow it heat through using only the heat in the pan. Be sure not to let this boil, or even to simmer, or the dish will curdle. To serve, mix with the spätzle and top with any remaining dill.

SHARPIE BIEROCKS

Until I embarked on the Great Chicken Chase of 2017 with my friend Jim Millensifer, I was only dimly aware of *bierock*. Jim lives in Kansas, arguably the hub of Bierock Nation. Pronounced "beer-rock," these little filled bread rolls are also called *runzas*, mostly in Nebraska. Russians have several names for these, and even Turks make a version. Whatever you call them, they're an amazing, handy, pocket lunch, like a Cornish pasty or empanada, only the starch is full-on bread, not a pastry crust.

Any meat you can imagine would go well here. I decided to make these with Columbian sharp-tailed grouse that Jim, Jim's friend Adam, and I shot in northwestern Colorado. After all, bierocks are Midwestern, and sharpies are typically a Midwestern bird, and, well, Jim introduced me to them.

For sharpies, you will want the breast meat from two or three birds, cut into dice the size of your pinkie nail. That makes about one pound; use that as a guide when you use other animals. Since the meat will cook fine in the pastry—and stay tender, too—there's no need to cook the meat before baking.

Serves 4 to 8 | **Prep Time: 2½ hours** | **Cook Time: 25 minutes**

DOUGH
1 cup warm water

1 packet yeast

¼ cup sugar

1 teaspoon salt

1 egg, lightly beaten

¼ cup soft butter

3½ cups bread flour, plus more for dusting

FILLING
1 pound tender meat, diced into small cubes

¼ cup butter

2 cups shredded cabbage

1 cup chopped sauerkraut

1 cup chopped onion

Salt and black pepper

1 teaspoon dried thyme

1 tablespoon mustard

2 tablespoons malt vinegar

¼ cup beer (lager or pilsner)

2 eggs, lightly beaten, for brushing the bierocks

2 tablespoons seeds (poppy, caraway, sesame, etc.)

Bloom the yeast in the warm water for 10 minutes, then mix together all the remaining dough ingredients in a bowl. Knead on a floured surface for 5 minutes, then cover and let rest 1 hour.

Make the filling. Heat the butter in a large pan, and cook the cabbage, sauerkraut, and onions over medium heat until soft, about 5 minutes. Add salt and black pepper to taste. Stir in the thyme, mustard, vinegar, and beer, and simmer until the liquid is all gone. Turn off the heat, cool, then mix well with the uncooked meat. Set in the fridge.

After the first hour has elapsed, punch down the dough, knead a few more times, then roll into a ball, cover, and let sit another hour.

When the dough has about 30 minutes to go, take the filling out of the fridge. It's important that it goes into the bierock at room temperature. Preheat the oven to 350°F. Grease a baking sheet well.

Cut the dough into eight pieces. Set the pieces you're not working on under plastic wrap or a damp towel. Divide the filling into eight parts.

Roll a piece of dough into a ball, then flatten it to about ⅓ of an inch thick. Roll the outer inch of the dough thinner, to about ¼ inch thick or even thinner if you can; this makes what will become the bottom of the pastry match better with the top. Add some filling, and bring the dough up all around it to seal. Set the dough seam-side down on a floured surface, and gently shape it into a flattened ball with your hands. Set on the greased baking sheet, and repeat with the other pieces of dough.

When all your bierocks are made and on the sheet, paint them all with egg and sprinkle with the seeds, plus a little more salt. Bake for 25 minutes, and cool a bit before serving. These are excellent at room temperature, too.

SAGE GROUSE, HUNTER'S STYLE

This is a dish inspired by a sage grouse hunt near Saratoga, Wyoming. My friend Jim, his friends Alex, Jim, and Jeff, and I all scored limits on that memorable day. On our walk through the sagebrush sea, I took note of a number of edible plants that we came across—desert parsley, little wild onions, and some watercress I saw growing in a creek near where we cleaned birds at the end of the day. So I decided to add those ingredients to a riff on Italian cacciatore. (If you want a real cacciatore, see Pheasant Cacciatore, page 97.) Tomatoes, sage (of course), and some diced Italian ham and white wine. It's a wonderful way to eat sage grouse legs.

Any legs will work with this recipe, from sage grouse to turkey, pheasant, or jackrabbits. In fact, there were so many white-tailed jacks where we were hunting that I was sorely tempted to use them, too.

Serves 4 | **Prep Time: 20 minutes** | **Cook Time: 2½ hours**

Legs from 4 or 5 sage grouse, about 2 pounds

Salt

¼ cup olive oil

¼ pound ham, cut ¼-inch thick and diced (or thick cut bacon, diced)

1 pound pearl onions, peeled

2 cloves garlic, minced

2 tablespoons chopped fresh sage

1 cup white wine

2 cups stock (grouse or other)

4 to 6 Roma tomatoes, peeled and torn up by hand

2 tablespoons chopped parsley

½ cup torn watercress sprigs

Black pepper to taste

Salt the grouse legs. Heat the olive oil in a large, lidded pot such as a Dutch oven, over medium-high heat. Brown the grouse pieces well. Don't crowd the pot; you may need to do this in batches. Remove the pieces as they brown, and set aside.

When all the grouse has been browned and set aside, add the ham and pearl onions to the pot and cook, stirring often, until lightly browned, about 5 minutes. Add the garlic and 1 tablespoon of sage, and cook another minute.

Add the white wine. Use a wooden spoon to scrape any browned bits off the bottom of the pot. Return the grouse to the pot. Boil the wine down by half.

Add the tomatoes and the stock, and mix well. Bring to a gentle simmer, and add salt to taste. Cover the pot, and cook on low until the meat is tender, about 2 hours or so.

When the meat is ready, fish out the drumsticks, strip the meat off them, and return the meat to the pot. I leave the thighs on the bone, but you can strip off all the meat if you want. Stir in the parsley, the remaining sage, and the watercress, and add freshly ground black pepper to taste.

Serve over polenta, or with pasta, rice, or just some crusty bread.

SAGE GROUSE ENCHILADAS

Hunting the sagebrush sea, you see a lot of green chile dishes at local restaurants, usually served with pork or chicken. But with the dark meat of sage grouse breasts, I think a red chile sauce goes best. Obviously, you can use whatever meat you like, but here I prefer a marriage between equals—strongly flavored sage hen and strongly flavored red chile sauce.

Be free with your choice of chiles—their weight is more important that the combination of varieties. And even the weight doesn't have to be precise.

Serves 4, and can be scaled up | **Prep Time: 90 minutes** | **Cook Time: 45 minutes**

RED CHILE SAUCE

½ pound dried red chiles (New Mexican, ancho, guajillo, etc.)

3 tablespoons lard or cooking oil

1 large white onion, cut in quarters

4 cloves garlic, whole and unpeeled

2 teaspoons cumin

2 teaspoons oregano, Mexican if possible

1 quart stock, preferably grouse stock

Salt (smoked salt if you have it)

Black pepper to taste

FILLING

Breasts from 2 sage grouse, about a pound

Salt (smoked salt if you have it)

About ½ cup red chile sauce (see above)

2 tablespoons chopped fresh sage

12 ounces shredded Monterey Jack and/or cheddar cheese (5 ounces for the filling, the rest as topping)

1 cup minced white onion

Fifteen 6-inch tortillas

Prep the chile sauce. Start by taking the stems off and opening the chiles to shake out the seeds. Flatten them as best you can. Heat a cast iron skillet—or better yet, a Mexican comal—over high heat. When it's blazing hot, toast the chiles. Press them down with a spatula for just a few seconds. When they blister, flip them and do the other side. Remove to a bowl.

When all the chiles have been toasted, char the quartered onion and the garlic cloves on the comal or skillet. You want some blackening. The garlic cloves will blacken first, so watch them.

Now that you have everything smoky and charred, tear the chiles in pieces. Chop the onion. Peel the garlic. Heat the lard or vegetable oil in a pot over medium-high heat. Add the chiles, onions, and garlic, and sauté for a minute or two. Add the stock, then the cumin and oregano, and bring to a simmer. Add salt to taste, and simmer gently until the chiles are soft, about 20 minutes.

Purée the sauce in a blender. This sauce can be made up to a week in advance and stored in the fridge.

Make the filling. Cut the grouse meat into pieces about the size of a fingernail. Salt well. Mix with about ¼ cup of the red chile sauce, the chopped sage, about 5 ounces of cheese, and the minced white onion.

Prep the tortillas. Heat the tortillas on a comal or other heavy skillet until they blacken a little. Put the warmed tortillas in a tortilla warmer, or stack them on a plate and put a bowl over them. Let them steam a few minutes before building the enchiladas.

Build the enchiladas. Pour a little red chile sauce into a casserole dish. Dip a tortilla in the red chile sauce briefly, and shake off the excess. Fill a tortilla with a little of the filling and roll it up, then place it seam-side down on the casserole. Repeat until you're done. You should get about 15 tortillas.

Pour more red chile sauce over the enchiladas and top with lots of the shredded cheese. Bake at 350°F for 25 minutes and serve.

CHAPTER 11

DOVES AND PIGEONS

For much of the United States, nothing says Labor Day like dove. Our warmer regions are havens for several types of doves, and the September 1 opener for the dove season marks the traditional start to the hunting season, much the same way sharp-tailed grouse and Huns do for the nation's northern Great Plains. A dove shoot—which is really what it is, since the hunting part is mostly about locating a place where doves want to be— is a social event, a time to laugh at each other's rusty shotgun shooting, trade plans for the coming hunting season's adventures, and, most of all, a time to barbecue.

You'll find most of my dove recipes in this book geared to this. For the most part, dove is either grilled or barbecued—it's just how you cook 'em. One reason is that doves (pigeons too) are lean, red-meat birds that really must be cooked rare to medium to be fully enjoyed.

That said, you can, of course, roast doves and pigeons, and deep-fried doves are pretty

damned good, too. I do include a few recipes for slow-cooked doves or pigeons, but in general, these birds are not at their best when done slow and low.

A word on pigeons. Hunters in the West have our lone surviving native pigeon, the band-tailed pigeon, *Patagioenas fasciata*. They're a trophy of a bird, as seasons are short and bag limits low. Often weighing more than a pound each, they should always be plucked and roasted whole.

But everyone has access to the common rock dove, *Columba livia*. Common pigeons are despised throughout the world, largely because they are perfectly cool with living in cities and eating Doritos and cigarette butts. I am not sure I'd eat those birds. But pigeons in rural areas eat mostly grain, which is why you find them in dairies and cattle feedlots. Common pigeons are wonderful eating, and they are, more or less, the size of partridges— about twelve ounces on the wing.

Readers in the United Kingdom will have wood pigeons available, *Columba palumbus*, which can be treated the same as either a band-tailed or common pigeon in the kitchen.

For the most part, you'll want to pluck your doves and pigeons whole; they are by far the easiest birds to pluck. I can pick a dove in about ninety seconds. Why do this? Because they look cool, the skin is tasty, and you then get to nibble on those little legs.

Doves generally don't live very long—it's not uncommon to bag a dove that's less than two months old—so they will be tender. Pigeons, on the other hand, can live a long time in the wild. It's the same relationship you see between cottontails and jackrabbits. Often, you can tell if you have old birds. Their feet look like they've been walked on for years and their keelbones are very stiff. Young birds have a flexible keel bone and are just fresher looking overall. Their feathers have khaki-colored tips,

too. (This is true in *all* young-of-the-year birds.) First-year birds also tend to have lighter-colored meat. But it's not an exact science. Incidentally, for non-hunters, you can buy squab in some fancier markets. A squab is just a young pigeon.

All these birds are meatier than they look. Their breast meat is very tightly grained and must not be overcooked, or it will resemble bad liver. They are birds to get down on, too: pick them up and gnaw. Sure, you can carve a pigeon and get all white linen, but I find it *so* much better eating them caveman style—juices flowing, and that crispy skin on the legs, which, to my mind, are the best part.

Figure on one to two pigeons or three to six doves per person. A single dove is a neat little appetizer—if it's a Eurasian collared dove or a big white-wing—but you'll want a whole lot of food coming behind it, or your guests will leave hungry.

Sprinkling smoked paprika on Doves a la Mancha (page 257)

HANK'S DOVE POPPERS

For more than a decade, I heaped hate on the venerable popper: a dove breast, usually skinless, nestled in a blob of cream cheese that is itself stuffed into half a jalapeño, all wrapped in bacon. Sometimes it's soaked in Italian dressing.

"Yech," my old snooty self sniffed. This was how Philistines ate. I plucked all my doves, preferring whole grilled dishes. And to be perfectly honest, I still do. But I have come to love the popper.

Dove poppers, you see, are more than just food. They're tradition. Dove poppers on the grill are to Labor Day in much of this country what candied yams or green bean casserole is to Thanksgiving—a dish laden with cultural weight, an edible touchstone.

I did not grow up dove hunting, or I might have realized this earlier. I didn't start hunting these tasty, speedy little birds until 2003, when Minnesota hosted its first dove season in generations. I got three, if I recall right.

Since then, I've hunted great blizzards of white-winged doves in Yuma, Arizona, and Brownsville, Texas, as well as many places less spectacular but still memorable. A safflower field just outside the Sacramento city limits is one such place, as is a vineyard in the Sierra Nevada foothills owned by my friend Bill Berryhill.

Dove hunting is about friendship and laughter—doves aren't terribly smart, but they are very agile, and a freaked-out dove can be among the hardest things to hit with a shotgun. This leads to a lot of hilarious misses on our part. I've seen doves reverse themselves 180° in a heartbeat, seemingly anticipating the cloud of pellets headed its way.

But we do tend to shoot our share, which leads to the next tradition: beer and barbecue. It's custom to eat your first day's doves on that same day with all your friends. Grilled, almost always.

And on that grill will always—always—be some poppers.

The origin of the popper is lost in the mists of history, but given what I know about American food traditions, it feels like a post-World War II creation, probably from Texas. No one seems to know for sure.

Everyone makes poppers differently. I myself simply couldn't bring myself to put cheese in my poppers; I find this ingredient to be the most off-putting part of the traditional dish. So I switched it up for roasted garlic, mashed into a paste with a touch of olive oil and salt.

But I realize that there's a reason for the cream cheese: to offset the heat of the jalapeño. So I went with the poblano, a milder chile that still has a touch of heat. And I roasted it, which I think makes for a better popper.

I also soaked the chiles in lime juice, because the Italian-dressing aficionados aren't wrong: there is so much fat in a popper that it needs acidity to balance it. Lime-juice-soaked poblanos do it for me.

Other than that, this is a pretty recognizable popper. Fun to eat, balanced with fatty, smoky bacon, zippy poblanos, deep savoriness from the garlic, and a nugget of meaty goodness from the dove. Oh, and if you use ham rather than bacon, it cooks a lot faster, which will keep your dove meat more rare.

So go out there and shoot well. Then, come back, pop open a cold one, and make some poppers.

Serves 8 | **Prep Time: 45 minutes** | **Cook Time: 20 minutes**

Boneless breast meat from 10 to 15 doves

1 pound thin bacon or thinly cut prosciutto ham

5 to 8 poblano or green Hatch-style chiles

Prepare the chiles. Blacken the skins of the poblano chiles on a grill or gas burner, put them in a bag, and let them steam for 30 minutes or so. Remove the blackened skin, stems, and seeds of the chiles, and soak them in the lime juice. Pickle them for at least 1 hour, and up to several days in the fridge.

Roast the garlic. While the chiles are blackening, preheat the oven to 350°F. Slice off the top ¼ of the heads of garlic and drizzle a little oil on the cut surface. Arrange the heads cut-side up in some foil. Close

(continued)

Juice of 6 limes

Salt

4 heads garlic

the foil and roast in the oven for 1 to 1½ hours. Remove, cool, and squeeze out the goodness into a bowl. Season with olive oil and salt. This can be done a day or two ahead.

Build the poppers. Lay down a slice of bacon, then a slice of poblano pepper about the same size. Smear some roasted garlic on the pepper, then put a dove breast on it. Salt the dove breast, then roll this up tight and stick a toothpick through to hold. Repeat until you've done all the breasts.

Grill over medium heat with the grill grate open. Take your time and turn the poppers often. They're done when the bacon or ham is crispy. Serve piping hot.

ROAST PIGEON

Here in America, everyone seems to think there's something dodgy about hunting and eating common pigeons, which are, after all, a non-native, borderline-invasive species, totally unprotected in most states. I have a thing for pigeons. I love hunting them, I love how fast they fly, how tough they are—pigeons don't die easily—and I love how they taste.

This recipe is an homage to my British ancestors. It's just a simple roast pigeon, served atop a bed of roasted root vegetables, with a little malt (or beer) vinegar splashed on and served, ideally with a British pale ale or a glass of claret.

As for the root vegetables, go for it—use whatever you want. The more the better, and the crazier the better. I've served this with salsify, parsley root, carrots, Jerusalem artichokes, and golden beets. Have at it.

Serves 2, and can be scaled up | Prep Time: 30 minutes | Cook Time: 1 hour

2 pigeons, plucked and whole

¼ cup melted butter or olive oil

Salt and black pepper

2 large carrots, peeled and cut into chunks

4 to 6 Jerusalem artichokes, cut into chunks

2 parsnips, peeled and cut into chunks

2 to 4 salsify roots, scrubbed and cut into 2-inch lengths (optional)

1 or 2 roots of Hamburg or root parsley, cut into chunks (optional)

3 tablespoons chopped parsley

Beer vinegar or malt vinegar, for garnish

Preheat the oven to 425°F. Put all the chunked-up vegetables in a small roasting pan and coat with about half the melted butter. Salt them well, and pop them into the oven to roast. Take the pigeons out of the fridge when the veggies go into the oven. Let the pigeons come to room temperature for 30 to 45 minutes.

Stir the root vegetables, which should be starting to get brown. Paint the pigeons with more melted butter, and salt them well. Pour the remaining melted butter into a small pan and get it hot. Sear the sides of the pigeons in the hot butter. You want to get the legs and wings halfway cooked before the birds go into the oven. This should take about 6 to 10 minutes. Don't sear the breast meat.

Check the vegetables. They should be pretty close to being done. If they are, remove them from the oven, transfer them to a bowl, and cover with foil. Turn the oven up to 475°F, or even 500°F if it will go that high. Wipe out the roasting pan. Let the pigeons rest for the 10 minutes or so this will take. When the oven is ready, put the pigeons into the roasting pan, breast-side up. Roast for 10 minutes.

Remove the pigeons from the oven and set them on a cutting board. Turn off the oven, pour the vegetables back into the roasting pan, toss with the chopped parsley, and set into the oven to re-warm and cook a bit further. Let the pigeons rest for 5 minutes before serving. Serve them surrounded by the vegetables, which you can season with a little vinegar if you want.

DOVES A LA MANCHA

If I have a signature dish, it's this one. I've been making it for more than a decade, and it's still my favorite dove recipe. Super simple, this lets you get all primal with your Labor Day bag of fat, juicy doves. Why? Because you pluck 'em, gut 'em, and then grill and eat the birds whole.

This recipe is crazy easy: oil the birds, salt them, stuff the little cavities with fresh herbs, grill, paint the doves with bacon fat (or duck fat), and sprinkle with smoky Spanish paprika.

Fair warning: if you make this, you may never go back to breasting out your doves.

Figure on two doves per person for a light lunch or an appetizer, or three to six for a main course. If you don't have access to doves, try it with pigeons, quail, woodcock, ptarmigans, or snipe.

Serves 4 | **Prep Time: 15 minutes** | **Cook Time: 10 minutes**

---

12 doves, plucked and whole

Kosher salt

3 tablespoons olive oil

12 bay leaves

12 to 24 sage leaves

About ¼ cup melted bacon fat, butter, or duck fat

Spanish smoked paprika

Freshly ground black pepper

Coat the doves with olive oil and salt them well. Stuff each cavity with sage and a bay leaf.

Get your grill hot, and clean the grates. Set the doves on the grill breast-side up, and cook them over medium-high heat, with the grill cover closed, for 6 minutes. Open the grill cover and turn the doves over so the top of the breast is wedged between grill grates. Paint the birds with some bacon fat. Let them cook this way for a minute or two, just to get a little color. Turn the doves on their sides, and grill for another minute or two—for each side. Paint with more bacon fat.

Dust with the smoked paprika and the black pepper and move the birds to a platter. Let them rest for 5 minutes. Eat with your fingers, and serve with a Rioja red wine, a California pinot noir, or an Italian Barbaresco—and a bowl to put the bones in. A simple tomato salad is a good accompaniment, as is a loaf of crusty bread.

DATELAND DOVE POPPERS

I don't much care for the standard jalapeño-cream cheese-bacon wrapped dove popper everyone seems to do, so I've gone my own way. I started with Hank's Dove Poppers (page 253), and after a great dove hunt in Yuma, Arizona, I got more inspiration. Holly and I had stopped at Dateland, a little roadside stop that features date shakes—my favorite kind of milkshake—as well as an array of various date products. I bought some medjool and honey dates.

I had an idea forming: doves and dates. Sweet and meaty. The dish had to be a bacon wrapped dove popper, but I didn't want it to be so one-note as just a date, a dove breast, and a slice of bacon. It needed something more. That's when I remembered something my friend Johnathan O'Dell told me about Dateland: in 1927, it was designated as a place to grow dates by the King of Morocco when his country was threatened by a date blight. So seed stock from the highest quality Moroccan dates was grown there, and since then a small but significant date industry has grown in Arizona and Southern California.

Morocco gave me the marinade: chermoula. Chermoula is an herby, citrusy, spicy mixture often used to marinate fish or meats. It has many variations, but any version would add a dimension to this dish. So I buzzed some chermoula together, marinated the dove breasts for a few hours, then built the poppers.

I settled on the small honey dates because they wouldn't overwhelm the dove. Medjools are too big, so if that's all you can find, cut them in half. I also left a lot of marinade on the doves for added flavor. And I half-cooked the bacon so the dove breasts wouldn't overcook by the time it crisped on the grill.

The result: exactly as I'd hoped. Fatty-smoky-crisp bacon, a soft and sweet date, and meaty dove laced with the bright, spicy marinade. Super good, fun to eat—but rich! Make these poppers for a party as an appetizer. Oh, and if you have leftovers for some reason, they're actually damned good right out of the fridge.

Serves 4 | Prep Time: 30 mins | Cook Time: 15 mins

---

12 to 16 dove breasts
  (24 to 32 halves)

12 to 16 small dates

1 pound bacon (not thick cut)

12 to 16 toothpicks, soaked in water

CHERMOULA MARINADE

2 tablespoons olive oil

Zest and juice of a lemon

1 bunch cilantro or parsley, chopped
  (about 2 cups)

4 teaspoons ground cumin

2 teaspoons paprika

1 teaspoon hot paprika, Aleppo
  pepper or cayenne

1 teaspoon salt

½ teaspoon black pepper

¼ preserved lemon, chopped
  (optional)

4 cloves garlic, minced

Put all the ingredients for the chermoula in a food processor or blender and buzz until smooth. Mix with the dove breasts, and set in the fridge, covered, for up to 8 hours.

Cook the bacon just until it gives up some fat and is limp. You want it about half-cooked, but not crispy. Set it aside to cool.

Slice the dates open vertically to remove the pit. Unfold the date to flatten it out. Take a dove breast, shake off excess marinade, and nestle it into the date. Bend the edges of the date around the breast.

Wrap a piece of bacon around the dove-date tightly, and secure with a toothpick. If you want, you can double up on the dove-dates if you want a bigger popper.

Get your grill hot, leaving one side with no coals or with no burners turned on. Set your poppers on the grill with the seam-side of the bacon facing down. Grill with the cover up, turning the poppers frequently to crisp the bacon on all sides. If you're worried the dove might not be fully cooked, set the poppers on the cool side of the grill when the bacon crisps, then cover the grill and cook for an additional 2 to 4 minutes.

DOVE CHILES RELLENOS

These aren't the chiles rellenos you get at cheapy, corporate Mexican(ish) places all over the country. It's a real-deal chile relleno that will knock your socks off. It's based on a Oaxacan version of the Puebla classic I found in Rick Bayless's book *Authentic Mexican: Regional Cooking from the Heart of Mexico*. But instead of a regular picadillo filling, I use dove meat.

Here's the story behind this dish. Holly and I were hunting doves in Yuma, Arizona, where the whole town celebrates the beginning of dove season to the point where several restaurants will cook your doves for you. The restaurant we went to served us a grotesque version of a popper that had the jalapeño, dove, cheese, and bacon entombed in a thick batter. Odd, dirty, yet strangely good for at least a few bites.

Driving home, Holly and I were rolling around ideas when she noted that a chile relleno is in many ways a lot like a popper, only nicer. And indeed, this is most definitely not a popper—for that, look to page 253 (Hank's Dove Poppers). But these rellenos do have a lot of the same flavors going on, and I can assure you it's worth the effort. You have the picadillo, which in Oaxaca has almonds and raisins but that I made all Arizona-like by substituting local dates and piñon pine nuts. The result is sweet-savory, with lots of texture.

You've got your cheese and your chile, too, and I suppose you could add chopped bacon into the poblano to get the full effect. But I like this chile relleno as it is. Everything about this dish sings Southwest, which is where it's at when it comes to dove season.

I'm not going to lie: making chiles rellenos isn't a quick process. But nor is it overly difficult. And some of the steps can be done a day or two in advance. My advice is to make a big batch of the filling and freeze it in recipe-sized portions; it's great as enchilada filling, too (see page 263). You can't really roast the poblanos too far in advance or they'll lose their integrity, but you can do them up to two days in advance.

You have some options with this recipe. First, the chiles. My pick is the poblano, which is traditional and easily obtainable in most supermarkets. Second choice would be the closely related pasilla chile, followed by a regular ole' green bell pepper, followed by Anaheims or Hatch chiles, which have thin walls that can break easily when you try to stuff them.

As for the meat, I used dove because I wanted to make this dish a hat tip to the Desert Southwest, where we were hunting doves. But you can use any meat whatsoever.

Serve these by themselves or with Mexican rice, along with lots of cold beer.

Serves 4 to 6 | **Prep Time: 60 minutes** | **Cook Time: 35 minutes**

FILLING

1 pound dove meat, roughly chopped

2 tablespoons lard or olive oil

1 cup white onion, roughly chopped

2 cloves garlic, chopped

1 teaspoon black pepper

1 teaspoon cinnamon

¼ teaspoon cloves

1 cup tomato purée

¼ cup chopped dates
   (or golden raisins)

Make the filling first. Put the dove meat and the onions and garlic in a food processor, and pulse it a few times, just to get a rough grind. You can also chop everything by hand.

Add the lard or oil to a frying pan over medium-high heat. Add the meat, onions, and garlic to the pan, and brown them for 5 minutes or so. Add the tomato purée, spices, and salt, and bring to a simmer. Simmer for 10 minutes, then add the pine nuts and chopped dates. Cook until the filling becomes a cohesive mass, about 10 minutes. Turn off the heat.

Make the sauce. Buzz the chiles, onion, and garlic in a blender, adding the tomato purée to combine. Heat the lard in a sauté pan over

(continued)

¼ cup chopped, toasted pine nuts
    (or slivered almonds)

Salt

SAUCE

3 to 5 chiles (serranos, jalapeños,
    or other hot chiles)

1 cup chopped onion

2 cloves garlic

One 28- to 32-ounce can tomato
    purée

2 tablespoons lard or olive oil

Salt

CHILES

6 to 8 big poblano chiles

⅓ pound cheese, either *queso para
    frier* or shredded Monterey Jack
    or similar

½ cup flour

1 egg for every poblano, separated

½ teaspoon salt

Oil for frying

medium-high heat until it's hot, then pour in the sauce. It will spatter, but stir it vigorously for a minute or two, then turn the heat down. Add salt to taste and turn the heat to its lowest setting.

Char the skins of the poblanos over a gas burner if you have one. This is the best method because it doesn't cook the peppers too much. If you don't have a gas range, use a grill or a broiler. When the skins are all blackened, put the peppers in a closed container, such as a bag, or in a bowl with a lid, and let them sit for 20 minutes before wiping the skins off with your fingers. Try not to use water to do this, as it will rinse away some of the flavor of the chile.

Now make a slit in each chile from the top to about 1 inch from the bottom. Carefully remove the seeds (you may need a paring knife to cut out the seed ball) and flush the seeds out of the inside of the pepper with running water; yes, this saps some flavor, but it beats picking out every seed by hand.

To make the batter, beat the egg whites with the salt until they just begin to hold a peak. Beat in one egg yolk at a time, then add a tablespoon or two of flour. Set aside.

Get your oil going. Add the oil to a heavy pot so that it reaches 1 inch up the side. Heat the oil to 375°F. This will take a bit of time.

While the oil is heating, stuff your peppers. Lay some cheese into each pepper and then stuff the filling into them. Keep in mind you'll need to reclose each pepper, so don't overfill.

Dust each pepper in the flour, then, when your oil is ready, coat with the batter. Lay a pepper or two in the hot oil, seam-side up. Fry until golden brown, about 3 minutes. Carefully turn and fry the seam side another 3 or 4 minutes. If you can't get all the peppers fried quickly, set the finished ones on paper towels in a baking sheet, and put the baking sheet in an oven set to "warm."

To finish, pour some sauce on everyone's plate and top with a relleno. Garnish with cilantro if you'd like.

DOVE ENCHILADAS

Yes, I know. Another Tex-Mex dove recipe. But since Texas and the Desert Southwest offer some of the best dove hunting in America, it's only natural. These enchiladas are from New Mexico, and I love them with dove—but literally any meat will work here.

You need just the breast meat from your doves for this, but if you want to go a step further, make dove stock for the green chile sauce. It's easy: roast the breasted dove carcasses in a 400°F oven until they're good and browned, about 45 minutes. Bash them up, cover in 5 cups of water, put a lid on the pot, and simmer gently as long as you can stand it, up to overnight. Strain and you're golden.

Once you get the process down, you can make big batches of dove enchiladas if you want. The green chile sauce keeps for a few days in the fridge, so can be made ahead. And once made, the enchiladas reheat well for leftovers.

A note on using other animals: if you use something that can be tough, like turkey thighs or jackrabbit legs, you should either dice the meat very small or braise it in some stock until tender and then shred it.

Serves 4, and can be scaled up | **Prep Time: 90 minutes, mostly for prepping the peppers**
Cook Time: 45 minutes

GREEN CHILE SAUCE

3 tablespoons lard or cooking oil

1 large white onion, chopped

4 cloves garlic, chopped

3 tablespoons all-purpose flour

1½ cups chopped roasted green chiles, about five

1 to 3 serrano chiles, minced (optional)

1 teaspoon epazote (optional)

1 teaspoon cumin

½ teaspoon ground coriander

2½ cups dove broth or chicken stock

Salt (smoked salt if you have it)

Black pepper to taste

FILLING

Meat from 15 doves, about a pound

Salt (smoked salt if you have it)

About ¼ cup green chile sauce (see above)

6 ounces shredded Monterey Jack and/or cheddar cheese (2 ounces for the filling, the rest as topping)

1 cup minced white onion

Fifteen 6-inch tortillas

Prep the green chiles. You need to roast your green chiles; I use New Mexican, Hatch-style chiles. This makes for a *picante* sauce. You can make it milder by using poblanos or even green bell peppers. If you've never roasted chiles before, see the recipe for Dove Chiles Rellenos on page 261.

Make the chile sauce. Heat the lard over medium-high heat, and cook the onions until soft, but not brown, about 5 minutes. Add the garlic, and cook another minute. Add the flour, and cook, stirring often, for 5 minutes. Add the remaining ingredients, stir well, and simmer gently for 20 minutes. Purée in a blender.

Make the filling. Dice the dove meat and salt well. Mix with about ¼ cup of the green chile sauce as well as about 2 ounces of cheese and the onion.

Prep the tortillas. Heat the tortillas on a comal or other heavy skillet until they blacken a little. Then put them in a tortilla warmer, or stack on a plate and put a bowl over them. Let them steam a few minutes before building the enchiladas.

Build the enchiladas. Pour a little green chile sauce into a casserole. Fill a tortilla with a little of the filling and roll it up. Place seam-side down on the casserole. Repeat until you're done. You should get about 15 tortillas.

Pour more green chile sauce over the enchiladas and top with lots of the shredded cheese. Bake at 350°F for 25 minutes and serve.

DOVE OR PIGEON JÄGERSCHNITZEL

Jägerschnitzel means "hunter's cutlets" in German, so why not adapt this Teutonic classic for dove breasts? At heart, jägerschnitzel is a thin cutlet of meat served with a mushroom gravy, or in this case lots of little, bite-sized cutlets. And while this is a great recipe for boneless dove breasts, any meat you can pound flat works.

What does it taste like? Damned good is what it tastes like. If your heat is high enough when you cook the dove cutlets, the center will still be pink, like a dove should be. And the mushroom gravy is, well, gravy—and who doesn't like gravy?

I like using chanterelles with jägerschnitzel, as this is traditional. If you can find them, use chanties; they taste wonderful, almost fruity, and look pretty on the plate. But don't let a lack of chanterelles put you off making this recipe. Any mushroom will do.

What to serve with this? Potatoes would be typical, but good bread or even rice would be fine. You want something to sop up all that sauce. A light red wine or a German beer would be what you'd want to drink here.

Serves 4 | Prep Time: 20 minutes | Cook Time: 20 minutes

Breast meat from 12 to 16 doves

Salt

1 to 1½ pounds chanterelles or other fresh mushrooms, cleaned and roughly chopped

1 cup chopped yellow onion

5 tablespoons bacon fat, lard, or butter, divided

Flour for dusting (optional)

2 tablespoons flour

1 cup stock (dove or beef)

1 or 2 tablespoons sour cream

2 tablespoons chopped parsley

Black pepper to taste

Place each dove breast between two pieces of plastic wrap and pound until it's about ¼ inch thick. Do this firmly, but don't wail on the meat or you'll tear it.

Set a large frying pan over high heat for 1 minute, then add the mushrooms to the hot, dry pan. Shake them around so they don't stick too much, and cook the mushrooms until they give up their water, about 3 or 4 minutes. Add 2 tablespoons of the bacon fat and the onions, and stir-fry everything until the onions begin to brown, about 4 minutes. Remove the mushrooms and onions and set aside.

Dust the dove breasts in flour if you want to. Add the remaining fat to the pan and let it heat over medium-high heat. Do not let it smoke. Sear the cutlets for 1 minute on the first side. Press them with a spatula to keep them from curling up. Flip the cutlets, and sear another minute for medium doneness. Remove the cutlets to a plate and put them in an oven set to "warm."

Add the 2 tablespoons of flour and mix with the fat in the pan. Turn the heat to medium and let the flour-and-fat mixture cook until it's the color of coffee-with-cream. Slowly pour in the stock, plus any juices that have come off the cutlets while they rested. You should now have a thick gravy. If it's thin, let it boil down a minute or two. If it's too thick, turn off the heat, wait for the sauce to stop bubbling, and stir in the sour cream. Add the mushrooms and onions back to the pan, and toss to coat in the sauce. Add salt and freshly ground black pepper to taste. Pour this over the cutlets and serve at once. Garnish with a little parsley.

DEEP-FRIED DOVES

I came up with the idea for this dish after reading a 1940s recipe for deep-fried doves in Roy Wall's *Fish And Game Cookery*. His recipe is old school, with the doves fried in shortening and served with a Southern milk gravy. Good, but not my style. I prefer this Cajun style, and as finger food, without gravy. You dredge the birds in corn flour—basically Louisiana fish-fry mix—with some Cajun or Creole seasoning and fry in peanut oil. Um-hmm.

Another alternative is to go Middle Eastern; Turkish, really. I like frying things in chickpea flour, which is available in good supermarkets and Italian and Indian stores. You could substitute some other earthy-tasting flour. You then lace the flour with a typical mixture of Middle Eastern spices: garlic, chile, cumin, sumac, and fenugreek. You could do any kind of spice mix you want. Just don't go with a thick batter, which gets in the way of enjoying the doves.

Doves are my usual bird for this recipe, but any small bird will work. Quail would be a great choice, as would partridge, snipe, rails, or woodcock.

What to serve this with? Rice is nice, like a jambalaya, or even just white rice. A salad is another good option, like a tomato salad or one with roasted red peppers. But mostly I just eat these as appetizers for a party.

Serves 4 | **Prep Time: 45 minutes** | **Cook Time: 20 minutes**

---

12 doves, plucked and whole

Salt

1½ cups fine cornmeal ("fish-fry" mix)

2 to 3 tablespoons Cajun seasoning

MIDDLE EASTERN OPTION

1½ cups whole-wheat or chickpea flour

1 tablespoon garlic powder

1 tablespoon sumac (optional)

1 tablespoon cumin

1 tablespoon cayenne (or to taste)

1 teaspoon fenugreek (optional)

Oil for frying (I use canola, peanut, or refined olive oil)

Wash the doves and set aside at room temperature for 30 to 45 minutes.

Pour the oil into a deep-fryer or heavy, high-sided pot such as a Dutch oven. A fryer will have a fill line, and the oil should be poured no higher than two-thirds of a pot's depth—half is better. Don't worry, you can reuse the oil. Heat the oil slowly, over medium heat, to 350°F. If you're using olive oil, keep it at 340°F.

Meanwhile, mix the flour or cornmeal and all the spices together in a bowl, and coat the doves. Make sure you get it into the cavity, too.

When the oil is hot, drop in a couple of doves at a time, and let them fry for 5 to 7 minutes, turning them to be sure they're golden brown all over. Let drain on a wire rack in an oven set to "warm." Serve with a bowl for the bones. And give your guests plenty of napkins.

CHINESE FRIED DOVES

OK, I'm not going to lie: this is an involved recipe, especially for an appetizer. But my friend Kian Lam Kho says this is one of his favorite things to eat and, given that he wrote my favorite Chinese cookbook, *Phoenix Claws and Jade Trees: Essential Techniques of Authentic Chinese Cooking*, I gave this recipe a go. I wasn't disappointed, and nor will you be. Kian uses squab (young pigeon) here, and if you do use pigeons, you'll need to quarter them. But small birds are better, like doves, quail, woodcock, small rails, or snipe.

Although I designed this version of the recipe as a main course for four people, twelve doves could easily be eaten by two people. Yeah, they're that good. My advice: double the recipe. It's going to take you a few days to get this all together anyway, so why not make a huge batch?

A word on the maltose syrup: this is a pretty common ingredient in Chinese cooking. It's used to lacquer Peking duck and the like. It's malt syrup, and it can be found in Asian markets and in some fancy supermarkets. For you brewers out there, maltose syrup is basically liquid malt extract. If you use that, thin it out a little with water before you paint the birds with it.

Serves 4 | Prep Time: 8 hours, mostly marinating time | Cook Time: 5 minutes

MARINADE

1 cup sake or other rice wine

¼ cup soy sauce

5 slices ginger, peeled and crushed with the end of your knife

3 green onions, sliced

One 2-inch piece of cinnamon

1 tablespoon sugar

DOVES

12 to 20 doves, plucked and whole

¾ cup maltose syrup (see above), or honey

1 tablespoon rice vinegar

About ¼ cup cornstarch, potato starch, or tapioca starch

Oil for frying

1 tablespoon five-spice powder

2 tablespoons kosher salt

Mix together all the marinade ingredients in a small pot, cover, bring to a boil, then let cool. Mix the doves with the marinade, and set the doves breast-side down in a lidded, plastic container, or put them all in a heavy sealable plastic bag. The longer you can marinate, the better. At least 4 hours, and up to 2 days. When you're done marinating, take the doves out and set them on a wire rack set over a plate uncovered in the fridge for at least a few hours, and up to 1 more day.

The day you're ready to make these, mix the maltose syrup or honey and the vinegar in a small bowl, and paint the doves with the mixture. Let this dry for 30 minutes, then do it again. Repeat this until you have at least three layers on the doves, and up to five. Putting the doves in front of a fan helps.

After the last painting, put enough oil in a large, heavy pot or deep fryer to deep-fry the doves. Preheat the oven to "warm," and set that rack over the plate inside; this is to hold the fried doves while you finish the batch. Heat the oil to 350°F.

Dust the doves in the cornstarch and fry for 4 to 6 minutes, or until they're golden brown. Mix the five-spice powder with the salt, and sprinkle it over the doves the moment they come out of the fryer.

DOVES WITH WHAT THEY EAT

What goes together in life goes together on the plate. It's a truism in the cooking world, and this maxim has been my guide for many years. Dishes like Grouse Northwoods (page 77) and Sharp-Tailed Grouse, Prairie Flavors (page 240) came out of a close observation of what an animal eats or the environment in which it lives and then translating that observation into a plate of food. This, ladies and gentlemen, is a plate of dove with what doves eat.

And what doves eat, by and large, are seeds. Doves have a great appreciation for our farm country, and they stuff their crops with safflower, sunflower, wheat, millet, corn, soybeans, and even peanuts. They're also partial to cowpeas, amaranth, sorghum, millet, Indian ricegrass, and many other seeds that we don't normally eat.

Having all this in mind, I had a vision of a dish. I'd make a quick broth from the carcasses of some doves, use that to cook some wheat berries, and make a pilaf based on the wheat (the most common crop that doves eat nationwide), that also featured a variety of other things doves like to eat. I'd dust the dove breasts in similarly dove-appropriate foods—wheat flour, corn flour, as well as some peanut flour, which is an amazing thing to flour meat or fish with.

Since sunflowers are a favorite dove food, the oil had to be sunflower oil. I used a refined one to fry the doves and a cold-pressed, unrefined sunflower oil for the pilaf. Finally, I added some Southwestern influences to the dish. After all, the Desert Southwest from SoCal to Texas is the hub of dove hunting in this country. So in went limes, cilantro, and a little chile.

The dish turned out to be a knockout, even better than I had expected. Frying the dove breasts in hot sunflower oil kept them pink on the inside, and every bite of the pilaf was exciting: sweet corn, hot chiles, tart limes, rich sunflowers and sunflower oil, fresh herbs, and edamame, chewy wheat berries.

And you know what's even better? This is pretty easy to make—just fried dove breasts with a simple grain salad. None of the ingredients except the peanut flour is hard to find, and you can skip the peanut flour if you like.

PILAF

1 cup wheat berries

2 cups stock (dove is preferred, but other stock will do)

Salt

1½ cups edamame (soy) beans, fresh or frozen

1½ cups sweet corn kernels

½ cup roasted, salted sunflower seeds

1 to 3 hot chiles, such as árbol or cayenne, thinly sliced

¼ cup chopped cilantro or parsley

¼ cup chopped chives

Zest and juice of 2 limes

¼ cup sunflower oil

DOVE

12 to 16 dove breasts (both halves)

Salt (smoked if you have it)

½ cup flour

½ cup fish fry (seasoned corn flour)

3 tablespoons peanut flour (optional)

Sunflower or other vegetable oil for frying

Pour the stock and another cup or two of water into a small pot, and add the wheat berries. Bring to a boil, taste for salt, then drop the heat to a simmer. Simmer the wheat while you prepare everything else. It should take about 30 minutes to become tender.

In another pot, bring a few cups of water to a boil, and salt it. Boil the edamame for 4 minutes, then drain and rinse under cold water. Put the cooked beans in a large bowl.

Add all the remaining pilaf ingredients to the bowl. When the wheat berries are tender, drain them (discarding the stock), and add them to the bowl. Mix well, and add salt and freshly ground black pepper to taste. Set aside.

Meanwhile, separate the little tenders from the dove breasts. Salt the meat on a cutting board, and let the salt penetrate for 10 to 20 minutes.

Heat the frying oil in a large, wide pan over medium-high heat. Mix the flour, corn flour, and peanut flour together. Dust the dove tenders in this, and fry for a minute or two. Move the tenders to the pilaf bowl and mix in.

Make sure the oil is hot, about 350°F. Dust the dove breasts in the flour mixture, shake off the excess, and fry in the hot oil. You should only need about 90 seconds to 2 minutes per side. Serve hot alongside the pilaf.

"Roast pigeons don't fly through the air."

—DUTCH PROVERB

HMONG SQUAB SOUP

I absolutely love Hmong food. It's like rustic Vietnamese: fresh, herby, sweet, sour, salty—often with a lot of game. This is a simple soup that hinges on good stock and fresh herbs. The better your stock, the better the soup will be. Homemade stock is best. For the tomato, I prefer canned, whole, peeled tomatoes, and I tear them up by hand. I just like the way it looks in the bowl.

You must use tender cuts of meat here because you're not cooking this soup more than twenty minutes, not enough time to tenderize anything that's tough. Doves are ideal, as are quail, cottontails, woodcock, snipe, and young pigeons. Incidentally, this soup is also dynamite with frog legs.

Serves 4 | **Prep Time: 30 minutes** | **Cook Time: 20 minutes**

2 to 4 pigeons, or 8 doves

¼ cup peanut or other vegetable oil, or lard

2 large cloves garlic, thinly sliced

¼ to ½ cup peeled ginger, thinly sliced

1 lemongrass stalk, outer leaves removed, cut into 3-inch pieces (optional)

1 quart chicken or other stock

2 cups water

Salt

½ to 1 pound Asian rice noodles (optional)

1 cup chopped tomato

1 cup coarsely chopped basil

1 cup coarsely chopped cilantro

1 cup coarsely chopped green onions

½ cup coarsely chopped mint

2 jalapeño peppers, thinly sliced

Black pepper to taste

Break the birds into pieces: leg/thighs, breast halves, wings if you feel like it. I like these all on the bone, because the best way to eat this soup is with chopsticks. But if you aren't into that, take the breast meat off the bone and consider skipping the legs, since they become fiddly without chopsticks. Salt the pieces well.

While the pigeons are absorbing the salt, get two other pots ready. Fill one with the stock and water, and the other with enough water to cook the rice noodles. Bring both to a simmer.

Heat the oil in a soup pot, your third pot, and stir-fry the garlic, ginger, and lemongrass over high heat until the garlic just starts to turn a bit tan, about 90 seconds. Add the bird bits and stir-fry 2 minutes.

Pour the simmering water and stock into the pot with the birds, cover the pot and simmer gently for 10 minutes. Add salt to taste, and then add the tomato. Now is a good time to boil your rice noodles, if using. Rice noodles need only about 3 minutes to cook. When cooked, move them to individual bowls.

Return to the soup, and add all the remaining ingredients. Simmer uncovered for 5 minutes, then divide the soup into the bowls. Serve with chopsticks and a spoon, and maybe some soy sauce or fish sauce on the side.

DOVE OR PIGEON TORTELLINI

Taking a bite from a lovingly made tortellini, filled with All That Is Good In Life, wrapped in a perfect pasta and bathed in a demure but harmonious sauce is as close as a cook can come to giving you that longed-for gift you never received.

This dish has a very Old World flavor, deep and warming. You taste the sherry and herbs in the filling, and the rosemary and juniper definitely come through in the butter. Damned good.

They are a labor of love, and they do take some time to make, but they're worth every moment.

Note that you'll need to cook these tortellini within a couple of hours of making them—or you can freeze them and have them ready whenever; frozen tortellini will keep three to four months before deteriorating. To properly freeze, put the whole baking sheet in the freezer for a few hours, then you can put them all in a freezer bag. Once they're made, this recipe comes together in minutes.

This is also a recipe you can use for any red meat: pigeon, squab, and dove of course, but duck, goose, sharp-tailed grouse, ptarmigan, and woodcock are all good substitutes. If you want to make tortellini with white meats, see the recipe for Tortellini en Brodo on page 122.

I like a medium-bodied red wine to drink with this, like a chianti or a French Côtes du Rhône. As for beer, go with something bold and malty like a Scottish ale, an English brown ale, or a German dunkelweizen.

Serves 4 to 6 | **Prep Time: 90 minutes** | **Cook Time: 10 minutes**

DOUGH

10 ounces all-purpose flour, about 2 cups

2 eggs

1 ounce water, about 3 tablespoons

FILLING

3 pigeons or 6 doves

Salt

3 tablespoons duck fat, butter, or olive oil

4 large cloves garlic, unpeeled

¼ cup sweet white wine or sherry

A small pinch celery seed

1 teaspoon minced fresh rosemary

Black pepper to taste

To make the dough, first make a well in the flour, then crack the eggs into the center of the well, and add the water on top of the eggs. Scramble the eggs with a fork and then incorporate the flour until you get a shaggy mass. Knead this well for 6 to 8 minutes, then wrap the dough in plastic wrap and set aside for an hour. Alternatively, if you have a vacuum sealer, you can seal the dough, which will hydrate the dough instantly.

Preheat the oven to 350°F.

To make the filling, heat the duck fat in an oven-proof pan. While the pan is heating, salt the pigeons well. Pat the birds dry, add them to the hot fat, and brown them well on all sides. Take your time to do this; you want them well browned. Once the pigeons are browned, add the garlic cloves to the pan, pop the pan into the oven, and roast for 30 minutes.

When the pigeons have cooked, remove them and garlic to a plate to cool. Set the pan on the stove (remember that the handle is hot!), and deglaze all that browned goodness with the sweet wine. Use a wooden spoon to scrape down the pan to incorporate everything. Let this boil for a few minutes, then turn off the heat. Pick off all the meat from the pigeons (use what's left for stock if you want), and remove the skins from the garlic.

Coarsely chop the meat and garlic and add it to a food processor. Add the celery seed, rosemary, and black pepper, as well as some of the liquid and fat from the roasting pan, and buzz everything into a fairly

(continued)

5 tablespoons unsalted butter

1 tablespoon fresh rosemary

8 juniper berries, mashed

Grated pecorino or Parmesan cheese, for garnish

smooth paste. Taste, and add salt if you need to. You might need all of the pan liquid, you might not. Eyeball it.

Roll out the dough in a pasta maker or with a rolling pin. I roll mine out to position 7 on my Atlas, which is two stops from the thinnest setting. You don't want it ultra thin or the filling will soak through. Use something round to cut dough discs about 3 inches in diameter—these are largish tortelli, not strictly tortellini. Put a heaping teaspoon of filling in the center of the disc, and fold it into a half moon, removing as much air as possible. You might need to wet the edges with a little water. Bring the ends of the half moon together and press them to seal. You might need to flip the edges up to get that shape. This recipe makes about 40 to 45 tortelli, or twice that many tortellini if you make them small. Set each one on a baking sheet that you've dusted with semolina flour or fine cornmeal.

To finish, melt the butter in a wide pan, and add the juniper and rosemary. Keep this over low heat, allowing the flavors to infuse in the butter, while you bring a pot of water to a boil. Boil the tortellini until they float, and then for 1 minute more. With a slotted spoon, remove the tortellini to the butter, toss to coat, and put them on the plate. Grate some cheese over them and serve at once.

NOTES ON FILLED PASTA

Filled pasta is an excellent use for any wild game. Game meats are, in general, heavy on flavor, but tend toward toughness. Grinding them with plenty of fat and herbs and other good things won't destroy that flavor, and it solves the toughness question.

A few words on making great filled pasta:

- Fat is critical; too little will make the mix crumbly and dry.

- How fine a grind? The smaller the shape, the finer it must be. A big raviolo or mezzaluna—where only two or three make a serving—can be a lot coarser in texture. Remember that it's the filling that counts, not the sauce. Make the filling so good that you want to keep eating it and eating it while you're making them, and you will have succeeded in making good tortellini.

- Sauces for filled pasta need to be simple so as to not compete with all that work you did making the filling. Basic tomato sauces, cheese sauces, good broth, or simply sage-and-butter sauce. This is what you want.

- What sort of pasta? Sometimes I like adding "rougher" flours to wild-game pastas because they're more rustic and marry better with game. I've used spelt, farro (another ancient wheat), barley, rye, chestnut, and even acorn flour for this. Semolina is a good middle ground. Eggs in the dough or no? Your choice. I've done both with good results. Eggy pastas don't store as long, but they're richer in flavor; they say "refined" to me more, and I use them a lot with vegetable fillings.

CHAPTER 12

SNIPE, WOODCOCK, AND RAILS

Ever since I started hunting I've wanted to chase the elusive, mystical woodcock, a bird so steeped in mythology it was once thought to spend its summers on the surface of the moon.

Timberdoodles, mud bat, bog sucker, wood elf—all names for *Scolopax minor*, the lewdly named American woodcock. OK, get your jokes out of the way. Lord knows I've told more than my share about this bird. But when you're done, you really ought to do everything in your power to actually eat one of these birds.

Many who have eaten them say that woodcock is the king of game birds, greater even than ruffed grouse or canvasback duck. The flavor of woodcock is strong, gamy-in-a-good-way, and like nothing else. Some say that when you bite into one that's been perfectly cooked—pink, and just a little bloody—the earth moves. That's a bit much, but only a bit.

Woodcock do not live west of the Great Plains, so when I hunt in the Upper Midwest, I do everything I can to get out and chase these fantastic birds.

First thing you notice when you're confronted by a roast woodcock is that it's an odd bird; the Native Americans say God made woodcock out of leftovers. Its breast meat is dark but its leg meat is light—the opposite of most every other bird we hunt.

They usually have a little fat on them, but nothing like a duck. Woodcock are small, the size of a squab, with spindly wings and chunky legs. They should be cooked medium, or even rare.

As for snipe? Well for starters, snipe are indeed a real bird. Let's get that straight at the outset. And no, you don't hunt them at night with pillowcases and salt. They're a small, sandpiper-looking bird that lives on the edges of marshes, sticking its needle of a beak into the mud to fish out yummy, wormy things. They're tough to hit with a shotgun—thus the term "sniper"—and, like the woodcock, happen to be wonderful eating. The Irish and the French know this intimately, and are perhaps the world's most avid snipe hunters. But the bird lives here in America, too, and is pursued by a small core of die-hard snipers. I happen to be among them.

Plucked snipe look much cooler when you leave the feet on.

What, you might ask, does a snipe taste like? It's hard to describe, because snipe aren't related to any other birds we normally eat. They're a little ducky, a little grousey. Dark, but not red meat like venison. Squirrel comes to mind as something close, but this won't help you if you're not a hunter. For non-hunters, the closest might be the "oyster" on a good, free-range chicken; this is the oval of meat where the thigh connects to the body of the bird.

Rails are a class of birds I have little experience with. Clapper, king, Virginia, and sora are the main species hunted, and they live in marshy areas all over the country. Mostly a Southern quarry, those in the know say they are best skinned and cooked with other meats, or in spicy dishes like gumbo. The meat runs from pink to dark, and the flavor is dove-like, or similar to a snipe.

In general these are all single-serving birds, and indeed soras and snipe are so small you want to serve everyone at least two, and four is a better serving for a main course.

ROAST WOODCOCK

Unless you find yourself with the rare luxury of lots of woodcock, there's only one real way to cook these birds: roast them simply and serve them on sturdy toast with Cumberland sauce. The Robber Barons loved roast woodcock, and if it was good enough for J. P. Morgan, Andrew Carnegie, and their fellow Gilded-Age tycoons, it's good enough for me. It's a simple, heavenly meal.

Count on two woodcock per person if you can spare them. One will whet an appetite but will leave you wanting more. Be sure to preheat your oven fully before putting the birds in, otherwise the bacon and the woodcock's skin won't crisp properly.

Serves 2 | **Prep Time: 30 minutes** | **Cook Time: 18 minutes**

WOODCOCK

2 to 4 whole woodcock, plucked and gutted

1 tablespoon lard or butter

2 slices thin bacon, cut in half

1 celery stick

Salt

2 thick slices sturdy bread

CUMBERLAND SAUCE

1 shallot, minced

½ cup Port wine

¼ cup glace de viande (page 57), or 1 cup low-sodium stock

A pinch of salt

½ teaspoon dry mustard

¼ teaspoon cayenne

Zest of a lemon

Zest of an orange

¼ cup red currant jelly

Freshly ground black pepper

Preheat the oven to 500°F. Most ovens will require a solid 30 minutes to get to this temperature. As the oven is heating, take the birds out of the fridge. If you want to truss the birds, tie some kitchen twine around their legs. It's traditional to leave the head on the woodcock and push the beak through the legs to truss it. This is too odd, even for me.

In a cast iron or other oven-proof frying pan, heat the lard over medium heat for a minute or two. Add the bacon pieces, and fry until halfway done. Remove the bacon and set aside.

Add the woodcock, and fry for 1 minute on each side without touching the breast. Remove the birds, and take the pan off the heat. Pour off all but a thin sheen of oil.

When the oven is good and hot, arrange the woodcock in the frying pan breast-side up, using pieces of the celery stick to keep them from falling over. Lay a piece of bacon over the breast of each bird and cook in the oven for 6 minutes.

Remove the bacon, and continue cooking the birds for another 9 to 11 minutes. Remove from the oven and sprinkle with the fleur de sel. Let the birds rest on a cutting board as you make the Cumberland sauce.

While the birds are cooking, slice the bread into thick slices. If you want to be fancy, you can cut the bread into rounds. Fry in butter until browned on both sides. Set aside.

To make the sauce, sauté the shallot in the pan you fried the bread in over medium-high heat for 90 seconds, just until it softens. Add the Port wine and use a wooden spoon to scrape up any browned bits stuck to the pan. Let this boil furiously until reduced by half. Add the *glace* (or stock), the salt, citrus zest, mustard, and cayenne, and let this boil for a minute or two. Stir in the red currant jelly and the black pepper. Let all this boil down until it's thick but still pourable. You can strain it if you want a more refined sauce.

To serve, set the woodcock on the toast and top with the sauce.

ROAST SNIPE

Snipe are different enough from woodcock to deserve their own roasting recipe. You can also use this recipe for small marsh birds like sora or Virginia rails.

Serve snipe as an appetizer, unless you're lucky enough to have lots around. And remember that snipe are pick-up-and-eat birds, so keep it casual. A dipping sauce is a good idea (like the sauce for the Honey-Mustard Pheasant Wings on page 105). Me? I prefer just a splash of good vinegar.

Serves 2, and can be scaled up | **Prep Time: 5 minutes** | **Cook Time: 10 minutes**

2 to 8 snipe, whole and plucked

Lard or butter

Salt and black pepper

High-quality vinegar (sherry, balsamic, or apple)

Celery sticks (to prop the birds in the pan while roasting, if needed)

Preheat oven as hot as it will go, hopefully 500°F or even hotter. Take the snipe out of the fridge, and smear them all over with lard or butter. Sprinkle salt inside the cavity and all over the birds. Let rest while the oven heats up, a solid 30 minutes.

Arrange the snipe in an oven-proof pan—cast iron is perfect—with a few tablespoons of water in it. You want just a little water in the pan, not enough to cover the bottom. This helps keep the snipe moist. Hold them upright with celery sticks if you need to.

Roast in the oven for 5 minutes. Take the birds out and baste them with more butter, lard, or olive oil. Roast for 3 to 7 minutes more, depending on how you like your snipe. I like mine medium, so I go for a total of 10 minutes in the oven.

Take the snipe out of the oven and move them to a cutting board. Let them rest uncovered for 5 minutes before serving. Sprinkle some good vinegar (or lemon) and black pepper on the snipe right before serving.

CLASSIC FRENCH SALMIS OF SNIPE

Mostly I roast snipe, but if I'm feeling nostalgic, I'll cook this traditional French recipe called a *salmis*, a two-hundred-year-old dish that is as good now as it was when we Americans were still pissed off at the English for burning down the White House in the War of 1812.

A *salmis*—pronounced sal-me—is a method used with all sorts of wild game; salmis of pheasant is a classic. To make one, you quickly roast a bird (or hare or rabbit) until it's not-quite-done, and then make a quick sauce with the bones. You serve the breasts with mushrooms and sometimes a nice piece of bread that's been fried in butter or duck fat.

Snipe are ideal for this, being small birds, easily cooked. But you can also do this recipe with woodcock, ducks, grouse, quail, pheasants, partridges, rabbits, and young hares or squirrels.

When you make this, I do recommend that you make the French sauce Espagnol, as it adds richness and body to the sauce, but you can make salmis with just stock, too.

Any mushroom will work here, but I like wild mushrooms. I used chanterelles in this case.

While thick pieces of toast are traditional, I like this with mashed potatoes or celery root. Serve a medium-bodied red wine with this, like a grenache, Chianti, California pinot noir. For beer, go with malty, like a brown ale, Belgian tripel, or Scottish ale.

Serves 4 | Prep Time: 15 minutes | Cook Time: 45 minutes

12 snipe, plucked and whole

Vegetable oil to coat birds

Salt

1 ¼ cup red or rosé wine

2 minced shallots

2 cups stock (beef, duck, or chicken), or 1 cup stock and 1 cup Sauce Espagnol (see next page)

4 tablespoons duck fat or butter (2 tablespoons for the sauce, 2 tablespoons for the mushrooms)

1 pound fresh mushrooms

1 teaspoon thyme

3 tablespoons minced parsley

If you're making the sauce Espagnol, do that first. Heat the duck fat or butter in a small pot, and add the flour. Stir well, and let this cook over medium-low heat, stirring often, until it turns the color of peanut butter. Add the wine (the mixture will sputter), and stir it in until combined. Turn the heat to medium-high, and mix in the tomato paste, thyme, and enough stock to make a thin gravy. Add salt and freshly ground black pepper to taste, and let this cook very gently over the lowest heat on the weakest burner you have.

Preheat the oven to 500°F. Coat the snipe with oil, and salt well. Put the birds in a cast iron frying pan or small roasting pan. Roast for 8 minutes. Remove the birds from the oven, and slice off the breasts and the legs. Set them aside for now.

Smash the rest of the carcasses in a mortar and pestle or in a pot using a potato masher. Put them in a medium pot, and cover with the wine, the minced shallots, and a pinch of salt. Bring to a rolling boil and boil for 5 minutes.

Add 1 cup sauce Espagnol and 1 cup stock; if you're not making the sauce Espagnol, use 2 cups stock. Boil this down by half. Set a fine strainer over a small pot, and pour the contents of the first pot into it. Boil the strained sauce down by one-third, then reduce the heat to low. Swirl in the 2 tablespoons of duck fat or butter, one tablespoon at a time. Keep warm.

(continued)

OPTIONAL SAUCE ESPAGNOL

2 tablespoons flour

2 heaping tablespoons duck fat or
butter

1 cup wine, white or rosé

1 heaping tablespoon tomato paste

½ teaspoon dried thyme

Salt and black pepper

About 1 cup stock (duck, beef, or
chicken)

While the carcasses are boiling, do the mushrooms. Set the mushrooms in a large frying pan or sauté pan, and turn the heat to high. Shake the mushrooms as they start to sizzle, and soon they will begin to give up their water; dry mushrooms will start to sear. When most of the water has boiled away or the mushrooms are searing, add the remaining 2 tablespoons of duck fat or butter and toss to combine. Add the salt and thyme and some black pepper, and cook over medium-high heat until the mushrooms start to brown, about 8 minutes.

To finish the dish, get a small pan very hot, and add a little vegetable oil to it. When the oil just barely starts to smoke, set the snipe breasts and legs in the pan, skin-side down. Sear until crispy, about 2 minutes. Or, you can use a torch to crisp the skin.

Toss the sauce with the mushrooms and spoon some on each plate. Set the snipe pieces on top of the sauce, and garnish with parsley. I like to serve this with mashed potatoes or thick pieces of toast fried in butter or duck fat.

"Everybody knows that the autumn landscape in the northwoods is the land, plus a red maple, plus a ruffed grouse. In terms of conventional physics, the grouse represents only a millionth of either the mass or the energy of an acre. Yet, subtract the grouse and the whole thing is dead."

—ALDO LEOPOLD, SAND COUNTY ALMANAC (1949)

WOODCOCK MICHIGAN

I call this dish Woodcock Michigan because the sauce was originally made with crabapple jelly from Michigan and homemade red wine vinegar from Michigan—and the woodcock I shot were from Michigan, so there you go.

You can make this recipe with woodcock, snipe, quail, ptarmigan, doves, or pigeons. It's important to use high-quality red wine or cider vinegar, and while crabapple jelly is hard to find, you can substitute any decent apple jelly, or even a little apple cider. If you can't get crabapple, one option is to add a few cranberries to the sauce along with the regular apple jelly. If you don't have bacon fat around, fry up some bacon and eat it, then make the sauce with the leftover drippings.

A word on the innards. They really do add a lot to the sauce, and since you strain them out at the end anyway, it should be no big deal even for squeamish eaters. So use them if you can. No innards? Buy some chicken livers and use them. Or use the giblets from other birds.

Serves 4 | **Prep Time: 30 minutes** | **Cook Time: 15 minutes**

4 woodcock or pigeons, or
    8 doves or snipe

Olive oil to coat birds

Salt

3 or 4 tablespoons bacon fat, divided

¼ cup minced onion or shallot

Hearts and livers from the birds,
    minced fine

½ cup stock (chicken or game)

2 tablespoons cider vinegar or
    red wine vinegar

2 tablespoons crabapple or apple jelly

4 pieces of thick toast

Parsley for garnish

Preheat your oven to 500°F, or as hot as it will get. Take the birds out of the fridge, and coat with oil. Salt well, and set aside at room temperature while the oven heats up. This should take 30 minutes or so.

Heat half the bacon fat in a small pot and sauté the onion and minced woodcock giblets until nicely browned. Add the stock, vinegar, and crabapple jelly and bring to a boil. Add salt to taste and let it simmer while you cook the woodcock.

Heat the rest of the bacon fat in a small, oven-proof pan—cast iron is excellent here—and brown the woodcock on the sides and breast. Put the birds, breast-side up, in the pan in the oven and roast for 10 to 18 minutes. Ten minutes will give you medium-rare meat. Remove the birds from the pan and set on a cutting board to rest.

Strain the sauce through a fine-meshed sieve and bring back to a boil. Put the toast on each person's plate (cut it into a circle if you want to be fancy) and put a woodcock on the toast. Pour the sauce over the birds, and garnish with parsley. Serve at once with a light red wine, a dry rosé or a hoppy beer like an IPA.

MICHIGAN WOODCOCK

THE FIRST TIME I ever hunted woodcock was in the closing stages of my first book tour, back in 2011. I'd been on the road for two months, and, like any tour, I had some serious stress to deal with. The hunt was at the tail end of that trip, and turned out to be a restorative experience.

My friend Brian Brenton had generously offered to show me the Michigan Northwoods, an offer I happily took up. I told him I had never killed a woodcock myself. "We ought to be able to fix that," Brian said.

We drove north past the little town of Luzerne and into the grouse woods. Brian was more interested in ruffed grouse, and as it happens, the two birds share the same sort of woods but inhabit different spots. Woodcock like life a little damper than grouse do. Both birds prefer thick cover.

Alders, black ash, birch, aspen. This is their home. As we walked through the woods, Brian's English pointer coursing around, Brian bent down to look at something. "Take a look at this," he said. "Put that in your blog." I looked. Bird shit. "That's classic woodcock. If you see that, the birds are around."

What did that woodcock eat to make such a shit? Probably earthworms. Timberdoodles love earthworms. They also eat other creepy crawlies like millipedes, beetles, snails, ants, and other assorted larvae. Another fun fact? They take a dump when they fly, so their guts are clean. Well, clean-ish. This is why some people like to roast their woodcock un-gutted. I'm not one of them.

Sure enough, Brian's dropping-fueled hunch was right. I heard a bird flush and say "peeent!" and saw the shape zig-zagging away from me through the saplings. Theoretically, this would be a tough shot, but I'd killed my share of snipe before, and they do the same thing, only faster. So I felt pretty calm. I missed with the first shell, but folded the bird on the second. Success! I rushed to the spot where it fell, but couldn't see the woodcock. Damn. Same as snipe. They blend in perfectly with the forest floor. I felt that flood of anxiety wash over me.

I hate losing birds, and I did not want my first-ever woodcock to be lost. Brian's pointer wasn't too interested in finding a dead bird, so we looked around ourselves. Brian himself soon found it, thank God. It felt good to have the bird in hand.

Hunting woodcock opens the mind the way steam opens the pores. As you make your way through the thickets—walking is too generous a term—your eyes dart around and your mind races as you try to solve the geometric dilemma of crossing tree limbs and stumps and brambles and fallen logs. You don't always succeed. On our second morning, I fell into a hole and bashed my knee on a stump. Occupational hazard.

As you move, you keep your head on a swivel and your ears pricked up. In that split-second you hear that basso thrum of a grouse's wings as it flushes, or the crackly flutter of a woodcock, you must raise your shotgun, find the bird, decide if you can shoot, pull the trigger, and be ready to follow through for a second shot, if you need it. Hunting woodcock occupies your entire existence. It is instinct.

Trouble lies in a relaxed mind. The only two woodcock I missed but should have killed were pointed by Brian's dog. I had only to walk up to the dog, who would then flush the bird, and I could shoot it at my leisure from close range. But for whatever reason, the ease of this whole scenario flustered me; it's the same with those "gimme" shots on ducks that I always miss. Don't think, Hank, just shoot!

I wound up with three birds over an afternoon and morning of hunting, and I could easily have shot a two-day limit of six had I been just a bit better (or luckier). I couldn't believe how many there were around. "I don't shoot woodcock unless I'm with someone who likes them," Brian said. "People up here don't really like 'em." It showed. The grouse, which is

the preferred quarry of Brian and most of the other local hunters, were so elusive that Brian only got one.

Driving back from the Northwoods, I thought about how to cook this three-bird bonanza. It didn't take too much thought. There was no way I'd do anything else but pluck them and roast them in a high oven.

But the sauce. That would be an ode to the Mitten State. Shortly after this hunt, I did a book event in Detroit, where I managed to pick up some homemade vinegar and a jar of wild Michigan crabapple jelly. Sweet? Tart? That's a classic French *gastrique*. Brillat-Savarin would have approved.

I roasted the birds and ate them with my hands, with a nice bottle of 2008 Beaujolais I was shocked to find in Ashley, North Dakota, where I ended up cooking the birds. They were orgasmic. Sweet-sour-savory sauce, woodcock fat running down my hands, crispy skin, and rich meat so jammed full of flavor that I just sat there gorged, after eating all three, one after the next.

That memorable meal made me feel like myself again. Home was in sight, and life was good.

SNIPE OR RAIL PERLOO

Low Country perloo, perlou, or pilau, as it is variously spelled, is a close cousin to Cajun jambalaya, basically a super flavorful, chock-full-of-goodness rice dish that is itself related to the biryanis of India and East Africa.

I wanted to include this recipe with the snipe and rail chapter, even though you can make it with basically any meat on earth, because, well, I know of no place where rails are more actively sought after than the Low Country of South Carolina and Georgia.

This version simply uses diced meat from the birds, but if you want to go old school, use whole birds simmered in water with some herbs (bay, thyme, black pepper, etc.) and pick the meat off the carcasses for this. Then strain the resulting broth and make the perloo with it.

Serves 6 to 8 | Prep Time: 30 minutes | Cook Time: 60 minutes

---

 2 tablespoons lard or vegetable oil

½ cup diced country ham

1 large onion, chopped

2 celery stalks, chopped

1 red bell pepper, diced

I green bell pepper, diced

1 tablespoon minced garlic

1 teaspoon cayenne

2 teaspoons dried thyme

2 cups long-grain rice

1 cup diced tomatoes

3 cups stock (chicken or game)

2 cups diced snipe, rail, or other boneless meat

1 pound shrimp (peeled, tails removed, and deveined)

½ pound smoked pork sausage like andouille, cut into coins

4 green onions, chopped

Zest and juice of a lemon

⅓ cup chopped parsley

Freshly ground black pepper

Hot sauce (I use Tabasco)

Heat the lard or vegetable oil in a large, heavy, lidded pot such as a Dutch oven. Add the diced country ham, and cook over medium-high heat until the ham begins to brown on the edges.

Add the onions, celery, and bell peppers, and cook, stirring often, until the edges of the onions begin to brown, about 6 minutes. Add the garlic, cayenne, thyme, and rice, and mix well. Cook, stirring, for 2 minutes.

Add the tomatoes, stock, and snipe, or whatever meat you happen to be using. Add salt to taste. Cover the pot, set the heat to low, and cook until the rice is nearly done, about 12 minutes.

Put the shrimp and sliced sausage into the pot. Don't mix them in just yet. Cover the pot and let this cook until the shrimp are done, about 5 minutes or so. Turn off the heat and let this sit about 5 to 10 minutes.

To finish, add the parsley, green onions, lemon juice, and lemon zest, and mix to combine. Serve with the hot sauce alongside.

GRILLED SNIPE BASQUE

As it happens, the area of France that borders Basque Country is a hotbed of snipe hunting. So I decided to create a Basque-style marinade for these little birds and grill them over a hot fire. What is a Basque-style marinade? Lemon, parsley, olive oil, espelette pepper, garlic, and one unusual ingredient—salted, preserved lemons.

You can buy preserved lemons online, but if you really want good ones, you salt them yourself. It's as easy as cutting a lemon into wedges and packing them all in salt. Put this in a Mason jar in the fridge, and they'll last a year or more. Skip it if you don't want to be bothered, but I will tell you it adds a lot to the flavor.

Espelette pepper is hot but not overly so. It can be hard to find, so use hot paprika one-to-one, or half the amount of cayenne.

This recipe is perfect for snipe, woodcock, doves, quail, partridges, pigeons—anything you can grill quickly over a hot fire. It's best with plucked birds, but will work with skinned ones, too.

Serves 4 as an appetizer | **Prep Time: 15 minutes, not including marinating time** | **Cook Time: 10 minutes**

---

8 to 12 snipe, whole

MARINADE

3 cloves garlic, smashed

½ cup chopped parsley

Juice of a lemon

½ preserved lemon, chopped
(optional)

2 teaspoons espelette pepper
or hot paprika

A healthy pinch of salt,
smoked if you have it

½ cup olive oil

Put all the marinade ingredients into a blender and purée. Coat the snipe with the marinade, making sure to get some into the cavity. Marinate in the refrigerator at least a few hours, and for up to two days.

When you're ready to grill, wipe off most of the marinade with your fingers; you want a little sticking on the birds here and there. Let the birds come to room temperature.

Heat your grill, and make sure the grates are clean. Set the birds on the grill breast-side up, and cook with the cover open for 3 minutes. Move them all to one side, nestling the legs between the grates so they get a bit of extra heat. Grill like this 2 minutes, then flip to grill the opposite side, doing the same thing with the legs.

Finally, flip the snipe breast-side down to grill directly for 1 to 2 minutes.

Remove the birds, and let them rest a few minutes before serving. These are best eaten with your fingers. Messy but tasty!

PART FOUR

GIBLETS AND CHARCUTERIE

CHAPTER 13

GIBLETS AND OFFAL

Heart, liver, kidneys, gizzards, even brains. Somewhere, someone eats every one of these wobbly bits off their upland game birds and small game. I'll be honest: in the small-game world, I largely stick to the innards of birds, which are called giblets. I use the offal from rabbits, hares, and squirrels far less frequently, primarily because the innards of rabbits and hares can be affected by parasites (see page 49), and I'd rather be safe than sorry. Keep in mind that offal from domestic rabbits is wonderful.

I do use squirrel hearts, livers, and kidneys, but I'm not one of those guys who likes squirrel brains in my scrambled eggs (it's a thing in Kentucky). Sorry, you'll have to go elsewhere for that one.

Giblets, however, shouldn't scare you. Other than the liver, they're all muscle meat, not so different from the breast or the thigh. And pheasant, grouse or turkey livers, whipped into a light, creamy mousse, are definitely something I can get behind.

But again, I'm not going to lie to you: gizzards on anything smaller than a grouse aren't worth messing with, so I rarely keep them. I like rabbit kidneys, but I usually just toss them into whatever braise or stew I'm already making. Hearts are always good, especially grilled (Grilled Hearts,

page 299) and livers go into either Liver Mousse (page 323) or Cajun Dirty Rice (page 297). I stick to a few simple yet accessible recipes for the offal of the creatures in this book, unlike deer or waterfowl, whose wobbly bits I enjoy more.

What follows are my favorite recipes for giblets and wobbly bits from upland birds and small game. Virtually all of them work with any of these animals, although I vastly prefer big turkey gizzards to dainty pheasant gizzards, both of which are perfectly edible.

But before we get to the recipes, you'll need to know a few tips and techniques to get the most out of your giblets.

ARE THESE PARTS SAFE?

Yes, with a few caveats. I've never heard of parasites in any heart or gizzard of a small-game animal or bird. Upland birds tend not to be heavily parasitized, but it can happen. Livers are one potential location for wee beasties, so inspect the liver carefully before saving it. If the liver has weird striations or whitish flecks or wormy looking things in it, toss it. Most liver parasites are visible.

If you feel like working with offal from rabbits or hares, just be careful. They can often carry tapeworm cysts in the gut cavity and flukes in their livers. I rarely keep anything other than hearts and kidneys from rabbits and hares. Squirrels seem to be less parasitized.

IN THE FIELD

In the field, you need to be ready to collect your wobbly bits before you go out hunting. Offal is very perishable and tends to get dirtier than the rest of the meat. Be prepared, and you'll be better off. I always bring a few items in my pack for this job:

- Sealable plastic bags.

- Paper towels. Wiping off excess blood is important. It can give the organ an off taste if left on too long. I also like to rest the innards on a paper towel on the grass to cool off before I put them into bags. You'll also use towels to wipe out the gut cavity of the animal.

- Water. In addition to what I'm drinking in the field, it's important to rinse off the bloody innards if you can. I'd avoid doing this in a stream because of the possibility of the meat picking up giardia or some other waterborne disease; hearts and livers are often served lightly cooked, and you want to be careful. Snow is fine to use, though.

- A cooler with ice if it's above freezing out. I keep this in the truck (with my extra water), but it's important to chill down the innards as fast as possible. They need to get cold faster than the rest of the animal.

Note that all this is for rabbits, hares, and squirrels, which you'll often gut in the field. Unlike big game, however, you can wait on all this until you get home if it's cold enough out, or if you can get the whole animal into a cooler quickly. Upland birds are almost always dealt with once you return from the field.

AT HOME

When you get home, you need to do some prep work before you can store your various bits. Rinse everything well under cold water, and carefully pick off any debris that might have attached itself to the organs. For hearts, try to wash out any blood clots in the arteries before you store them. Once they're all rinsed, you can store hearts and kidneys straight away.

For the liver, trim off any membranes and connective tissue and discard. Be careful around the gall bladder, which is an evil-looking greenish organ nestled between the lobes of the liver. If you break it, bile will spill everywhere—nothing that cold running water can't fix, but it's nasty anyway.

Kidneys come encased in fat. I rarely eat this fat, as it's very waxy. Peel away the fat, and keep the kidneys whole for storage.

Gizzards need to be cleaned. Wash them well, and take a look at them. You'll notice that a gizzard is two semicircular halves of meat around a fleshy center. Inside that center is a sack of grit; the bird uses this to grind seeds into a paste. The best way to clean a gizzard is to take a sharp paring knife or other small knife and slice each half of meat carefully away from this center. The meat arcs around the center sack—remember that when you're cutting. Do a few and you'll get the hang of it.

Discard the center and, if you want, slip the point of the knife under the silverskin on each side of the meat and remove it. You don't have to do this if you're slow-cooking gizzards.

When everything is cleaned up, I tightly wrap each kind of giblet in plastic wrap, then put the little bundles in a heavy freezer bag. They'll keep that way a year or so.

CAJUN DIRTY RICE

This should be your starter dish when you're working with offal or giblets. Dirty rice is so good, so accessible—all the giblets are minced small—that you'll find yourself storing giblets just to make this. Seriously.

Any sort of livers and wobbly bits will work here. I normally use giblets, but offal from rabbits, squirrels, and hares works, too. The trick to good dirty rice is to get a succession of crusts on the bottom of the frying pan that you scrape away with a wooden spoon. Each crust adds a little more flavor; it's a technique you see a lot in Italian ragus, which are long-cooked pasta sauces.

Serves 6 | **Prep Time: 20 minutes** | **Cook Time: 20 minutes**

1½ cups long-grain rice

3 tablespoons butter, lard, or vegetable oil

½ to 1 cup livers

½ to 1 pound of ground meat from gizzards and hearts or any other ground meat

Salt

1½ cups broth appropriate to the animal you're using

½ cup finely chopped onion

2 celery stalks, finely chopped

½ cup finely chopped green pepper

1 to 3 hot chiles, finely chopped

2 cloves garlic, minced

1 to 2 tablespoons Cajun seasoning

1 teaspoon dried oregano

4 green onions, chopped

Cook the rice as usual. Move the cooked rice to a sheet pan and lay it out to cool. You need to start with cool rice. You can do this step a day ahead if you want.

If you're using gizzards, clean them of grit and that silver membrane, and either chop fine or, if you have a meat grinder, grind them (if you do have a grinder, this is preferable to chopping). Alternately, you can use any ground meat. Either finely grind or finely chop the livers.

Heat the duck fat over medium-high heat, and, when it's hot, add the ground gizzards and the chopped livers. Toss to coat in the fat and then let them sit a bit to develop a crust on the bottom of the pan. Stir only occasionally, as you want to develop a good crust. If your Cajun seasoning isn't salty, salt the meat now.

Pour about ¼ cup of the broth into the pan, and use it to scrape up the browned bits on the bottom. Add the onion, peppers, celery, and garlic. Mix to combine, and cook for a solid 3 to 5 minutes, until the vegetables are soft.

Sprinkle the oregano and the Cajun seasoning over the giblet mixture and let a crust form on the bottom of the pan again. When it does, add the rest of the broth and the rice, and mix to combine. Scrape the bottom of the pan again. When the liquid has almost totally evaporated, mix in the green onions. You're ready when the liquid has all evaporated. Serve hot.

Serve this on its own for a light dinner, as a side dish to gumbo, or alongside roast birds.

CORNED GIZZARDS

Giblets are probably the least-used parts of the birds we bring home, and this is a shame. Even many who happily eat chicken giblets at the holidays or as a bar snack wrinkle their noses at eating the heart, liver, and gizzard of their wild birds. I have no idea why this is; it sure ain't because of flavor.

Allow me to give you an iron-clad, no-fail recipe for gizzards that will turn haters into lovers. I'm talking about corned gizzards. Yep, corned, as in corned beef. A simple brine followed by a simple bath in a slow cooker will turn out some of the finest meat in the wild world. The flavor is virtually identical to corned beef, and you can control the normally crunchy texture of the gizzard by how long you cook them.

This is my favorite way to eat waterfowl gizzards, and it works well with the gizzards from pheasants, large grouse and turkeys. Sliced thin and tossed with a simple sauté of wild mushrooms, a bitter-greens salad, or with sauerkraut and German spätzle, it's a killer dish!

Everything in this recipe is easy to find, with the possible exception of the pink curing salt. I buy mine in bulk online, but any butcher shop will have it, as will any place that makes its own smoked sausages. You can also use Morton's Tenderquick in a pinch; follow that product's instructions for corned beef to know how much of the stuff you should use. You can also skip the curing salt altogether, but the gizzards won't get that pretty rosy color.

Serves 8 | Prep Time: 12 hours, brine time | Cook Time: 12 to 24 hours in the crockpot

---

1 pound cleaned gizzards

¼ cup kosher salt

½ teaspoon Instacure No. 1 (curing salt, available online or at butcher shops)

1 quart broth (chicken or game)

2 bay leaves

Dissolve the salt and curing salt in 1 quart of water. Submerge the gizzards, and let them brine in the fridge for at least 6 hours, and up to 12. The longer they stay in the brine, the saltier they will get. I like to do this before I go to bed, and then I start the cooking before work the next morning.

When you're ready to cook, remove the gizzards from the brine and discard the brine. Put the gizzards in a crockpot and cover with the broth. Add water if they're not completely submerged. Add the bay leaves and set the crockpot to high. My crockpot will never hit a simmer, even at high, and this is what you want. So set your slow cooker at whatever setting will be nice and hot but not simmering. Cook the gizzards for at least 6 hours (they'll still be crunchy, though), and as many as 24 hours if you want silky, tender meat.

If you do this in the oven, submerge the gizzards in the broth in a small, lidded pot. Set the pot in a 190°F oven, and cook at least 6 hours, and up to 12 hours. You can also do this on the stovetop with the pot set over a small burner set on low; it's a bit harder to control temperature this way, however.

Once the gizzards are corned, they'll keep up to 2 weeks in the fridge, so long as you keep them in the broth that you cooked them in.

GRILLED HEARTS

If you've never eaten the hearts of poultry before, this recipe would be a good place to start. It's simple, quick, and flavorful. The hearts are brined for a short while to season them and to keep them tender over the hot fire, then they're skewered and grilled.

You can make this dish as fancy or as humble as you want. I have a rosemary bush in my front yard, so I like to take some long sprigs, soak them in water, and use them as skewers. If you don't have your own rosemary bush, use regular metal or bamboo skewers instead.

If you can grill over hardwoods—apple, oak, hickory, maple—you'll notice a huge difference in flavor. Even some wood chips thrown in a charcoal fire or on top of the burners in a gas grill will make a difference.

Any sort of sauce works well here, even just a squeeze of lime. But I love Japanese yakitori sauce with this. Nothing in it is hard to get in most supermarkets, and, while this recipe makes quite a lot of sauce, it keeps in the fridge a long, long time.

Serve these with lots of crusty bread and a good rosé or a light red wine, like a grenache.

Serves 4 as an appetizer | **Prep Time: 2 hours, most of it brining time in the fridge** | **Cook Time: 5 minutes**

HEARTS
¾ to 1 pound hearts

2 tablespoons vegetable oil

YAKITORI SAUCE
1 cup mirin, Japanese sweet rice wine

1 cup soy sauce

½ cup sake

1 tablespoon brown sugar

½ to 1 teaspoon ground black pepper

1 bunch green onions, chopped

2 garlic gloves, crushed

A 1-inch piece of ginger, sliced

½ cup stock or broth

Add all the yakitori sauce ingredients to a pot and bring to a boil. Let it cool to room temperature. Pour into a plastic container with a lid, and add the duck hearts. Let the hearts brine in this for a few hours, and up to overnight.

When you want to grill your hearts, remove them from the sauce. Bring the sauce to a boil, then simmer until the liquid is reduced by about one-third. Pour through a fine strainer. You can serve this warm or at room temperature, and any extra will keep for months in the fridge.

If you're using wooden skewers, soak them in water while the hearts brine. Start your fire, and get the grill good and hot. Make sure it's clean.

Pat the hearts dry with a paper towel. Toss with the oil, and push onto skewers. Leave a little space between each heart.

Right before you lay the skewers on the grill, oil the grates. Use a pair of tongs to pick up a paper towel, and dip it into some vegetable oil. Wipe down the grill grates with the oiled paper towel, and lay the skewers on them. Grill over high heat with the grill cover open for 2 minutes per side.

Serve the yakitori sauce on the side. You can slice the hearts in half if you think they might be too big for one bite.

CLASSIC GIBLET GRAVY

If you're roasting birds, you can't go wrong with giblet gravy. And hell, if you're roasting rabbits, you can do the same thing with their innards. I find this to be most satisfying when done with roast pheasant, wild turkey, or grouse. You'll want to reserve the necks, gizzards, hearts, and livers of your birds. You can omit the liver if this makes you happy.

For variations, you can skip the mustard and add a shot of bourbon and a glug of maple syrup. Or you can add some caramelized onions to the finished gravy, which is awesome puréed, or not.

Serve 6 to 10 | **Prep Time: 20 minutes** | **Cook Time: 2 hours**

Giblets from 1 turkey or from 3 to 6 pheasants or grouse

2 tablespoons butter

1 cup chopped onion

½ cup chopped carrot

½ cup chopped celery

1 tablespoon minced garlic

1 bay leaf

1 teaspoon dried thyme

5 cups stock (game or chicken stock, water, or a combination)

2 to 3 tablespoons flour

Salt to taste

2 teaspoons mustard

Heat the butter in a medium pot set over medium-high heat. When hot, add the giblets to the pan. Brown the giblets on all sides.

Add the onion, celery, and carrot, and sauté until the onions turn translucent, about 5 minutes. Mix in the garlic, and cook another minute.

Add bay leaf, thyme, water, or stock, and bring to simmer. Simmer gently with the pot partially covered for 2 hours.

Strain the giblets and stock through a fine-meshed sieve into a bowl. Set aside the stock. Remove the giblets. Pick the meat off the neck and mince everything else.

If you've been roasting birds, finish the gravy when the birds are resting on the cutting board after they're done. Add the flour to the roasting pan set it over two burners of the stovetop, and turn the heat to medium. Whisk the flour into the drippings. Let this cook until the flour browns, about 5 to 15 minutes depending on how dark you like your gravy. Stir this constantly.

If you haven't been roasting birds, heat another 2 to 3 tablespoons of butter or other tasty fat (pheasant fat, anyone?) in a medium pot and brown the flour in that. Then proceed with the remainder of the recipe.

Pour in the stock and minced giblets, stirring constantly. The mix will seize up at first, then loosen gradually. You want it the consistency of cream. Bring this to a simmer, and cook it until it thickens to your liking.

Stir in the mustard, and add salt to taste. Serve it as-is, or purée the gravy in a blender.

CRISPY BIRD SKIN

A lot of times, you don't need the skin on your birds, but let's face it: crispy chicken or turkey skin is one of the reasons we eat those birds—and the skin of their wild cousins is every bit as good. With pheasant, turkey, or grouse breasts, you'll notice that once the breast is removed and taken off the bone, the skin no longer covers about a third of the meat. This is very different from, say, a duck. Consequently, I pull that skin off my pheasant breasts and cook it separately.

What do you do with this crispy skin? Eat it as a snack, of course. But you can also put it in tacos, where they may become your all-time favorite taco filling.

Oh, and the smoked paprika is just what I happen to put on them. Cajun seasoning or any seasoning mix you want will do.

Serves 2 | **Prep Time: 5 minutes** | **Cook Time: 45 minutes**

Skin from 2 pheasants or grouse, or 1 turkey

Salt

Smoked paprika

There are two ways to get crispy skin. The easiest is to put a little oil in a pan and fry the skins, starting fat-side down. You'll need to flatten the skin with a spatula until it settles, as the skin will want to curl up. Fry until crispy like bacon, then, the moment it comes out of the pan, salt it and hit it with something tasty like smoked paprika. This is best for smaller birds.

For the other crispy-skin method, lay the skin as flat as possible fat-side down on a baking sheet. Salt it well, and cover with another baking sheet; I grease the underside of the top baking sheet to make sure the skin won't stick. Bake at 375°F for 30 to 40 minutes, depending on thickness—pheasants, 30 minutes; turkeys, 40 minutes. Remove the top sheet, and sprinkle with the paprika. Note that this method is the only way to do crispy turkey skin. The result is a nifty, glass-like pane of crispy turkey "bacon."

GIBLET BOLOGNESE SAUCE

Many years ago, when I first started making Bolognese sauces for pasta, I began hearing of people who put chicken livers in their version. As it happens, this is apparently a well-known variant of the classic Bolognese sauce, which is itself the godfather of our meat sauces here in America.

More important than any claim to authenticity is that this is a great way to use innards from your animals in a way that everyone will enjoy. It's a lot like Cajun dirty rice in that the bits are finely chopped or even ground, so you don't get big honkin' globs of liver in your sauce.

This is basically a traditional meat sauce, best simmered a long time to let the flavors meld. If you like spaghetti and meat sauce, you'll like this version. Like most sauces and stews, this one is best a day after it's made. It will keep for a week in the fridge.

Spaghetti, tagliatelle, pappardelle, or any substantial, short pasta shape would be a good choice for the pasta. Nothing too delicate, like vermicelli. Polenta would be another great choice.

1 ounce dried mushrooms

1 small onion, peeled and coarsely chopped

1 celery rib, chopped

1 large carrot, chopped

1 large garlic clove, chopped

1 pound various giblets: hearts, livers, gizzards, minced or ground

4 ounces ground meat (any kind)

¼ cup olive oil

Salt

A few gratings of nutmeg, about ½ teaspoon

2 bay leaves

1 quart whole tomatoes, crushed by hand

1 cup sweet sherry or Marsala wine

⅓ cup heavy cream

Black pepper to taste

Grated cheese for garnish

Break up the mushrooms, and submerge them in 1 to 2 cups of hot water. Let them sit while you proceed.

Pulse the onion, celery, carrot, and garlic in a food processor until you get somewhere between a fine mince and a paste. Don't purée it. Set the vegetables aside in a bowl for now.

Heat the olive oil in a large Dutch oven or heavy, lidded pot set over medium-high heat. When the oil is hot, add the giblets and the ground meat. Brown them well, sprinkling some salt over them as they cook. When they're close to being done, stop stirring them so a crust, what the French call a *fond*, forms on the bottom of the pan. Brown is good, black not so much. So watch your heat. When it forms, remove the meats and set aside.

Add the vegetables to the pot. Let the moisture from the vegetables soften the meat crust in the pot. Salt them as they cook. Use a wooden spoon to scrape up all the browned bits. Cook over medium heat until the vegetables soften well, and then let another crust form.

While the vegetables are cooking, mince the mushrooms. Keep the mushroom soaking water, and strain it if there's debris in it. When the crust has reformed in the pot, add the mushrooms and the cup of sherry. Use the wooden spoon to scrape up the browned bits again. Let all the sherry cook away until yet another crust forms.

Add the nutmeg, bay leaves, cloves, and 1 cup of the mushroom soaking water. Scrape up the crust one last time. Bring the sauce to a simmer, and add the juice from the jar of whole tomatoes. Crush the tomatoes by hand into the pot. Return the meats to the pot, stir well, add salt to taste, and simmer, partially covered, for at least 90 minutes. You want the gizzard bits to be fairly tender.

To finish, get your water boiling for the pasta. Turn the heat to low on the sauce, and add the cream. Bring the sauce back to a bare simmer, and when the pasta is ready, grind black pepper over the sauce. I like to put the pasta in a large bowl, add one ladle of the sauce over it, and toss to coat. I then give everyone some pasta and add a bit more of the sauce on each person's plate. Grate some cheese over everything and you're good to go.

CHAPTER 14

SMALL-GAME CHARCUTERIE

Curing small game and making rabbit or poultry sausages is similar to doing the same thing with pork. For starters, all these meats tend to be lean. And when you do find fat on, say, a wild turkey or a pen-raised pheasant, it's too low in saturated fat to be of use in any type of sausage other than a hot dog or some other emulsified sausage.

Mostly these meats lend themselves to smoking. Smoked pheasant and turkey are wonderful, and hard-smoked wings from turkeys make a great addition to beans or a pot of collard greens.

Pâté, rillettes, and terrines are also great uses for small game and upland birds. Pâté and rillettes are long-cooked, shredded or pounded meat mixed with some other fat, like pork fat or butter. A terrine is, more or less, a fancy meatloaf you eat cold with pickles and mustard.

Know that while I do identify particular animals for each recipe, most of the sausages and cured-meat recipes in this section work with most anything; a hare terrine can easily be a pheasant, turkey, or even woodchuck terrine. Grouse rillettes can become quail rillettes or rabbit rillettes with no trouble at all. You get the point.

SAUSAGES

Sausages are not something you typically think of when you think of small game. After all, with the exception of turkeys, they are all, well, small. And unless you shoot a bunch of turkeys, you'll probably want to eat them in ways other than sausage. Still, poultry and rabbit sausages are a thing, and the red meat of a jackrabbit is perfect for sausages.

SPECIAL EQUIPMENT NEEDED

You will need some special equipment to make sausages. You can hand-chop or grind meat in a food processor and stuff by hand with a funnel, but unless you're an expert, this results in an inferior sausage and is far more work. At a minimum, you'll need a meat grinder attachment for a stand-up mixer.

If you're serious about making sausages, you'll want some extra gear. Here's my set-up:

- Hog, sheep, and/or beef casings, available at butcher shops or online from places like The

Sausage Maker or Butcher & Packer. I rarely use synthetic casings.

- A dedicated sausage stuffer. Avoid both the KitchenAid attachment and those cornucopia-shaped stuffers. You can get good stuffers online or in sporting goods superstores like Cabela's.

- A wooden rack to hang sausages to dry.

If you're a beginner, start by making sausage patties, not links. Remember that you can also wrap your sausage meat in blanched cabbage or chard leaves, roll the meat in bulgur wheat and make Lebanese kibbeh, wrap it in caul fat (available from good butchers, although you might need to order ahead), or stuff it into grape leaves. Homemade sausage is also a great filling for bierocks (see Sharpie Bierocks, page 245).

If you do plan on stuffing your sausages, hog casings are the easiest to buy. Nearly every good butcher has them, and they're inexpensive. Most come heavily salted in plastic tubs and must be soaked in warm water for a half hour or more to reconstitute them. You also can use narrow sheep casings or very wide beef casings, but you may need to special order them from your butcher or buy them online. You can buy artificial casings made from edible collagen, but I only use them for Slim Jim-like snack sticks.

SAUSAGE BASICS

The leanness of small game and upland birds can be a problem when you decide to make sausages. You'll always need to add some sort of fat to the mix. Pork fat is the standard. You can use beef fat, but I don't much like it, and it will make your poultry sausages taste like beef; this is OK with hare sausage, however. Pork fat is softer than beef fat and far more neutral tasting. Good pork fat can be had in any decent supermarket and in all butcher

shops. It's usually cheap, too. Your first choice should be back fat, which is easier to cut and slightly harder than the fat in the shoulder, which is the next best thing. Pork bellies are OK, but there is enough meat in them to influence the flavor of your sausage—not necessarily a bad thing, but you should be aware of it before you toss some bellies into the grinder.

Sausage is traditionally made with the random trim and wobbly bits of an animal. But, with small game, you're basically using whatever meat you can get off the carcass that isn't loaded with sinew. Normally, that means breast meat of most upland birds, as well as thigh meat from larger ones like pheasants and turkeys. With mammals, get what you can get. Usually it's the hind legs and backstraps.

Make sure your meat and fat are *very* cold when you grind it. Ideal temperature is around freezing, about 32°F or thereabouts; the salt with the meat will prevent it from freezing solid. If you're doing multiple grinds, put the meat and fat in the freezer for an hour or so between grinding. This helps prevent smear, where the fat breaks down and coats the meat. If this happens, you will never get a good bind on the sausage, and it'll be crumbly, like bad cat food.

While you mix the meat, you still want to see individual little pieces of fat, like the marshmallows in Lucky Charms cereal. I often mix by hand now, and I know by feel when the mix has bound—your achingly numb hands will feel only the undifferentiated mass rather than lots of discrete bits of meat. You should be able to pick up an entire five-pound batch and it will hang together.

When making links, thread a length of casing on your sausage stuffer, then make one big coil of sausage at once. After you have big coils, *then* link them. For fresh sausages, I pinch off six- to eight-inch links with my fingers, then roll them in opposite ways. I roll the first link away from me, the next link toward me. That helps the links keep their shape while you dry them.

In a word, control. Old style, traditional recipes use teaspoons and tablespoons for ingredients, and that's perfectly fine for seasonings like pepper and herbs and garlic. But for salt, it just won't work—and it's more than just a flavor issue; it's one of safety.

Salts are not equally ground. A tablespoon of, say, Morton's kosher salt will not be the same amount of salt that you'd get in a tablespoon of Diamond Crystal salt and definitely won't be even close to a tablespoon of table salt. For the record, I use Diamond Crystal kosher salt.

I can tell you that the difference between thirty-four grams of salt and thirty-eight grams of salt in a five-pound batch of sausage is very noticeable—despite the fact that, depending on which brand of salt you use, each could be a couple of tablespoons. What's more, when you're curing meats, you need a set percentage of salt to be safe; normally it's about 2.5 percent. You can't get there accurately with tablespoons.

This becomes even more important with curing salts, sodium nitrite and sodium nitrate. These powerful salts are measured in tiny amounts, with six grams being the standard for my recipes. Hard to do with a teaspoon. Put too much in your meat and it can make you sick. So get the scale, OK?

Drying links helps the sausages tighten up in their skins, which improves the texture. I use a wooden clothes rack to hang my sausages, and it works like a charm. Hang your links a for a few hours at room temperature, and then let them sit overnight, uncovered, in the fridge, surrounded by paper towels to soak up any stray moisture. Even better is to let them hang at around 33°F to 40°F overnight. Can you eat them the first day? You bet, but the texture and flavor will improve the second day.

ADVANCED SAUSAGE-MAKING TIPS

Once you have several batches of sausages under your belt, you can start thinking more about perfecting your craft. Here are a few advanced tricks and tips I've learned over the years.

- When making fresh sausages, use fresh ingredients if possible: fresh herbs, fresh garlic, etc. You will notice the difference.

- When you do use dried spices (seeds like black pepper, fennel, coriander, etc.), toast them in a dry pan first. It makes them taste stronger, even weeks later. Don't toast dried herbs, though, or you'll burn them.

- Salt your meat and fat and let it sit in the fridge for a day or even two before you grind. This helps develop myosin, the protein that binds the sausage to itself.

- Work with never-frozen meat if possible. Never-frozen meat will bind to itself better than thawed meat. And "hot-boned" meat—meat butchered *before* the animal goes into rigor mortis—will get you the absolute best bind.

- Stuff your sausage rather loosely when making the initial coil. This gives you more wiggle room to make links. If your initial coil is too taut, you won't be able to twist them enough to keep the whole coil from unraveling. They can (and do) burst when this happens.

- Vary the length of your sausage links depending on how rich they are. This is, of course, a matter of opinion, but I think leaner links ought to be long and skinny and fatty ones shorter and plumper.

- The liquid you use to moisten your links matters a lot. The exact same sausage recipe made with red wine will taste different with white wine. Vinegar will change it again, as will water or fruit juice or liqueur; I've added ouzo in a few of my recipes. Remember that especially acidic liquids can break the bind in the meat, so use them sparingly.

- Consider using binders like dry milk powder or something like C-Bind from The Sausage Maker, which is made from carrot fiber. These help bind and help the links retain moisture, even if you overcook them. A little goes a long way.

- The most important thing to learn is balance. Make enough sausages, and after a while you'll develop an eye for how much spices or herbs would overpower the meat, how long to make links, etc. A good sausage has all flavor elements in harmony. Savory is easy; so is salty. Sour can come from vinegar, sweet from any number of sources. Herbs need to play well with one another, as do spices.

My final bit of advice: *write everything down*. If you don't keep accurate notes, you'll never be able to tinker with your recipes, and, most importantly, you'll never be able to recapture those moments of perfection.

PROVENÇAL PHEASANT SAUSAGES

This is an herby, bright sausage that highlights white meat like pheasant or turkey breast. I make it with pheasant breasts mostly, but any white meat will work. You can play with the amount of herbs in here, and their ratios, but the point is to taste the herbs. These are best cooked on the grill and eaten with bread or a summer salad.

3 pounds pheasant meat

2 pounds fatty pork shoulder or belly

34 grams salt

2 teaspoons dried thyme

3 teaspoons chopped lavender blossoms (optional)

1 tablespoon chopped rosemary

1 tablespoon chopped sage

1 tablespoon chopped garlic

2 tablespoons chopped basil

1 tablespoon freshly ground black pepper

Zest of 1 lemon

Hog casings

Get out about 15 feet of hog casings and soak them in warm water.

Cut the meat and fat into chunks that you can fit into your meat grinder. Mix the salt with the meat and fat until every piece has a little salt on it. Refrigerate overnight if you can, but let it marinate at least an hour or so; this helps develop myosin in the mixture, which helps the texture of the finished sausage. Just before you grind, put the meat in the freezer until it's between 28°F and 35°F. Put your grinder parts (auger, dies, blades, etc.) in the freezer, too, and put a bowl in the fridge.

When you're ready to grind, mix all the herbs, lemon zest, and black pepper with the chilled meat and fat. Grind the mixture through the coarse die (6.5 mm) on your grinder. If your meat mixture is still at 35°F or colder after grinding, you can go right to binding. If it has warmed up, you'll need to chill everything down again. Use this time to clean up the grinder.

Once the meat is cold, put it in a large bin or bowl, and add ¾ cup of ice water. Mix well with your (very clean) hands for 2 minutes—a good indicator of temperature is that your hands should ache with cold when you do this. You want to mix until the meat binds to itself. You can also do this in a stand mixer set on its lowest setting, but I find you don't get as good a bind as you do when you do this by hand.

To make links, put the loose sausage into a stuffer and thread a casing onto it. Stuffing sausage is easier with two people, one to fill the links, the other to coil, but I do it solo all the time. Stuff the links well but not super tight; if they're too full, you won't be able to tie them off later. Don't worry about air pockets yet. Stuff the whole casing, leaving lots of room on either end to tie them off; I leave at least three inches of unstuffed casing on either end of the coil.

To form the individual links, tie off one end of the coil. Now pinch off two links, each about 6 inches long. Rotate the link between your hands forward a few times. Look for air pockets. To remove them, set a large needle or a sausage pricker into a stovetop burner until it glows (this sterilizes it), then pierce the casing at the air pockets. Twist the links a little and gently compress them until they're nice and tight. Repeat this process with the rest of the sausage, alternating your twist forward, then backward.

Dry your sausages overnight before you seal and freeze them.

SHEBOYGAN WHITE BRATS

It was Wisconsin where I first learned to love the brat. Bratwurst was a new thing to me, child of Jersey that I am, but here in this new land, it was as common as the Italian sausage I knew and loved back home. It was 1992, and I was living away from the East Coast for the first time. I ate an awful lot of brats and drank an awful lot of beer when I was a student at UW-Madison.

Then I moved back to Long Island, and there I met a woman who would ultimately become my wife for a time. Ironically, she was from Wisconsin, and when it came time to meet her family, I found myself back on familiar ground. It was her uncle—a gruff older man, probably in his sixties, a true blue-collar, stand-up guy, deer hunter, family man, lover of Friday night fish-fry—who first showed me how to make this sausage. One day, he invited my wife and me down to his workshop-basement. It was time to make sausage. Brats, to be exact. And not just any kind of brat. It was the classic "white brat" made famous in nearby Sheboygan.

Sheboygan brats owe their origin to the classic German bratwurst, possibly the Nürnberger variety, which looks and tastes similar. No two recipes are alike, but they all tend to have marjoram, ginger, nutmeg, black or white pepper, and occasionally mustard seed, caraway and other spices. Many recipes have a bit of egg and or cream in them, too.

His recipe had most of these ingredients, although no egg or caraway. We made a big batch, easily thirty pounds, and it was made with the traditional mix of pork and veal. No matter what meats you use, a Sheboygan brat is light in color, medium-coarse rich, and bright with that medieval spice mix that feels like it's been around for a millennium.

Grill these brats and serve them on a roll with mustard and sauerkraut or caramelized onions. There ain't nothing better when the Badgers or Packers are playing. Of course, you can eat them rooting for another team, too, I suppose.

Makes about 4 pounds | **Prep Time: 90 minutes, depending on how experienced you are**

---

3 pounds boneless white meat

1 pound pork belly or fatty pork shoulder

25 grams kosher salt

2 grams black pepper, about a teaspoon

1 gram dried marjoram, about a teaspoon

5 grams ground ginger, about 1½ teaspoons

2 grams freshly ground nutmeg

50 grams dry milk

3 grams caraway, about a teaspoon

2 grams mustard seed, about a teaspoon

1 egg white

½ cup heavy cream

Hog casings

Soak about 10 feet of hog casings in warm water.

Cut the meat and fat into chunks that you can fit into your meat grinder. Mix together the salt, pepper, marjoram, ginger, and nutmeg, then mix this with the meat and fat until every piece has a little on it. Refrigerate overnight if you can, but let it marinate at least an hour or so; this helps develop myosin in the mixture, which helps the texture of the finished sausage. Just before you're ready to grind, put the meat in the freezer until it's between 28°F and 35°F. Put your grinder parts (auger, dies, blades, etc.) in the freezer, too, and put a bowl in the fridge.

When the meat has chilled, grind two-thirds of the mixture through the coarse die on your grinder, and the rest through the fine die. This creates a more interesting texture. If your meat mixture is still at 35°F or colder after grinding, you can go right to binding. If it has warmed up, you need to chill everything again. Use this time to clean up the grinder.

Once the meat is cold, put it in a large bin or bowl and add the dry milk, caraway, mustard seed, egg white, and heavy cream. Mix well with your (very clean) hands for 2 minutes—a good indicator of

(continued)

temperature is that your hands should ache from the cold when you do this. You want to mix until the meat binds to itself. You can also do this in a stand mixer set on its lowest setting, but I find you don't get as good a bind as you do when you do this by hand.

You now have bratwurst. To make links, put the loose sausage into a stuffer and thread a casing onto it. Stuffing sausage is easier with two people, one to fill the links, the other to coil, but I do it solo all the time. Stuff the links well but not super tight; if they are too full, you won't be able to tie them off later. Don't worry about air pockets yet. Stuff the whole casing, leaving lots of room on either end to tie them off; I leave at least three inches of unstuffed casing on either end of the coil.

To form the individual links, tie off one end of the coil. Now pinch off two links of about six inches long. Rotate the link between your hands forward a few times. Look for air pockets. To remove them, set a large needle or a sausage pricker into a stovetop burner until it glows (this sterilizes it), then pierce the casing at the air pockets. Twist the links a little and gently compress them until they're nice and tight. Repeat this process with the rest of the sausage, alternating your twist forward, then backward.

Hang your links for an hour or so to dry. Once you've taken the links down, they can be refrigerated for up to a week, or frozen for up to a year.

HARE SAUSAGES CATALAN

Jackrabbits are perfect for sausages. Plentiful, with no seasons or limits, and with a mild red meat that plays well with pork fat. Hare meat can be used in any venison or beef sausage recipe (I have plenty in my book *Buck, Buck, Moose*), but I especially like the way the flavors come together in this Spanish recipe for a simple *butifarra*.

Could you make this with a lighter meat? Sure. But it's at its best as a red-meat sausage.

Makes 7½ pounds of sausage | **Prep Time: 90 minutes, depending on your experience**

4 pounds hare meat

3 pounds pork shoulder

½ pound pork fat

45 grams salt

45 grams sugar

14 grams freshly ground black pepper

10 grams freshly ground white pepper

7 grams ground allspice

3 grams ground cloves

¼ cup sherry, chilled

Hog casings

Soak about 20 feet of hog casings in warm water.

Cut the meat and fat into 1-inch chunks. Mix together the salt, sugar, both peppers, allspice, and cloves, then mix this with the meat and fat until every piece has a little on it. Refrigerate overnight if you can, but let it marinate at least an hour or so; this helps develop myosin in the mixture, which helps the texture of the finished sausage. Before you grind, put the meat in the freezer until it's between 28°F and 35°F. Put your grinder parts (auger, dies, blades, etc.) in the freezer, too, and put a bowl in the fridge.

When the meat has chilled, grind the mixture through the coarse (6.5 mm) die on your grinder. If your meat mixture is still at 35°F or colder after grinding, you can go right to binding. If it has warmed up, you need to chill everything again. Use this time to clean up the grinder.

Once the meat is cold, put it in a large bin or bowl, and add the chilled sherry plus ¾ cup of ice water. Mix well with very clean hands for 2 minutes—a good indicator of temperature is that your hands should ache from cold. You want to mix until the meat binds to itself. You can also do this in a stand mixer set on its lowest setting, but I find that you don't get as good a bind as you do when you do this by hand.

To make links, put the loose sausage into a stuffer and thread a casing onto it. Stuffing sausage is easier with two people—one to fill the links, the other to coil—but I do it solo all the time. Stuff the links well but not super tight; if they're too full, you won't be able to tie them off later. Don't worry about air pockets yet. Stuff the whole casing, leaving lots of room on either end to tie them off; I leave at least three inches of unstuffed casing on either end of the coil.

To form the individual links, tie off one end of the coil. Now pinch off 2 links, each about 6 inches long. Rotate the link between your hands forward a few times. Look for air pockets. Remove them with a clean needle or sausage pricker. Twist the links a little, and gently compress them until they're nice and tight. Repeat this process with the rest of the sausage, alternating your twist, forward then backward.

Dry your sausages overnight before sealing and freezing.

PTARMIGAN GRAVLAX

I learned about this recipe in a cool little book called *Icelandic Food & Cookery*, by Nanna Rögnvaldardóttir. It's normally done with Icelandic ptarmigan, which is *Lagopus muta*, the rock ptarmigan. Unless you hunt your own, your best bet is to buy Scottish grouse, which are *Lagopus lagopus scotia*, a very similar bird. Any ptarmigan works, as would a sharp-tailed or sage grouse or prairie chicken. This is a red-meat bird preparation.

Once cured, serve this with a vinaigrette on top of a green salad, or with pickled berries or chopped apples, and maybe a drizzle of honey or maple syrup. It's also good in a sandwich.

Serves 4 as an appetizer | **Prep Time: 2 days**

4 ptarmigan breasts, off the bone and skinless, tenders removed

4 tablespoons kosher salt

2 tablespoons sugar

2 tablespoons minced fresh parsley

1 tablespoon minced fresh lovage or angelica (optional)

2 tablespoons fresh thyme leaves

2 teaspoons cracked black peppercorns

2 teaspoons cracked white peppercorns

10 juniper berries, crushed (optional)

1 garlic clove, crushed

1 tablespoon honey

Mix everything but the ptarmigans and honey in a shallow bowl. Roll the ptarmigan breasts in the mixture, making sure every bit gets covered.

Lay the breasts in one layer in a container, and sprinkle over any remaining herb mixture. Drizzle the honey over everything. Cover and refrigerate for 36 to 48 hours. Flip the breasts twice a day, and remove any brine that develops.

To serve, scrape off most of the herb mixture, then cut on the diagonal into thin slices.

PHEASANT OR TURKEY CONFIT

Many of you know about duck confit (pronounced "con-FEE"). It's a classic French method of slightly curing meat, then poaching it gently in fat until it's meltingly tender. With ducks or geese, it's a natural: I've confited domestic duck legs with only the fat on the legs themselves—no added fat needed! Upland game birds, however, being lean, require special care.

You should know that the process takes hours, or even days, if you're looking to preserve the meat for months. So why bother with it? Because the end result is so wonderful that you'll change your perspective on eating pheasants. Done this way, the legs and thighs of a ringneck are far better eating than the breast meat. Really.

Here's why. Start by thinking about people for a moment. The older we get, the more interesting we are. Chatting with an eighteen-year-old isn't nearly the same experience as drinking whisky with someone in her fifties, right? Well, pheasants are the same way. The meat of an old rooster or tom, which can be several years old, will be far more flavorful and memorable than the legs of a domestic chicken, which is typically less than two months old.

But in this case, as in most cases, flavor comes at a price. Sinew. Tendons. Tendrils of tissue so tough you can use them as dental floss. It's as if all that deliciousness is imprisoned by those sinews. Confit is a way to deal with this.

By slowly cooking the legs and thighs, you break down an awful lot of connective tissue. By cooking them in fat or oil, and not a broth, you infuse a normally lean bird with luxurious fat. Not a bad thing to my mind.

Still, I'm not going to lie to you. Nothing on this earth will break those tendons down completely. That means the legs of pheasants and turkeys (not so much with quail, partridges, or grouse) will still be best eaten shredded off the bone. But fear not. Serve the thighs in one piece, shred the leg meat, and put it into, well, anything. A bitter green salad is a nice choice, but then so is a taco. Or you can shred, reform into patties, and make into "pheasant cakes" that are so good you'll wonder why on God's Green Acre you never saved the legs from your pheasants. The possibilities are boundless.

I use a modified sous vide method for this since it uses less fat than submerging the legs in 4 to 5 cups of fat or oil. I save up chicken fat or pheasant fat and combine it with butter, but you could also use lard or olive oil. I don't recommend using duck fat, which is traditional with confit, because I don't want a ducky flavor with upland birds. But if this doesn't bother you, go for it.

Of course, you can use this technique with lots of animals, and I find these flavors work well with any chicken-like bird, as well as with rabbits and squirrels.

Once made, this confit will last, sealed in its bag, for a couple months in the fridge. It can also be frozen for up to a year.

Makes 6 legs of confit | **Prep Time: 12 hours, passive curing time** | **Cook Time: 8 hours**

---

2 pounds legs and thighs of pheasant
  or some other creature

¼ cup kosher salt

1 tablespoon dried thyme

1 tablespoon freshly ground black
  pepper

Zest of a lemon, minced

2 bay leaves

1 cup olive oil, lard, or butter

This recipe works best with a vacuum sealer. If you don't have one, you should get one; they're are endlessly useful. But alternative directions are at the end.

Mix together the salt, thyme, black pepper, and lemon zest. Pack the pheasant legs with the mixture. Press it into the skin and the exposed meat, and make sure every part has some on it. Refrigerate for at least 6 hours, and no more than 24 hours. The longer you go, the saltier it will get—and the longer it will preserve.

(continued)

Rinse the cure off as above, then pat dry thoroughly.

Totally submerge the meat in oil—you'll need 4 to 5 cups—and put, uncovered, in an oven set on "warm," or not hotter than 200°F. Alternatively, you can do this on a stovetop with a weak burner set on low, or with a flame tamer. Watch that the oil never sizzles. Cooking time will be about the same. When you're done, filter the oil through cheesecloth, and you can use it again.

When you're done curing the legs, rinse them off, then pat dry with paper towels. Put on a rack to dry further while you make the vacuum bags. Make two vacuum bags, each large enough to hold 3 legs or wings. Put a little butter, lard, or oil into the bottom of each; I add about 2 to 3 tablespoons. Add the pheasant legs and the bay leaves, then divvy up the rest of the fat between the two bags.

Seal the bags, and place in a large pot (the largest you have) that's two-thirds filled with water that is somewhere around 170°F to 180°F, which is below a simmer. You need a large pot to keep the temperature stable; the smaller the pot, the faster the water temperature will change. Poach the legs for 4 to 8 hours, flipping every half hour or so if they float. Young, tender birds (or pen-raised birds) will need only 4 hours, old pheasants might need the full eight hours.

Remove the bags from the water and plunge them into a large bowl of ice water. When they're cool, store in the fridge.

When you're ready to eat your confit, you'll probably want to crisp it up. You can sear it in a pan, but that method spatters a lot. I prefer to roast the leg/thighs, skin-side up, in a pan in a 400°F oven. No need to preheat the oven, just pop the legs in and cook until it's as crispy as you like, anywhere from 15 to 45 minutes.

"A man has to hold his mouth open a long time before a roasted partridge flies into it."

—AFRICAN PROVERB

SMOKED PHEASANT OR GROUSE

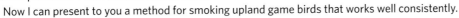

Smoked pheasant can be either the best expression of the bird or the worst, a dessicated husk, usable only as a flavoring for broth. I've had it turn out both ways, I'm sad to say. After my failures, I got back on the horse and smoked another pheasant. Then another. And another.

Now I can present to you a method for smoking upland game birds that works well consistently.

The issue with wild birds like pheasants, chukars, and grouse is that they work for a living. They can be old and tough, and smoking doesn't do a lot to tenderize them.

But brining does. A salt soak is vital with pheasants. Skip this, or short it, and you'll be sorry.

I brine my pheasants for at least six hours. This is a long time for a bird that typically weighs somewhere between two and three pounds plucked and gutted. But the salt brine needs time to work its magic. Brines help meats retain more moisture as they cook. Brine too little and you get a dry bird. Brine too much and you get a salt lick. In this case, you want to take the brining process to the edge of "too salty."

Beyond that, smoking a whole pheasant is pretty easy—brine, dry, then smoke over hardwood. I like a bit of sweet with my smoke, so I use heavy syrup—boiled down maple syrup in this case. You could use molasses, honey, treacle, or thick birch, hickory, or corn syrup. You just want it to be thick, because thinner sweeteners and syrups, like regular maple syrup, will just bead on the surface of the pheasant.

If you plan on smoking partridges or grouse, reduce the brining time to four to eight hours, and keep an eye on your smoking time. Turkeys will need more like twelve hours to brine, and probably an extra hour in the smoker. Regardless of species, you want the breast meat to hit an internal temperature of about 150°F.

Eat the breasts of the smoked pheasant right off the smoker for dinner, or you can let it cool and slice it for sandwiches. Gnaw on the thighs for a snack, and use the rest of the carcass for smoked pheasant soup, the recipe for which is on the next page.

Serves 4 to 6 | Prep Time: 30 minutes | Cook Time: 3 hours

---

2 whole pheasants or grouse

¼ cup kosher salt, about 2¼ ounces

¼ cup brown sugar

4 cups water

2 cups maple syrup, boiled down to 1 cup

Dissolve the salt and sugar in the water. Find a lidded container just about large enough to hold both pheasants. Cover them with the brine and let this sit in the fridge for 6 to 12 hours.

Remove the pheasants from the brine and pat them dry. Set on a cooling rack, and let them dry overnight in the fridge. Alternatively, set the birds under a ceiling fan or in a breezy place, and let them dry for 1 to 3 hours. This drying process is an important step. If you skip it, the smoke won't adhere well to the pheasant.

Smoke the pheasants over the wood of your choice—I prefer apple, hickory, or pecan—for at least 3 hours, and up to 5 hours. You want a relatively warm smoke, between 200°F and 225°F. Let the pheasants smoke for 1 hour before painting on the maple syrup, then baste with the syrup every 30 minutes afterward.

When the pheasant breast meat reaches an internal temperature of 150°F, take the birds out of the smoker. Put them on a cooling rack, and baste them with maple syrup one more time. Wait at least 20 minutes before eating. They are excellent cold, too.

SMOKED PHEASANT SOUP

What do you do with the rest of the pheasant after you've carved off the breasts? Make this soup. The carcass makes a fantastic soup base, and all that meat gets shredded off so you don't waste it.

There's a certain jazz involved with the rest of the soup. I use rice, but any grain you'd like to eat will do. Just be sure to cook the grain separately in the broth—if you cook it in the soup, the grains will turn the clear broth cloudy. Button mushrooms are easy to get, but any mushroom will do. I roast them in the oven first and then add them to the soup. Doing this will give you a better texture. Finally, you want a pungent green thing. Mustard is my choice, but arugula, watercress, or turnip greens are all good alternatives. Finish the dish with a squeeze of lemon juice at the table.

Note that if you were to smoke a whole turkey, this soup would be awesome with the drumstick and wing meat.

Serves 6 to 8 | **Prep Time: 3 hours, mostly to make the broth** | **Cook Time: 20 minutes**

BROTH

2 quarts water or stock (any kind)

Carcasses of 2 smoked pheasants or grouse, chopped into a few pieces

SOUP

1 pound fresh mushrooms, cut into bite-sized pieces

2 tablespoons melted butter or olive oil

1½ cups rice

Salt and black pepper

¾ pound mustard greens, chopped small

¼ cup finely chopped chives

Juice of 1 or 2 lemons

Start by making the broth. Heat up the premade stock or water to the steaming point, then add the chopped up smoked carcasses. If you want, feel free to add a chopped onion, carrot, and celery if you have them lying around. Let this steep at the steaming point—don't let the broth simmer or boil—covered, for 2 to 4 hours. Then strain the broth. Put a sieve over a large bowl. Set a piece of paper towel in the sieve, then ladle the broth through this into the bowl. Keep the strained broth warm.

While the stock is cooking, preheat the oven to 375°F. Toss the mushrooms with the melted butter or oil, and salt them well. Set them in a roasting pan, and grind some black pepper over them. Roast for 15 minutes, and then turn off the heat. Let the mushrooms continue to roast as you do other things. They can sit in the oven for up to 3 hours.

About 30 minutes before the broth is ready, pour off 2 cups and put that into a small pot. Add the rice and another cup of water and bring it to a boil. Cover the pot, lower the heat to its lowest setting, and cook the rice. When the rice has absorbed all the water, about 15 minutes, turn off the heat, but leave the lid on the pot.

While the rice is cooking, fish out the legs and carcasses of the birds and pick off as much meat as you can.

To finish the soup, add the chopped mustard greens to the strained broth and let them cook until wilted, about 5 minutes. Put some shredded meat, rice, and mushrooms in individual bowls, and ladle over some of the broth and greens. Sprinkle chives on top and add lemon juice and black pepper to taste.

SMOKED WILD TURKEY BREAST

Anyone who's ever cooked any sort of turkey, wild or domestic, knows that the breast meat can get dry in a hurry. As with most of the smoked meat recipes in this book, brining is the secret to a moist turkey breast.

After the brine, you need to dry the turkey breast to form what's called a pellicle on the surface of the meat. A pellicle is a thin sheen or skin of denatured proteins that, when it dries out a bit, becomes tacky. This allows smoke to adhere to the meat far better than if you put wet meat into a smoker. This is an important step in smoking often ignored.

I like smoking over fruit woods (cherry in this case), but you can use whatever—oak, hickory, walnut, beech, alder, mesquite.

To give the turkey one last punch, I paint it with something sweet. I use honey here, but maple syrup, birch syrup, a fruit syrup, or even molasses would work. The combination of sweet-salty-smoky-meaty is irresistible.

You'll notice that I truss and trim my wild turkey breast here. I do this to get a more compact shape that cooks and slices easily. To trim, I slice off the thin triangle of turkey breast that lies over the tail end of the breast—you'll notice that all bird breasts have a thick and a thin end, and you're trimming the turkey's breast so you have, more or less, a big cylinder of meat that you can truss properly. If you don't trim, you can't truss very well.

Do you need Instacure, the curing salt? I like it, as it adds some flavor to the turkey, makes it a little "hammy," and helps prevent botulism. I use a Bradley smoker that doesn't get hot very quickly, so I like the added protection of the curing salt. If you have a smoker that gets to temperature quickly, you can skip the curing salt.

Once made, the smoked turkey will keep in the fridge for a week or so and can be frozen (vacuum-sealed is my preference) for up to a year.

Makes one turkey breast | **Prep Time: 2 days, brine time** | **Cook Time: 4 hours, more or less**

---

1 skinless turkey breast, trimmed (see note above)

2 quarts water

½ cup kosher salt

4 teaspoons Instacure No. 1 (curing salt, available online or at butcher shops—optional)

¼ cup sugar

⅓ cup honey, maple syrup, or other syrup

Mix together the salt, curing salt, water, and sugar until the salt and sugar dissolve. Submerge the turkey breast in the brine, making sure it's totally covered; you might need to weigh down the turkey to keep it submerged. Cover, and put in the fridge for 2 days.

Take the turkey breast out of the fridge, and truss it with kitchen twine like you'd truss a roast. Trussing gives you a more compact piece of meat that cooks more evenly and is easier to slice when done.

Dry the turkey breast to form the pellicle, a sheen that allows the turkey to better take on smoke. You can leave the breast on a rack, uncovered, in the fridge overnight, or you can put it on a rack in a cool, breezy place for a few hours. Either way, be sure turn the turkey few times while you do this. Don't skip this step!

Smoke the turkey slowly at about 200°F until it reaches an internal temperature of about 160°F; this takes about 4 hours with my smoker. Let the turkey smoke undisturbed for an hour, then paint it with honey every 45 minutes or so until it's done. When the turkey is ready, take it out of the smoker and set it on a rack. Paint it one more time with the honey, and serve any way you like it: warm for dinner or cold for sandwiches.

SMOKED TURKEY DRUMSTICKS OR WINGS

As you probably know, turkey drumsticks and wings are tough as nails. Although you can certainly braise these bits until the meat gets tender, you can also go with the toughness and smoke the hell out of turkey, then use the wings or drumstick like a ham hock for flavoring beans, broth, stewed greens, or soup. This also works well with sage grouse legs and wings.

Makes 4 turkey wings | **Prep Time: 3 days, brine time** | **Cook Time: 4 hours smoking time**

3 tablespoons kosher salt

2 tablespoons brown sugar

1 teaspoon garlic powder

1 teaspoon dried thyme

1 teaspoon crushed juniper berries (optional)

¼ teaspoon Instacure No. 1 (curing salt, available online or at butcher shops)

4 to 8 turkey drumsticks or wings, separated into drumettes and tips

Mix together the kosher salt, sugar, garlic powder, thyme, juniper, and curing salt. Massage the mixture evenly into the turkey wings, then put the wings into a container just large enough to hold them. Cover and refrigerate for at least 24 hours, or up to 3 days.

Rinse off the cure. Pat dry, and arrange on a cooling rack. Put the rack in a cool, breezy place (or in front of a fan), and let the wings dry for an hour or two.

Smoke the turkey wings at 250°F for at least 4 hours, until they're heavily smoky and well cooked. They may take up to 8 hours. You want them firm, smoky, and a little dry. Let the wings cool, then seal them in butcher paper or a vacuum-sealed bag. They will keep in the fridge for 10 days or in the freezer for up to 1 year.

"The partridge loves peas, but not those that go into the pot with it."

—SENEGALESE PROVERB

LIVER MOUSSE

I'm normally not a huge fan of liver pâté, but this one I like. It's light and airy, and is great spread on toast with some pickles. Any liver will work here, but if you happen to use very dark livers, which will have no fat in them, I'd soak the livers overnight in milk before proceeding with this recipe, the inspiration for which I got from *The Meat Hook Meat Book: Buy, Butcher, and Cook Your Way to Better Meat*, by Tom Mylan.

Once made, this mousse will keep a week in the fridge. It does not freeze well.

Serves 6 to 8 as an appetizer | Prep Time: 10 minutes | Cook Time: 20 minutes

¾ cup minced yellow onion

2 tablespoons poultry fat or butter

Salt and black pepper

2 sprigs fresh thyme

2 sprigs fresh rosemary

6 fresh sage leaves

¼ cup brandy

1 pound small game livers, whole

¼ cup white wine

½ cup heavy cream

2 to 3 ounces cream cheese,
   cut into chunks

Cook the onion in a small pan with 1 tablespoon of the butter or poultry fat over medium heat. Salt it as it cooks, and sauté until the onions begin to brown. Grind some black pepper over them. Add 1 sprig of each of the herbs and half the sage. Mush them down into the pan. Add the brandy, mix well, and boil it away. This should take about 4 or 5 minutes. Discard the herbs, and move the contents of the pan to the bowl of a blender.

Add the other tablespoon of poultry fat or butter to the pan and sauté the livers over medium-high heat. You really only want to cook them about 90 seconds to 2 minutes per side; you want the livers to still be pink in the center. Salt them as they cook.

Pour in the white wine, add the remaining herbs, and boil this away. Don't let the livers stick to the bottom of the pan. Discard the herbs, and let the livers cool.

Put the livers into the bowl of the blender and start buzzing them. After they've begun to purée, slowly pour in the heavy cream and add the pieces of cream cheese. Add a little more black pepper. Purée the whole thing, and adjust for salt.

If you want to be fancy, push this purée through a fine-meshed sieve before packing it into ramekins. Sometimes I do this, sometimes I don't.

GROUSE RILLETTES

Rillettes are like the best pâté you've ever eaten. Most pâté is ground, but this is shredded meat that's been slow-cooked in butter. I prefer the slightly funky meat of grouse legs, but any animal in this book can be made into rillettes. If you use meat that has bones, increase the amount by about how much you think the bones might weigh—this isn't an exact science, so your guess is probably fine.

You'll want some pork belly or fatty shoulder, plus some plain bacon. Don't use bacon with maple or peppercorns on it.

If you can't find either Chinese five-spice powder or French *quatre epices*, look for "pumpkin pie spice," which is basically the same thing. Hate those flavors? Leave it out, and add more black pepper and herbs.

Rue is impossible to find unless you grow it. It's an intensely aromatic yet bitter herb that goes quite well with fatty things. Parsley or sage is a good alternative.

Serve your rillettes with good bread or on crackers. I like to add either a bit of mustard or something pickled.

Serves 6 to 8 as an appetizer | **Prep Time: 10 minutes** | **Cook Time: 3 hours**

½ pound boneless meat

¼ pound fatty pork

¼ pound bacon

6 ounces good unsalted butter

1 teaspoon dried thyme

2 bay leaves

A pinch of Chinese five-spice powder
　　or French *quatre epices*

Salt

Freshly ground black pepper

About 1 teaspoon chopped rue or sage

Brandy or bourbon

Cut the meat, fatty pork, and bacon into small pieces about an inch long.

In a pot, melt the butter with about ½ cup of water, and add the meats, thyme, and bay leaves. Slowly cook this until everything wants to melt, at least 3 hours, and maybe four. You can do this on the stovetop or in a 250°F oven. Check on things every 30 minutes or so to make sure they're not sticking to the bottom of the pot.

When everything is basically falling apart, take it off the heat and remove the bay leaves. Shred the meat with forks, and when it is a bit warmer than room temperature, start beating in the seasonings: five-spice powder, salt if needed, black pepper, and the herbs. When it tastes as you want—it should be a little salty, but not overly so—add a splash of brandy or bourbon, and pack the rillettes into a bowl or ramekin.

Cover the bowl, and refrigerate overnight before eating. If you want, you can store these in the fridge for a month or two by packing the rillettes into a squat half-pint Mason jar, then melting butter or lard over the top to seal it. Put the lid on and you're good for weeks. Whenever you break into them, however, you'll need to eat your rillettes within a few days.

HARE TERRINE

A terrine is essentially refined meatloaf. It's made in a loaf pan or, traditionally, an enameled iron terrine pan. Most are 1½ quarts and are sold online or in places like Williams Sonoma. But this can be done in a regular loaf pan, too. There are country terrines, which is what this is, and there are fancy ones that are emulsified like mortadella, with things like nuts and fruits suspended inside.

Terrines are easier than they look, and they're a great way to wow party guests, or really anyone at your table. Like French *glace de viande* (Small-Game Glace de Viande, page 57) this is an old-school food that somehow got lost in the fog of modernity. Terrines last a couple of weeks in the fridge, and they freeze well. You can eat a slice as a snack, a light lunch, or a cold supper.

First, any meat works here. I chose hare (jackrabbit) because it's plentiful and traditional. But any of the animals in this book will work, as will venison or waterfowl. In fact, mixing meats is encouraged, especially if you add chunks of tender meat in the terrine, which cooking schools call "interior garnish."

Make this terrine on a weekend, or when you have some time in the kitchen, because the first few times you make one, you'll want to work slowly.

Serves 8 to 10 | **Prep Time: 1 hour** | **Cook Time: 90 minutes**

¾ cup dried berries (cranberries, blueberries, lingonberries)

1 cup brandy

1.6 pounds hare meat

¾ pound pork fat

28 grams salt

3 grams Instacure No. 1 (curing salt, available online or at butcher shops)

2 slices of bread, crusts removed

½ cup milk

¼ cup heavy cream

2 eggs, lightly beaten

6 grams freshly ground black pepper, about 2 teaspoons

1 tablespoon butter

1 tablespoon minced garlic

1 tablespoon minced shallot

1 cup sherry

⅓ cup pine nuts, toasted

Soak the berries in the brandy overnight.

Cut the meat and fat into pieces that will fit into your grinder. If you want, save out about ¼ pound of the pork fat, and dice it small for adding later; doing this makes the interior of the terrine more interesting to eat. Regardless, mix the salt and the Instacure with the meat and fat, and refrigerate overnight if you can. If you can't refrigerate overnight, leave this in the fridge at least 1 hour. This pre-salting helps develop myosin in the meat, which helps the terrine bind to itself.

Just before you're ready to grind, put the meat mixture into the freezer. Put your grinder parts—auger, die, blade—into the freezer, and the tray and bowl into the fridge. Let this chill until the meat is down to about 33°F.

Meanwhile, tear the bread into bits and soak it in the milk and cream. When it's soaked, mash it all into a paste with a fork. Mix the eggs in, and set this in the fridge.

In a pan, heat the butter and sauté the garlic and shallot until they're just beginning to brown, about 3 minutes on medium heat. Add the brandy from soaking the berries (you'll use the berries in a moment) and the sherry. Boil this furiously until thickens and it gets syrupy. Turn off the heat, and move the mixture to a bowl to cool.

When the meat is nice and cold, grind it, along with the bread-paste mixture, through your coarse (6.5 mm) die. Check the meat temperature, and if it's 38°F or cooler after grinding, go right to the second grind. If not, freeze everything again until its temperature drops to below 38°F.

When the meat is adequately chilled, grind half of it through a fine die (4.5 mm).

Now get a big bowl. Mix all the ground meat—which now has the bread-paste mixture in it, too—with everything from the pan that had the shallots and brandy in it, along with the brandy-soaked berries and the pine nuts. Basically, you're mixing everything together now.

Mix well with your (very clean) hands for 2 minutes, until it all comes together in a big mass. Your hands should ache from cold doing this. Alternatively, you can put everything in a stand mixer with the paddle and mix on low speed. But I find that doing it by hand works better.

You basically have a bitchin' meatloaf now. To give it the terrine consistency, you need to cook it in a *bain marie*, as the French call a hot water bath.

Heat your oven to 325°F. Set a large roasting pan inside. Get a big pot of water boiling.

Line your terrine pan, or a bread loaf pan, with plastic wrap so that you'll be able to cover the top with the wrap at the end. Now pack your meat into the pan. You want to really pack it in hard, so you get no air pockets. I find that slapping it in, bit by bit, then pressing it down, works best. Once your pan is full and even on top, cover the top with the plastic wrap and put the lid on, if you have one.

Pour the boiling water into the roasting pan that you've put in the oven. Place the terrine in the middle. Bake this until the center hits 155°F, which can take from 60 to 90 minutes.

Remove the terrine, let it cool, and chill overnight before serving. If you can, place a board or other weight on the terrine to compress it while it's still hot, and keep that on overnight.

It all sounds complicated, and it will be the first time you make it, but if you break it down into steps, making a terrine is basically making a meatloaf or meatball mixture, stuffing it into a rectangular pan, cooking it gently, compressing it if you can, chilling it, then eating cold.

ACKNOWLEDGEMENTS

This is my fourth wild game cookbook, and it may well the best of the bunch. And when I say "my," I really mean "our." No book is a solo effort, and this one is no exception.

First and foremost, I have to thank Hunter Angler Gardener Cook nation. Many thousands of you, some of whom I've only interacted with online, some of whom have become fast friends, have enriched this book. You've offered me ideas, provided me with inspiration, served as a sounding board for my various schemes and plans, tested my recipes, taken me out into the field, opened up your homes, and even gave this book its name; thanks to Dan Denn of Hadley, New York for that one.

I also want to call out a few folks who have helped me get the field experience necessary to write a book about varieties of upland birds and small game that range from Labrador to Alaska to Arizona and Florida. Thanks go out, in no particular order, to Brian Brenton of Michigan; Nate Grace of Massachusetts; Johnathan O'Dell, Mike Scott and Wade Zarlingo of Arizona; Cory LeHew and Sam Weston—young Cheech and Chong—from Utah; Evan Oneto, Matt Ames, Joe Navari, Matt Greene, Kevin Taylor and Josh Stark of California; Randy King of Idaho; Alan Davis of Delaware; Jim Millensifer of Kansas; Larry Robinson and Jesse Griffiths of Texas; Joe Keough of Ohio; Jonathan Wilkins of Arkansas; Chris Hastings of Alabama; Todd Baier of Montana; and, most of all, Chris Niskanen of Minnesota. You created a monster, Chris. Now you gotta live with it.

Pheasant, Quail, Cottontail has been something of a family affair: my sister Laura designing, her husband Richard Feit editing, my sister Elizabeth illustrating, and my partner-in-crime Holly doing more of the best wild-game food photography in the business. Getting the full band together like this has been a goal of mine for a long time; I knew that together we could create a book far greater than the sum of our individual skills. And we did.

Finally, I am most grateful for the partnership I've forged with Quail Forever and Pheasants Forever. I am proud to work with these twin habitat organizations (I am a life member of Quail Forever) to do my small bit to help restore, maintain, and expand habitat for all our upland birds. Giving back so that pheasants, quail, and grouse will have a place to live on this increasingly crowded earth means enough to me to put my money where my mouth is: I am donating a portion of the proceeds from each book sold to QF and PF. It's the least I can do.

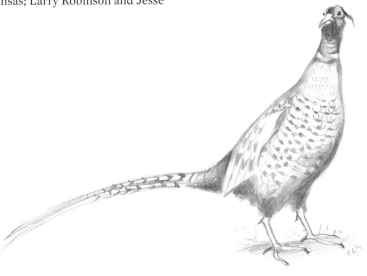

HOW TO GET INVOLVED

Giving back to the animals we hunt has become more and more important in this digital world, where people would rather stare at a screen than go outside. The organizations I list below are all working very hard to preserve, restore, and expand habitat not just for the game animals we pursue, but for every other plant and animal that make up the ecosystems in which those animals live. I am a member of them all, and I urge you to consider joining one or more. Most charge less than $50 for an annual membership, and in most cases, 90 percent of that money goes right back to habitat. Money well spent.

Pheasants Forever and Quail Forever

Pheasantsforever.org
Quailforever.org

These organizations focus on habitat for ringneck pheasants and all our native quail. Both are national (and Pheasants Forever also operates in Canada), and money donated to a local chapter stays there, so local dollars can help local birds.

National Wild Turkey Federation

Nwtf.org

This group works to expand and protect habitat for wild turkeys all over North America. And since turkeys largely live in forests, NWTF is a leader in protecting our forest land.

Ruffed Grouse Society

Ruffedgrousesociety.org

This group focuses on both the ruffed grouse and the woodcock, and operates mainly in the Midwest and the East, although they have chapters in Alaska and Canada. The RGS is also a leader in protecting forest land.

North American Grouse Partnership

Grousepartners.org

This group focuses on the plight of our prairie grouse: sage grouse, prairie chickens, and sharp-tailed grouse. Of these, only the sharpie is considered to have a stable population; the others are in desperate need of help from us to forestall massive habitat loss. This group also keeps tabs on ptarmigan and blue grouse in the West.

SELECTED READING

Consider this a guide to getting deeper into this topic rather than a comprehensive bibliography. These are books that helped me understand the various arcana of charcuterie, butchery, and overall game cookery.

Bent, Arthur Cleveland. *Life Histories of North American Gallinaceous Birds*. New York: Dover Publications, 1963.

Cameron, Angus, and Judith Jones. *The L.L. Bean Game & Fish Cookbook*. New York: Random House, 1983.

De Gouy, L. P. *The Derrydale Game Cookbook*. Latham, MD: Derrydale Press, 2000.

Dickson Wright, Clarissa, and Johnny Scott. *The Game Cookbook*. Latham, MD: Kyle Books, 2005.

Fearnley-Whittingstall, Hugh. *The River Cottage Meat Book*. London: Hodder and Stoughton, 2004.

Griffiths, Jesse. *Afield: A Chef's Guide to Preparing and Cooking Wild Game and Fish*. New York: Welcome Books, 2012.

Hasheider, Philip. *The Complete Book of Butchering, Smoking, Curing and Sausage Making: How to Harvest Your Livestock and Wild Game*. Minneapolis: Voyageur Press, 2010.

Kho, Kian Lam. *Phoenix Claws and Jade Trees*. New York: Clarkson Potter, 2015.

Knight, John Alden. *Woodcock*. New York: Alfred A. Knopf, 1946.

Kochilas, Diane. *The Glorious Foods of Greece: Traditional Recipes from the Islands, Cities, and Villages*. New York: William Morrow, 2001.

McGee, Harold. *On Food and Cooking: The Science and Lore of the Kitchen*. New York: Scribner, 2004.

Mettler, John. *Basic Butchering of Livestock & Game*. North Adams, MA: Storey Publishing, 2003.

Rinella, Steven. *The Complete Guide to Hunting, Butchering, and Cooking Wild Game: Volume 2: Small Game and Fowl*. New York: Speigel & Grau, 2015.

Schwabe, Calvin W. *Unmentionable Cuisine*. Charlottesville, VA: University of Virginia Press, 1979.

Shaw, Hank. *Hunt, Gather, Cook*. Emmaus, PA: Rodale, 2011.

Sheraton, Mimi. *The German Cookbook: A Complete Guide to Mastering Authentic German Cooking*. New York: Random House, 1993.

RECIPE INDEX BY ANIMAL

🕊 QUAIL, PARTRIDGES, AND CHUKARS

🐇 **RABBITS**

🐦 **SHARPTAILS, SPRUCE
GROUSE, SAGE GROUSE,
PTARMIGAN, AND PRAIRIE
CHICKEN**

GENERAL INDEX

Boldface page references indicate photographs.

HANK SHAW is the author of three award-winning cookbooks—
Hunt, Gather, Cook; *Duck, Duck, Goose*; and *Buck, Buck, Moose*—
as well as the James Beard Award-winning website Hunter
Angler Gardener Cook (huntgathercook.com). Shaw has been
featured on numerous television shows, including the Travel
Channel's *Bizarre Foods* and CNN's *Somebody's Gotta Do It* with
Mike Rowe. His work has appeared in *Food & Wine*, *Organic
Gardening*, *Field & Stream*, *Garden & Gun*, *Petersen's Hunting*, and
The Art of Eating. He hunts, fishes, and forages near Sacramento,
California. He can be reached at scrbblr@hotmail.com.